Endorsements

There is absolutely NOTHING ordinary about Charla Pereau, except that her name may not be a household word. That's because she is one of the most unassuming, humble women I know. And that is exactly why God has been able to use her life in such an incredible way. Her story is a real-life God-adventure that will continue to change lives for all eternity. I have been to the Baja mission and loved it so much I took my children back.

If you are looking for a story to build your faith and challenge the depth of your commitment, THIS IS IT! Charla is proof that with faith, nothing is impossible. I *highly* recommend this book!

Terry Meeuwsen
Co-Host, *The 700 Club*
Founder, Orphan's Promise

This book is a collection of testimonies from many people who have participated in the calling and vision of a simple woman, and it represents just a small portion of the fruit from seeds she's planted. Some 50 years ago, Charla got the call from the Lord and said yes. In the most unlikely place, she heard children laughing. The rest is history. My wife, Nancy, and I had the privilege of participating for more than 40 of those years to help make that vision become reality.

The Lord wants to use all of us, and He opens doors to accomplish His calling. Charla, a most humble, God-fearing woman, had gifts only the Holy Spirit can give. Only eternity will show us how many people she touched and blessed.

Two of Charla's quotations will always stay in my heart. She said to me, "God has a plan for your life, Hans." And over the mission's dining room door is a sign that reads, "You will never be the same." Both statements are so true. God wants to use you as well. How do YOU respond? Hopefully, "Here I am, use me."

Hans Benning
The Benning Academy of Music Foundation
Long-Time Mission Volunteer

I've been honored and blessed to know Charla and Chuck for more than 28 years. They've tutored me in real Christian living through their lives, their service to others, and the way they continue (even in their later years) to reach out and touch so many people. As I read this book, I was brought to tears. I've witnessed and participated first hand in so many of the things their stories described, and thought finally others would now see what an amazing ministry Charla and Chuck have had.

I recommend this book to anyone who wants to see what REAL CHRISTIAN service and sacrifice looks like and the blessings it brings.

Barry Wineroth
Director, Short-Term Mexico Outreach
Youth with a Mission (YWAM), Chico, California

When our daughters and their families came to visit and we all sat around the table, we each remembered Charla Pereau and her husband, Chuck, who changed the lives of thousands and thousands of people in Mexico. We can't stop from telling the stories and crying as we think about how God chose them and used them to bless our people and also our lives.

We have benefitted greatly for more than three decades because of their preaching the gospel to those in need, not only with words but also through their example. We give thanks to God for them. They are a blessing to many people and to my family specifically.

Mario Cordoba
Mission Pastor

Having followed Charla's ministry for nearly 50 years, I can readily confirm the exciting events that are reported in this amazing volume of inspiring, informative, and innovative missions.

Dr. John W. Lucas
Founder/President, MEA Worldwide
Calgary, Alberta, Canada

Sequel to the Angel Award-Winning Book
Charla's Children

Charla

An Ordinary Woman with Faith
in an Extraordinary God

Charla Pereau
with Twila Belk

Cover design by Bob Ousnamer
Cover photo: Terry C. Barnes

Photos of Mario and Graciela Cordoba, Hans and Nancy Benning, Peter Bianchini, Leland and Marcia Lantz, Dirk and Mary Kos, Carl and Jan Holter, and Dr. John and Doris Lucas are all used with their permission. Foundation for His Ministry (FFHM) has given permission to use all of the other photos, which are provided from its ministry archives.

Charla, An Ordinary Woman with Faith in an Extraordinary God
by Charla Pereau with Twila Belk

ISBN: 978-1-952369-95-7
LCCN: 2021914874

Published by EA Books Publishing, a division of
Living Parables of Central Florida, Inc. a 501c3
EABooksPublishing.com

This book is dedicated to the six children who were raised in our family: Colleen Andrea, Charles Dana, Craig Bradley (who is now in heaven),
Richard "Dickie" Gregory (who came to us at age 14), Charles Curtis (our adopted Zapotec baby), and Greg Gunther (who also was 14 when he came to us).

They sacrificed much to have a father and mother who divided their time and energy between them and many children in Mexico. My deepest prayer is that God will bless them, their spouses, their children, and their children's children in ways that only He can do.

"Now to him who is able to do immeasurably more than all we ask or imagine, according to his power that is at work within us, to him be glory in [our family], the church and in Christ Jesus throughout all generations" (Ephesians 3:20–21, NIV).

Charla

A Note from the Writer, Twila Belk

In a God-ordained way, I became the writer for Charla's book. I didn't know her. I hadn't heard of her. And I had no idea how big her story was.

Everything happened so quickly. Within a matter of weeks from our initial conversation, I was on an airplane to Mexico and about to begin the experience of a lifetime. I'm grateful that my daughter, Laney, was able to join me.

As I started collecting information and doing my research, I became overwhelmed with awe. Who is this woman? I wondered. My admiration only grew while observing the surroundings and interviewing people during our time in Mexico.

It didn't take long after meeting her for us to get a glimpse inside her heart. We listened as she told us her favorite God stories and watched her interactions with those around her. She peppered her conversations with "Praise God," "Hallelujah," and "Jesus."

Before dozing off at night, praises, songs, and prayers flowed from her lips. (Laney and I were in the bedroom across from her. We heard.) She awoke in the mornings singing. It's a natural part of who she is.

One thing I noticed is that she's not a woman big on words and certainly not one who enjoys the spotlight, but she absolutely adores the Mexican people. A touch of the head. A lingering hug. A blessing. A sincere interest in their lives. She claims she has trouble remembering names, but not once did she forget a person or what God had done in that person's life.

On our ride somewhere between Tijuana and Colonia Vicente Guerrero, she said, "The place where Angel works is up ahead. I'd like to see him." Janelle Keller pulled the van onto a deeply rutted dirt road in front of a few tiny buildings. Because of the sparsely populated area, the fact that Charla even knew where we were impressed me. She went inside to see if Angel was there and waved us in. Her face beamed with joy—the joy of a proud mama—as she chatted with him in his little workshop.

Angel was one of the first children at Hogar Para Niños and is very dear to her. He came to the home severely disabled and couldn't walk. To get from place to place, he dragged himself along the floor. Thanks to Charla's and Chuck's efforts, he underwent multiple surgeries in the United States, which eventually enabled him to ambulate with the help of crutches. The day we saw him, he worked from a wheelchair.

As Charla told us anecdotes from his childhood, he smiled broadly and pointed to a picture hanging on the wall. It was the two of them together. I easily understood why he called her Mama Charla.

By the time our trip was over, I lost count of the number of times I heard those two words. Grown men wrapped their arms around her and buried their heads in her shoulder. They lingered in her embrace. Those men were once hardened criminals, gang leaders, practitioners of witchcraft, addicts, or delivered from some other horrible circumstances. They became like children in her presence, their gratitude abundant.

At the home for children in Oaxaca, I saw young girls squeal with glee when they met her, as if they were with a celebrity. Charla gathered them close and showered them with the love of a grandmother.

We attended an evening service at the Baja mission church, and she tried to stay in the background. But that didn't last long. The pastor announced from the pulpit that she was there, and crowds huddled around her afterward. Beautiful indigenous people, hunched over from years of hard labor, hugged her, thanked her, and gave glory to God for her help in changing their lives.

The respect, honor, and admiration the Mexican people showed her spoke volumes.

As she introduced the individuals we met and filled me in on some of the details of their lives, I witnessed her delight. In some ways it reminded me of the pleasure a grandmother has when pulling out a stack of pictures to brag on her precious grandchildren. She doesn't seem to be an emotional woman, yet several encounters caused her to reach for a tissue. The memories had overwhelmed her.

During our week and a half together, I learned about her fearlessness—how she walked ten miles into a remote region of the Oaxacan mountains to get answers after villagers martyred one of Foundation for His Ministry's missionaries. And then there was the time she crossed a raging river while holding onto a rope and carrying $10,000 on her head to save the Bible institute. Those and other reports of her standing in the face of danger convinced me that she has legions of angels at work on her behalf.

I listened as people told me about the role she played in lining up medical treatments and/or medicines that saved their lives. And I heard many accounts about the opportunities she made available for higher education or employment.

While we were in Oaxaca, we had the privilege of flying into the mountains in a tiny Missionary Aviation Fellowship (MAF) plane. We had planned to visit Modesto, one of FFHM's missionaries, in a hard-to-reach area that is hostile to the gospel. My daughter sat next to the pilot, Charla and I were in the middle seats, and Edgar Rivera was behind us.

Unfortunately, we couldn't land because of inclement weather, but the memory of the experience will stay with me forever. As we flew through the clouds hovering over the mountains, Charla's hand was raised in prayer the entire time. She was busy interceding and speaking blessings over the Oaxacan villagers—her "children" and "grandchildren" below.

Laney took a picture out the front window. When she looked at the photo on her phone, she discovered it had captured a reflection of our airplane with a full rainbow encircling it. I knew then that we were experiencing a holy moment. "It's like we're in the shadow of the Almighty," Laney said. We all had a profound awareness of God's presence.

The appearance of the rainbow that day reminds me of God's faithfulness and His many promises. I can't help but think of the countless ways He's proven Himself to Charla over her almost nine decades of life. As you read the following pages, you'll understand what I mean.

In the back of her Bible, the names of her children, grandchildren, and great grandchildren are written, along with a special scripture God gave her on the day of each one's birth or adoption. She prays that scripture regularly over them. In a similar way, the names and faces of her Mexican family are written on her heart. She holds them up to her heavenly Father in constant prayer and intercedes for their specific needs.

Many years ago, Evangelist Dick Mills gave her a prophetic word: "Your children and grandchildren will know the Lord." That is her hope for her Mexican "children" and "grandchildren" as well. That is why she does what she does.

When she was just a 13-year-old girl, Charla boldly proclaimed, "I want to do great things for God!" She has, and she continues to do so.

Several people during our trip referred to her as the Mother Teresa of Mexico. My daughter, whose hero is Elisabeth Elliot, spoke of her as Elisabeth Elliot 2.0. Charla would probably say that she's just an ordinary woman who places her faith in an extraordinary God.

Because I'm a writer and speaker who loves what I call braggin' on God, I often refer to myself as the Gotta Tell Somebody Gal. Charla's is a story I'm thrilled to tell. It's one that shines the light on God in a huge way. But her story doesn't end with the last word in this book. Her "children" and "grandchildren" in Mexico will be living it throughout eternity.

I hope you are as blessed and encouraged as I was in learning about Charla and what faith in an extraordinary God can do.

Twila Belk
(www.gottatellsomebody.com)

Contents

Introduction

My husband, Chuck, and I never dreamed that we'd adopt a raven-haired, bronze-skinned Zapotec baby or that it would lead to a deep compassion for our orphaned, abandoned, impoverished, and disadvantaged neighbors south of the border.

We never dreamed when we made our first trip to Colonia Vicente Guerrero on October 1, 1966, that we would become the founders of a multifaceted ministry that reaches people in the Baja Peninsula, the mainland of Mexico, and even the mountains of Oaxaca.

We never dreamed that what started as a small orphanage would evolve into a mission that includes several homes for children in need, a huge outreach to migrant workers, a high-tech medical facility, schools, churches, a Bible institute, a day care center, prison ministries, a drug and alcohol rehab, a learning environment for those with special needs, literacy training, evangelism to people groups that have never heard the name of Jesus, and so much more.

We never dreamed that we would face such horrible, heart-wrenching trials as babies dying, floods washing our buildings away, corrupt people trying to take advantage of us, arsonists and earthquakes, or that some of our Bible school students would become martyrs for the sake of Christ.

And we never dreamed that we would experience the all-encompassing, supernatural power of Almighty God in so many ways.

We've had highs. We've had lows. We've seen God. We've felt His embrace. And we are in awe.

We thank God for what He has done in us and through us over the years. It's not that we have phenomenal abilities. We don't. He's shown us that He's much more interested in our availability, and that's what we've offered Him. We're just ordinary people who trust in an extraordinary God. And He's proven again and again that when ordinary people allow God to use them, miracles are possible.

God has blessed us with faithful volunteers, generous donors, devoted missionaries, and dedicated staff. They deserve credit for all that's been accomplished. Without their service and support, we wouldn't have a story.

And speaking of stories . . .

Bethany House Publishers published my first book, *Charla's Children*, in 1981. After a few years, the rights reverted back to us, and we self-published it in 1987 with some changes and additional chapters. Praise God, it has sold nearly eighty thousand copies! The book highlights God's incredible hand at work in the development of Hogar Para Niños, our home for children that came about through a vision He gave me.

One of our Foundation for His Ministry (FFHM) friends entered *Charla's Children* in the book category for the 1988 International Angel Awards, a prize given annually for excellence in moral quality media. Two weeks prior to the gala event at the prestigious Beverly Wilshire Hotel on Rodeo Drive in Beverly Hills, we were notified that our little book was in the top fifty finalists out of seven thousand entries.

With such well-known authors as Charles Swindoll, Josh McDowell, Jack Hayford, Dr. James Dobson, Charles Colson, Lloyd J. Ogilvie, and other big names being considered, not once did I think I could win. So, I decided to skip the festivities, especially since the ticket price was $80. Yes, eight zero. (Do you know how many children you can feed with that amount?)

Lu Ann White, our administrative assistant and bookkeeper at the time, pushed me to attend. "You could win," she said. At her insistence, I sent in the money, while grumbling to myself that there's no way a self-published book stood a chance with such high-profile competition. I also considered taking along a doggy bag!

The night of the ceremony, I left my car on a nearby residential street and walked a half mile to save myself the $10 parking fee. Once inside the luxurious room, I was ushered to a table with a group of people I didn't recognize. Then I soon learned that the smiling, bursting-with-charm lady sitting across from me was the famous entertainer Dolly Parton, who had been nominated for her televised Thanksgiving special.

Last on the program that evening were the nominees for the print and book category. The presenter was Clayton Moore, also known as The Lone Ranger (my hero), dressed in full costume. I scarcely paid attention to his words because I was so enamored with him.

The gentleman sitting to my right nudged me. "You've won," he said. "You need to go up and accept your award."

My first reaction was laughter. "That's not possible," I said. But the laughter quickly turned to tears. I made my way to the platform to receive the coveted trophy. Still in a state of shock, I forgot to give my thank-you speech after they handed me the seven-inch silver angel. I wished I had asked the Lone Ranger for one of his signature silver bullets. He always left one behind as a token.

I never dreamed that I'd win an Angel Award, and I never dreamed that I'd later receive an envelope with a check for $10,000 as part of the prize. But God knew. He's worthy of all the glory.

Ever since *Charla's Children* came out, I've promised to write a sequel, but numerous obstacles have kept it from happening. Now, as my life here on earth is winding down, I'm determined to tell more of the stories and to share about some of my early influences that played a part in who I am today. I hope this book will be an encouragement to you.

The account of His Ministry in Mexico is much bigger than the pages you're reading can contain. I've struggled just trying to decide what to include.

I appreciate and agree with what John said in the twenty-first chapter of his gospel, after testifying about Jesus's frequent supernatural deeds. "Jesus did many other things as well. If every one of them were written down, I suppose that even the whole world would not have room for the books that would be written" (John 21:25, NIV).

God has revealed Himself to us repeatedly. Here are four of many important truths He's emphasized through His actions on our behalf: (1) Nothing is too small for His attention, (2) nothing is too big for Him to accomplish, (3) His timing is perfect, and (4) He knows just what we need.

While reading the scriptures, I've noticed how much the psalmist David delighted in exalting God. It's something I love to do as well. In Psalm 34:1–3 he said, "I will praise the LORD at all times. I will constantly speak his praises. I will boast only in the LORD; let all who are helpless take heart. Come, let us tell of the LORD's greatness; let us exalt his name together" (NLT).

As I tell of the Lord's greatness in the following pages, I invite you to exalt His name with me.

I regret that I can't name every person who has been involved in His Ministry over the years—that would be an impossible task—so I've chosen to tell you about only a representative handful. But God knows who our faithful, unsung heroes are, and He smiles.

Laying the Foundation for His Ministry

Early Influences

“**H**ave you always wanted to be a missionary?” “What led up to your involvement in Mexico?” “Why do you care so much?” Those are just a few of the questions I receive from curious people. The answers go all the way back to my childhood.

As I reflect on my formative years, I can point to many influences that shaped my beliefs and passions, gave me an empathetic heart, and helped lay the foundation for the multifaceted ministry happening in Mexico today through FFHM.

One of those influences was my maternal grandmother. Although I never met her, the lessons she instilled in my mother through example and experience live on in me.

Every Memorial Day, my mother took me to the cemetery to visit the gravesites of relatives. We stopped and lingered at each one while Mother shared interesting historical tidbits. I loved hearing anecdotes of my extended family, but the information about my grandmother is what I enjoyed the most.

Her small granite tombstone intrigued me because of the six simple words engraved there: SHE HATH DONE WHAT SHE COULD.

“What does that mean, Mama?” I asked during one of our visits.

Mother used the opportunity to tell me a Bible story from the fourteenth chapter of Mark. It was about a special woman with an alabaster jar of expensive perfume. She humbly approached Jesus, broke the jar, and poured the contents over His head. But some of the bystanders thought the woman was foolish and rebuked her for wasting the valuable oil.

After Jesus told the naysayers to leave her alone, He said, "She has done a beautiful thing for Me, and she has done what she could." He acknowledged that her gift to Him was costly, but she had offered it as an act of worship and to prepare Him for burial.

I especially like what Jesus said next. "Truly I tell you, wherever the gospel is preached throughout the world, what she has done will also be told, in memory of her" (Mark 14:9, NIV). I could hardly imagine the joy I'd have to hear those words spoken about me!

The tombstone's inscription meant so much more after hearing the stories Mama told me about Grandmother. I determined then that I wanted to become a person who did what she could.

My grandmother and grandfather, a hard-working farmer, were highly respected in the Lapeer, Michigan, area. In addition to the many hours he spent toiling on his farm, Grandfather and his team of fine horses helped other farmers clear their land. He earned ten cents for every tree stump he pulled.

People throughout the county knew Grandmother for her good works and leadership. She was an avid supporter of the Woman's Christian Temperance Union and an advocate of women's suffrage and prison reform.

They faithfully attended First Methodist Episcopal Church with their family of thirteen children. Through my grandparents and church, my mother, Olive, learned about God and His ways.

Mama married Edward Davis, the postmaster in Detroit, when she was 17. At that time, the post office frequently received General Delivery mail for people who didn't have a permanent address. One day Reid Lunsford, a young hobo, came in and inquired about his mail. As other hobos did, Reid had been riding the rails and hitchhiking his way across America in search of a job and a better life. "Do you have anything for me from Georgia?" he asked.

Through their conversation, Edward learned that Reid had left Georgia with a broken heart. He had professed his love for his sweetheart, Frances, and proposed marriage, but because he was "from the other side of the tracks," her parents disapproved of their relationship. They flatly objected and refused to give them their blessing. That's what put him on the hobo trail.

Edward saw something special in Reid and invited him home for a hearty, home-cooked meal. He and my mother always had room for one more. As Reid and Edward got to know each other over time, they became the best of friends.

Reid grew up in a poor family, and his education ended after the sixth grade. Yet he had read all four hundred of the books in the school's library. Edward could tell that the call of God was on his life, so he encouraged him to apply for seminary at Mercer University in Macon, Georgia. Miraculously, the school accepted his application, and he went on to become a Southern Baptist preacher. Also, miraculously, his sweetheart's parents changed their minds and approved of their relationship. He and Frances were married in 1925 in Macon.

Shortly after that, Edward had an appendectomy that led to peritonitis. He died at the young age of 27, leaving Mother on her own at 23 with two small children. Mother notified Reid, and he hitchhiked from Georgia to preach the eulogy at his best friend's funeral in Michigan.

Because she didn't have insurance or widow's benefits, Mother had to rely on her resourcefulness to support her family. For income, she drove a horse-drawn wagon to deliver milk in Detroit, which allowed her to take the children with her.

As a major industrial city, Detroit's railroads bustled with freight train activity, and the hopper cars were often overloaded with coal. Mother and her little ones gathered what fell to the wayside and used it to heat their home. She was also a remarkable seamstress and sewed for others to earn extra money.

Mother didn't have much, but she used what she had to help others, and she gained a reputation for "taking in strays."

When my grandmother died, two of her teenaged daughters still lived at home. My widowed mother took in her sisters so they could finish their education, and her family of three became five.

A plague of diphtheria (a highly infectious respiratory disease) caused the death of many people in Michigan during that time. Mother opened her arms, her heart, and her home to three orphaned neighbors.

She now carried the responsibility for seven children, and our family's legacy of caring for the fatherless and orphaned began. It continues to this day.

In 1931, during the depths of the Great Depression, Mother married Charles Slocum Davis. His original surname was Slocum, but he legally changed it to Davis later on. That worked well for Mother, who was able to keep her previous married name.

Charles was a Roman Catholic with an Irish background. A Methodist Episcopal farm girl from Michigan marrying a Roman Catholic man crossed great denominational lines. It was unheard of in those days!

I came along on July 4, 1932. My parents expected a boy and planned to name him Charles, after my father. Instead, they got a surprise—me. After some quick thinking, they changed the name to Charla and gave me the middle name of Joann. My family often called me Jo.

Mother sent Reid Lunsford a telegram announcing my birth. (Most homes didn't have telephones in 1932, especially in rural areas.) Once again, he hitchhiked to Detroit and dedicated me to the Lord when I was eight days old. What an interesting mix of denominations—a Southern Baptist preacher, a Catholic father, and a Methodist mother!

That was the first time my father and Reid had met, and Mother was a bit concerned because Baptists and Catholics didn't always get along. But their love for books created a bond between them. Father showed off his bookcase filled with a variety of fascinating titles, Reid made a selection, and they hardly spoke a word until 3 a.m. when they retired. They became friends for life.

In those days, whenever a Catholic married a non-Catholic, the couple had to sign an agreement to assure that any children born to them would be educated in the Catholic faith and raised according to its teachings. Because of that, I attended the early morning Latin mass at the Catholic church. Then I would continue on to Sunday school with my mother, which allowed me to learn wonderful stories from the Bible.

Childhood left me with some good memories and others not so good. The fourth of July, my birthday, was always a special occasion. We watched the fireworks display in Eastwood Amusement Park from a second-story window of our home in Detroit, and Father would say, "Do you see that, Joey? They're celebrating your birthday!"

Eventually, I realized the fireworks were actually meant to commemorate the birth of our great nation, and that made my birthday even more meaningful. All these years later, whenever I see fireworks light up the sky, I remember those merry times with my father.

My going-to-school memories, however, aren't so happy. I started first grade in 1938 (we didn't have kindergarten at the time), and by mid-term most children could rattle off the alphabet with ease. After all, it was written above the blackboard that we stared at every day! But when my turn came to recite the ABCs in front of the class, I stood up and said, "ZYXWVUTSRQPONMLKJIHGFEDCBA." The other children laughed, but the teacher just sat in stunned silence.

Humiliation and ridicule seemed to be an inseparable team during most of my elementary years. At least once every few days I had to sit in a corner and face the wall, wearing a tall, pointy dunce cap. Other times my teacher picked up a piece of chalk and drew a circle on the blackboard. She commanded me to keep my nose in that circle while she continued teaching class. I had to stand on my tippy-toes to reach it! Her back-of-the-head eyes stayed plenty busy alerting her to any failure on my part to abide by her orders.

Learning didn't come easily for me. More than once, my father told me, "You're going to have to work extra hard, Charla, because you're not very smart."

For some reason, though, the lessons Mother taught me weren't as hard to grasp. Maybe it's because she lived out what she believed.

On one occasion, our family received a large box of groceries as a gift. I watched as Mother arranged the various canned goods in an unusual manner on the kitchen table. "Why are you sorting the groceries that way?" I asked.

"I want to determine a tithe of this gift to give to the poor," she said.

That seemed so strange to me, and I couldn't believe what she was saying. "Are there any people poorer than we are?"

Mother motioned to ninety percent of the groceries on the table and said in a convincing voice, "Look at all we have. We're blessed." From her, I learned the value of tithing.

In the bleak post-depression days, our cupboards and icebox were seldom full, but Mother was such a marvelous cook and hostess that we didn't realize our lack. When supper was little more than bread and milk, she set the table with a candle or fresh flowers, and cloth napkins.

She celebrated every conceivable holiday with a memorable dessert. On Groundhog Day, we had cupcakes covered with chocolate coconut. For Abraham Lincoln's birthday, she served a cake topped with a Tootsie Roll cabin and flag. On March 17th, we ate green potato soup followed by a cake decorated with shamrocks.

When Mother said, "Save your fork," we knew the best was yet to come. (And years later, when God called her home for His great banquet in heaven, I made sure she held a fork as she lay in her coffin. Those who knew her understood the significance.)

Mama was extraordinarily beautiful, and I often felt ugly and awkward compared to her. It didn't help that my feet were already an adult size ten when I was only in my early elementary school years. To find shoes that would fit, we had to go to the Fyfe Building in downtown Detroit. It was one of Detroit's first high-rises and named after a merchant who made his fortune in the footwear business. Although it claimed the honor of largest shoe store in the world at that time, the only shoes that worked for me were of the Cuban-heeled variety worn by nurses or people with disabilities. They were hideous!

To make matters worse, my legs wouldn't fit under the desktop at school. My feet—with the embarrassing shoes—dangled into the aisle for the whole world to see. My teacher insisted I put them back where they belonged, but that was an impossible task. She finally realized the problem and called the custodian to the classroom to remove the shelf from underneath my desk. I was mortified.

My oversized feet were a disadvantage at school, but they certainly gave me an advantage on the ice. Each winter, the neighborhood children gathered at the vacant lot with their shovels and piled up sod to form a dike. A couple of firemen would arrive in their truck and flood the field after that to create the Manning Avenue ice skating rink. When my brother Warren got a pair of black shoe skates, I fell heir to his clamp-on blades and amazingly learned to skate quite well. In fact, I was so good that I was the only girl allowed to play hockey with the boys.

On my ninth Christmas, I received quite the surprise—an upgrade from the blades. (Many of our earlier Christmases had been dampened because of my father's drinking habit. But our celebrations changed forever after he met two men named Bill and Dr. Bob. I'll tell more about that in the next chapter.)

Before dawn that morning, I crept down the stairs, trying my best to avoid the step that always creaked. I beheld the beautifully decorated tree with tissue-wrapped presents under its boughs—the usual book from Aunt Goldie and the flannel pajamas Mother lovingly made for each of us every year on her treadle sewing machine. But this year, a large square package covered in red paper also bore my name. It was from Santa Claus. I ran my hand over the tissue in an effort to see if the box had writing on it, to no avail. The rest of the family would have to awaken before I could learn of its mysterious contents.

Finally, after what seemed like an eternity of waiting, my mother passed the gift to me. Never could I have imagined what it held—a brand new pair of white Sonja Henie figure skates! (Sonja Henie was a Norwegian Olympic skating star and a favorite of mine.) I could hardly wait to try them out on the ice.

When the time came, and I was able to sit on the banked-up sod surrounding the rink, I opened the box in front of everyone there with an air of pride. My buddies had never seen white ice skates. "You can't play hockey with us wearing those dumb-looking skates," they said.

I sure showed them. Not only could I play hockey, but I also learned to figure skate quite well—which played nicely into snagging the man I would marry seven and a half years later.

I was good when it came to skating, and I received a lot of enjoyment from it, but I continued to struggle with anything related to school. Why was it such a challenge for me? I wondered.

One day, each of us students had to fill out a form asking about our race. That meant nothing to me, but I was too afraid to ask the teacher for clarification. So, I went to the giant dictionary on a pedestal at the front of the classroom to look up the word *race*. There I saw *dog race, horse race,* and *human race*. Now I get it, I thought, and wrote down *human* as my answer.

My teacher called me aside and said loud enough for the whole class to hear, "Well, I might have known that you're a part of the human race." I was so clueless; I had no idea she was belittling me.

Every Monday we received a list of new spelling words for the week. On Thursday nights, Mama drilled me on them and then gave me a paper to study on the way to school the next morning. No matter how much I practiced for the tests or how hard I tried, I rarely spelled more than eleven or twelve correctly. My grade was always an F. I couldn't understand why nobody ever congratulated me for learning a dozen new words.

I'd often come home crying. I ran through the house and up the stairs to my bedroom, where I buried my face in a pillow. "I quit," I said between convulsive sobs. "I'll never learn. What's the use of even trying?"

Mother was never too far behind. In her quiet, consoling way, she'd remind me, "Charla, it's always too soon to quit." She had a way of knowing what to say.

I badly wanted to give up on school and my studies—it was too difficult for me—but with other things I was determined to make a difference, just like my grandmother did. Sometimes I felt like I could take on the world.

On December 8, 1941, our family was gathered around the dining room table listening to the radio when the President of the United States, Franklin D. Roosevelt, interrupted the broadcast. He spoke these somber words: "Yesterday, December 7, 1941—a date which will live in infamy—the United States of America was suddenly and deliberately attacked by the naval and air forces of the Empire of Japan."[1] He went on to say that many American lives had been lost because of the bombing of Pearl Harbor.

---

1 https://www.archives.gov/publications/prologue/2001/winter/crafting-day-of-infamy-speech.html

A holy hush came upon us as we realized that our country was going to war. I was a young girl and knew nothing about Pearl Harbor or Japan, but I sensed the seriousness of the situation. I broke the silence and boldly declared, "We must win this war!" My parents and siblings laughed, which distracted from the gravity of the occasion, but I meant it.

I soon discovered that bacon fat—something most people had—contributed to the manufacturing of explosives. So, I grabbed my little red wagon by the handle and walked through my neighborhood every Saturday morning. I stopped at each house, knocked on the door, and gave my best let's-help-our-soldiers speech. "Do you have any spare bacon fat you can donate to help us win the war?" I asked. The neighbors smiled at my efforts and gave generously of their fat. My weekly haul was then turned in to the local meat market.

Shortly after that, I also learned tin cans could be used in the production of ammunition. I added the searching for discarded cans in Detroit alleyways to my Saturday routine. It was a "she hath done what she could" project for me, and I continued to do it until we moved to Richmond, California, a few years later.

Life took a dramatic turn for me when I got to the fifth grade. I had a teacher who disregarded my dismal academic record that implied I was mentally retarded—a term used at the time to indicate severe learning disabilities. Today, teachers and medical professionals would recognize my challenges as dyslexia and dysgraphia, conditions in the brain that make reading, writing, and spelling difficult.

Miss Devries saw my potential and took a different approach to teaching me. She promised that if I would read Felix Salten's book *Bambi*, she'd take me to the soon-to-be-released motion picture by the same name that was scheduled to show at the elegant Fox Theatre in downtown Detroit. That was just the incentive I needed. I was so excited, I actually finished the book! As I sat with her during the matinee, I stared in awe at the beautiful chandeliers in that huge theater, amazed to have won such a prize.

My now favorite teacher began supplying me with short missionary classics distributed by Moody Press. With great interest, I read stories about David Livingstone, Mary Slessor, Hudson Taylor, Gladys Aylward, and so many more. As soon as I finished one book, Miss Devries gave me another. Those inspirational biographies planted the seeds for my missionary desires.

From that point on, I excelled in school and graduated at the age of 16. Because of my unpleasant early experiences, I realized the importance of literacy. Providing others with opportunities to receive a good education has since become one of my greatest passions. I know the difference it can make in a life.

Another life-changing factor for me came at the age of 12, just as my spiritual sensitivity was heightening. I received a special invitation from Reid Lunsford to spend the summer with his family. He now lived in Asheville, North Carolina, and oversaw the ministry of the Eliada Orphanage, home to more than one hundred children. Much to my surprise, Mother put me on the bus in Detroit and allowed me to make the 700-mile trip alone.

That adventure taught me a great deal about people and about myself. While there, I spent a lot of time with the orphans who lived at the facility and made some fascinating observations. They came from diverse backgrounds, but they were just like other children. In fact, they were just like me. The only difference is that they didn't have the advantage of loving parents. I returned home with a new perspective and a lasting impression on my heart.

Little did I know at the time what an impact Reid—the man who dedicated me to the Lord as an infant—would have on my life. He mentored and guided me up until the time he died from a terminal disease. My husband, Chuck, and I visited him frequently in his beloved desert home in Phoenix, Arizona.

Because of Reid's love for the desert, I took advantage of the oil painting classes our church offered in 1966 and created a picture of an agave (a desert cactus) for him. The paint on my artwork wasn't even dry when we received the call from a family member. "Come now," they said. "His departure is very near." Reid was still coherent when we got there and delighted with the painting.

As we gathered with family around his hospital bed in the living room, Chuck began to sing the treasured old hymn "In the Garden." When he sang the words "and the voice I hear . . . the Son of God is calling," an angel appeared in the room. Some in the group saw it; others felt its presence. And Reid went to his eternal home with a heavenly escort.

Unfortunately, Reid died just a few months before Chuck and I made our initial trip to the Baja Peninsula in October 1966 that brought about our ministry in Mexico. When negotiations began toward the purchase of the mission property in Colonia Vicente Guerrero in spring of 1967, the hills of Baja were covered with agave. I thought of Reid and had a strong sense that the trip was preordained.

He never got to see the children's homes or churches or Bible school or the rest of the fruit. He never knew the outcome of his investment in my life. But God knows and I know. Much of the work we do through Foundation for His Ministry is due to his mentorship and prayers for me over the years.

I often wondered what became of the agave artwork after Reid died. Much to my surprise, when I spoke at the Lutheran Church of Joy in Glendale, Arizona, in 2012, Reid's daughter June came to the service. She had with her the painting I hadn't seen in more than forty-six years. It now hangs in a spare bedroom of our house and serves as a precious reminder of Reid's inspiration and God's blessing.

Today, as I reflect on my early influences, I see clearly how God's hand worked in my life, preparing me for what was to come. He didn't waste a thing. These insightful words written so long ago come to mind: "And we know that in all things God works for the good of those who love him, who have been called according to his purpose" (Romans 8:28, NIV).

I determined at a young age that I wanted to be like my great grandmother—a woman who did what she could.

When I entered first grade, I was 6 years old. Because I was dyslexic, I memorized the alphabet from right to left. One day, the teacher called on me to recite it, and I did—from Z to A. I didn't know why the other students laughed.

I painted this landscape for Reid Lunsford in 1966. More than four decades later, his adult children gave it back to me. It was a precious gift because I thought it was lost.

Alcoholics Anonymous and the Salvation Army

When I was a young adult, I asked my mother, "Mama, why on earth would an upright Methodist Episcopal farm girl from Michigan marry an Irish Roman Catholic alcoholic?"

She snappily responded with, "I didn't know he drank!"

Father couldn't let her have the last word. "Any man who would marry a widow with seven children in the heart of the Great Depression had to be drunk!" He followed with, "But you know, Charla, I was wild about your mother and always have been."

The conversation was funny at the time, but as a child living with an alcoholic, not so much.

My father got his first taste of the bottle as a teen, and before long he was hooked. He developed an addiction by the time he turned 25. Early in my parents' marriage, his alcoholism became progressively more and more destructive.

On Christmas Eve in 1936, Mother gave him $5 and sent him out to find a Christmas tree. "Get the best one you can, Charlie," she said, "and don't pay more than a dollar." As he was about to leave, she called out from the kitchen, "Take Charla with you."

I bounced down the front steps, so excited to have a little excursion with my father. I couldn't wait to find the perfect tree and then decorate it once we got home. However, we never made it to the Christmas tree lot.

Father got sidetracked with the need for liquid fortification before we could even start our outing. "Let's make a quick stop first," he said, and we entered Paddy's Saloon. He located an empty stool for himself and lifted me to the bar top, where I snacked on O-KE-DOKE cheese-flavored popcorn while he touted the greatness of the Irish with the other boozers.

One drink led to two, and two led to three. And on it went. Eventually, he ran out of money and was quite drunk when the bartender threw him out for starting "Irish arguments."

We walked across the dirty-slushy Detroit street and reached the curb on the other side. Then my father stumbled and fell face down in the gutter. Horrified, I cried out to passersby because I couldn't lift him myself. "Help me! Please help me!" I said in my loudest 4-year-old voice.

As I paced around my father, I could hear their whispers. "Tsk, tsk, tsk." They shook their heads in disgust, wrapped their coats tighter around them, and walked by. Some even went to such great lengths as crossing the street just to avoid us.

I didn't know what to do, and I felt so alone. The only thing that seemed right was to bury my face in my hands and cry. So that's what I did. Eventually, I lifted my head and saw a kind man wearing a uniform standing beside us. He looked like a soldier, but in those days the only uniformed men on the streets of Detroit on Christmas Eve were from the Salvation Army.

That gentle soul was like none other. He lovingly reached down into the gutter, rescued my father, and helped us home. Then our Good Samaritan disappeared as quickly as he appeared.

Sadly, we didn't have a festive tree decorated with tinsel and lights to gather around that Christmas morning, but Mother made sure we still had the traditional flannel pajamas. And much to our delight, my adopted Aunt Ruth showed up at our home, surprising us all by wearing a cotton batting beard and her old red coat with cotton basted on the front. She came through the door saying, "Ho, Ho, Ho," and gave each of us a red and white candy cane.

"Santa's" visit turned what could have been a gloomy holiday into a memorable occasion. Every year since then, Santa has made an annual appearance at our Christmas celebrations, always cheerfully acknowledging the true reason for the season.

A few years went by, and Father's desperation only got worse. By the fall of 1939, Mother had nearly given up hope. Then one day she went to the mailbox, and her weekly copy of *Liberty*, a popular general interest magazine, was there.

She glanced at the cover and saw these words in big, bold letters along the bottom edge: "Alcoholics and God." Quickly, she flipped through the pages until she found the article written by Morris Markey. The first sentence said, "Is there hope for habitual drunkards?" As she continued reading, she learned about two men from Akron, Ohio, who claimed to have found a cure for alcoholism. It was the first national publicity for a new group called Alcoholics Anonymous.

Mother contacted Dr. Bob Smith, one of the co-founders of the organization. He insisted she take my father to Akron without delay. Convinced she might have found the answer they needed, she loaded up the old Pontiac and headed to Ohio with Father that weekend. Once there, she turned him over to the care of Dr. Bob and his partner, Bill Wilson, and within a few days of working with them, he was sober!

Soon after returning to Detroit, my parents opened their home on Manning Avenue to host some of the first ever areawide AA meetings. By early 1940, the gatherings had outgrown their basement, and three new groups were started throughout Detroit. Salvationists from the citadel heard of their success and invited my father to come share with them about what was happening with the fast-growing movement.

When the time came to do that, he left the *Detroit Times*, where he worked as the foreman of the press room, and walked a short distance to Michigan Avenue to skid row and the citadel, grateful for the opportunity. As he approached, he heard a booming voice coming from the Salvation Army mission. Curious, he peered inside and became captivated by an animated and rotund older gentleman who was telling fascinating stories of his life, his failures, and his miraculous redemption.

Henry F. Milans, who had been preaching at the Detroit mission for weeks, shared about his success as a prominent New York newspaper editor when in his early twenties. He talked of his lovely wife and fine home. And then he told about his penchant for drink. Like with so many others, one was never enough. By the time he turned 30, his alcoholism had destroyed his career and marriage. Blacklisted, penniless, drunk, and out of work, he ended up at the New York Bowery, trading all his possessions—including his shoes—for "whiskey credit."

In 1908, doctors at Bellevue Hospital in New York diagnosed him as hopelessly incurable and released him to live on the streets. Then he heard about a Boozer's Convention put on by the Salvation Army. He attended the nightly meetings, and on Thursday—after a full week of learning about the power of God—the Holy Spirit convicted him. With a contrite heart, he repented of his wrongdoing and asked God to rescue him from the grips of alcohol and the pits of despair. And God did a miracle in his life.

As my father listened to Henry, he realized he wanted that same power at work in his life. He left the back of the room and fell to his knees in penitent form. After praying for deliverance from his sin, he experienced his own miracle that night. Alcoholics Anonymous had helped him get sober; the Salvation Army led him to God.

Once Father got home, he shared the story with Mother. She was overjoyed! "I want to meet that man," she said. "I need to express my gratitude."

When they went to the Bowery to talk with Henry, Mother learned he was 79 years old, nearly blind, and living alone in a Detroit hotel. She couldn't tolerate the thought of that.

"You absolutely must come home and live with us," she said. Because of her insistence, he moved in with our family on Manning Avenue and became Grandpa Milans to me.

By the time of his death in 1946, he had earned the moniker of "The Correspondent Evangelist" for the thousands of letters he wrote reaching out to alcoholics and their families throughout the United States and abroad. And he's among only a small group of individuals around the world to be awarded with Salvation Army's highest honor—Order of the Founder.

He taught me a lot while he stayed with us, and his tenderhearted compassion during some of my most difficult years was instrumental in forming my character.

In the spring of 1945, as World War II was nearing its end, my father received a job offer from Mare Island Naval Shipyard, and our family moved to Richmond, California. It wasn't too long after we arrived that my parents started up new AA meetings in the area.

We lived across San Francisco Bay from San Quentin Prison—a maximum-security correctional facility, and one of the most famous in the United States. The warden at that time was Clinton Duffy, a big proponent of prisoner education, rehabilitation, and reform. Knowing alcohol and addiction played a huge role in crimes committed, he wanted to get to the heart of that problem. He discovered AA and started the first prison group in the world. Over time, the program resulted in drastically reduced recidivism rates.

Warden Duffy met my father at an Alcoholics Anonymous meeting and asked him to be involved at the prison. Until they moved to Los Angeles in 1946, my parents hosted AA groups for hardened criminals, allowing them to offer hope, develop redemptive relationships, and experience the joy of changed lives.

I know my empathy for alcoholics, addicts, and prisoners—and my desire to help them—is in large part due to my childhood years. I sat in a front row seat for the show of destruction and despair that comes through addiction's control. And I saw first-hand the transformation that happens when God's power is given full reign.

The important work of Alcoholics Anonymous and the Salvation Army brought light into my family's darkness. My desire is to keep that light shining for others in a similar place.

Henry Milans

Henry Milans of the Salvation Army came to our house and lived with us for six years. He led my dad to the Lord and was like a grandpa to me.

Great Things for God

The move to California at the age of 13 was tremendously difficult for me. For one thing, the weather didn't cooperate with my young lifestyle. It was rarely warm enough to swim or cold enough to ice skate. I liked to do both. And now I was well more than two thousand miles away from sixty-eight first cousins on my mother's side. She had a wonderful, tight-knit family who lived on rural Michigan farms, and I loved being with them. I missed the times we had together.

I was painfully shy, but eventually I met a girl who had recently been released from a Japanese internment camp. We became friends, and one afternoon she invited me to her humble abode. By the time I began my walk home, the Bay Area air was cold. I can't remember whether I'd forgotten my coat or what, but I had a good case of the shivers and looked for a place to warm up.

I noticed a little Baptist church with a light on. *I'll step into the narthex for a few minutes before going the rest of the way home.* It was an innocent thought.

As soon as I entered the building, a man standing near the door shoved a hymnal in my hands and ushered me to a front-row seat where a service was already in progress. (Because of the way I was raised, I had no idea churches had evening services, nor had I ever seen a hymnal!) How did I get into this mess? I wondered.

My parents expected me home at a certain time. The sky was getting dark. And I didn't know how to leave without calling attention to myself. So, at that moment, I prayed probably the sincerest prayer I've ever prayed. "Help! Get me out of here!"

Just then the pastor got up and started preaching. He gave a message I'd never heard before about the love of God. God's love can't be earned. It's not about being good or bad. It's totally engulfing and unconditional.

As I listened, I thought about what that meant to me: It doesn't matter how often I go to confession. It doesn't matter how many candles I light. It doesn't matter how many good works I do, like trying to win the war. What matters is that God loves me *just as I am*. That was a whole new concept for me.

At the end of his sermon, the pastor invited anyone who wanted to know more, or who wanted to pray, to come forward. I didn't understand everything, and I had no idea what was happening inside of me, but something drew me to the altar. On that cold California night in a Southern Baptist church, I obeyed the Holy Spirit's wooing, prayed with the pastor, and gave my heart to God.

I left there basking in God's transforming love, and I had no doubt in my mind that I was born again.

I could hardly wait to tell my parents about my experience, so I ran the last couple of blocks until I reached our home. (We lived in a long barracks building provided by Kaiser Shipyards.) Bursting through the door, I called out in search for my father. "Dad . . . Dad?" I found him where I suspected he'd be—in the living room chair reading a book.

Without even telling him where I had been, I exclaimed, "Daddy, I want to do great things for God!"

He slid his reading glasses to his forehead, looked at me intently, and said, "What?"

"I want to do great things for God," I repeated.

And my father—someone who worshiped the God of the universe, the God who created all things and held all things together—asked, "What makes you think you can do anything for Almighty God, Charla? He doesn't need your help."

I don't know what I expected him to say, and I sure didn't know how to describe what happened to me in that service. But I wanted him to understand that I had just experienced the love of God in a powerful way, and I desired to do something about it.

Mother heard us talking and came in from the kitchen. She'll understand, I thought. She's always reading her Bible and her little devotional book called *The Upper Room*. So, I said, "Mother, I want to do great things for God."

"You can start by making your bed," she said. Obviously, she didn't get what I was trying to say. Besides that, I already did make my bed!

As I tried to sleep that night, the events of the day replayed in my mind, and I pondered my newfound passion to serve the Lord. I'm sure my parents wondered about a lot of things too, especially since they still had no idea where I had been or what had happened.

The next morning, without mentioning our earlier discussion, my mother said, "Charla, do the kindest thing you can do today, and you will always be in the center of God's will."

At the time I thought it was an oversimplification of what I meant. I was a new person in Christ, and I longed to accomplish great things for God! But over the years I've learned that what she said made a lot of sense. Embracing a child, writing a letter, visiting a prisoner, or even touching someone's shoulder while praying for them can make an eternal difference.

My family moved again in 1946—this time to the San Fernando Valley in Southern California. My father gave me permission to attend any church I wanted. Because of my special experience at the little Baptist church in Richmond, I started out my hunt with First Baptist Church in Van Nuys. But the message disappointed me. I went to the

Methodist church where my mother attended, and it didn't meet the need.

I visited church after church trying to find one that talked about, and demonstrated, the amazing love of God—the most transforming power on earth. I finally decided that maybe there's no place quite like the place I first met Jesus.

Then a girlfriend invited me to a Saturday night social event, sponsored by a Lutheran church. When I found out it involved ice skating, I said, "Yes, yes, yes, I'd love to go! I haven't skated since we moved from Michigan, and that was a long time ago."

We met at the church, and on my way to the office to check in, I saw the most handsome guy I had ever seen standing in the doorway. I mean, he was drop dead gorgeous! Immediately, my heart started racing. I was spellbound. Right then and there I made one of the most important decisions of my life—that I would become a Lutheran!

Somehow, I finagled a ride to the skating rink in the same car as "Mr. Wonderful." We got acquainted, and he made it known that he was a pro when it came to skating. I learned differently when we got on the ice.

He couldn't even stand without falling! I suppressed my giggles and kindly ushered him off the rink. Later, he said, "Well . . . I can roller skate. I thought ice skating would be similar."

After I got home that night, my father asked where I'd been. "I went to an ice-skating party with Emmanuel Lutheran Church's youth group in North Hollywood. It was fun. I think I might visit there tomorrow morning."

And my father, raised a staunch Catholic who was well aware of the long-time feud between the Catholic and Lutheran denominations, said in a snarky voice, "I suppose you'll visit a synagogue next." I just ignored him.

My fondness for Mr. Wonderful, also known as Chuck Pereau, grew quickly. The more time I spent with him, the more I admired his good heart and strong work ethic.

Originally from Rolla, Missouri, his parents had moved their family of six siblings to St. Louis in hopes of finding work, but the Great Depression made that difficult. At the young age of 7, Chuck chipped in to help with the finances by vending newspapers on the streets.

Because of available jobs at Lockheed Aircraft Corporation in Burbank, his family moved to California in 1943. There, he became a pinsetter at a bowling alley when he was 13. (That was before mechanical pinsetters were used.) He stood at the end of the alley and manually cleared fallen pins, returned balls to the players, and reset the pins to their correct position. Many times, he worked past midnight. In the spring of his seventeenth year, he started doing construction work. All his earnings went to his parents.

Some of Chuck's high school buddies invited him to play baseball at Emmanuel Lutheran Church's field in North Hollywood. It was a lighted field, which was rare in the 1940s. Chuck loved baseball, so he readily accepted the invitation. Following the game, the pastor, Norman Hammer, took Chuck aside and talked to him about Jesus. That night, Chuck entered into a relationship with the pastor and, even more important, with the Lord. He then started attending the Lutheran church where I first saw him.

Over time, Pastor Hammer got to know him well. He recognized his potential and started preparing him for ministry. Although Chuck already had a good job in construction, the pastor encouraged him to attend the Lutheran Bible Institute in Seattle, Washington.

I heard about his plans and had an immediate interest in attending the same school. My parents were disappointed in my decision, especially since I turned down a scholarship opportunity elsewhere, but I had to follow my heart. I couldn't let the man of my dreams go without me, could I?

To be honest, the instructors at the Bible institute were boring. But every Tuesday morning, Reverend Rieke, a local pastor, came to teach a class on missions. It was the highlight of my week. He told stories that reminded me of the books I had read in fifth grade, and I longed to learn more from him.

He started each class with a song titled "Lord, Lay Some Soul Upon My Heart." He sang it acapella and often wept as the words—a prayer—flowed from his mouth.

Pastor Rieke had a global concept of God. His God was big. And his God had a plan to reach the entire world with His amazing love. Although I had experienced the transforming love of God for myself, Pastor Rieke's teachings gave me a new perspective. His desire to reach the lost became my burning desire as well.

I'd sit in class and pray, "Lord, give me a passion like Pastor Rieke's to reach the world for You. Your love is the only thing that will make a difference in people's lives. Your love is what will change the world."

The spark that caused me to want to do great things for God as a 13-year-old girl was kindled in Bible school and has since become a full-blown blaze.

To this day I wake up each morning with Pastor Rieke's precious song on my heart. It's my earnest plea that God would love others through me and help me to win souls for Him.

At the age of 13, I boldly proclaimed, "I want to do great things for God!"

A New Family Member

A month after we came home from Bible school, I said to Chuck, "Are you going to marry me, or not?" He said yes, and on July 21, 1949, we got on a Greyhound bus and eloped at the Gretna Green Wedding Chapel in Yuma, Arizona. He was 19 and I had just turned 17.

We both signed up for fall classes at Los Angeles Valley College (LAVC), a newly opened community college in the east central San Fernando Valley. At the time, our only transportation to school (or anywhere) was a Cushman motor scooter.

We paid $85 a month to live in a guest house in Reseda, California, but it didn't have heat or hot water. It didn't even have its own bathroom. We had to cross the patio and enter our landlord's home to use his. That got old fast.

A "for sale by owner" ad in the *Van Nuys Green Sheet* caught our attention. It was for a GI home in Sylmar, the northernmost neighborhood in Los Angeles. We took a look at the jim-dandy home, and it was love at first sight. The problem, though, is that we would need a $400 down payment and an escrow payment of $48. We had only $200. We also needed to secure a mortgage. Pride prevented us from going to our parents for money.

On our way home, I saw a Bank of California sign at the corner of Reseda Boulevard and Sherman Way. The word "loans" popped out at me. I went to the bank the next morning at ten and waited in line to apply. A man standing in front of me politely asked why I was there. I said, "I want to buy a house."

"You know, you have to have collateral or access to collateral for the bank to make such a loan," he said.

"What do you mean? We're going to pay it back with interest." At 17, I was too young and naïve to understand how complex financial matters worked. (Years later I went into real estate, but that's another story.) I filled out the loan application, and somehow it was approved. Perhaps the stranger in line co-signed for me. To this day I still don't know.

Thankfully, a dear friend from Emmanuel Lutheran Church loaned us the remaining funds needed for a down payment. I can't remember how we got escrow money, but it all came together for us to purchase the house.

Although we were grateful for Chuck's part-time job as a custodian at the school, we were so poor we lived on catsup and split pea soup. Our dire circumstances caused many tears during our first years together.

Chuck felt called to ministry, so after completing a year at Los Angeles Valley College, we met with a pastor for counseling. The pastor said, "Chuck, if God has genuinely called you into the ministry, you wouldn't be happy doing anything else but preaching the gospel."

"I really love doing construction work," Chuck said, "and especially cement work more than anything."

"Then God has not called you into the ministry." The pastor's wise counsel was liberating. Chuck soon started a job doing cement work, and in less than two years he had a contractor's license.

What the pastor didn't know—and maybe Chuck didn't even realize at the time—is that God *had* called him to ministry, but not in the usual form. (When a person has a servant's heart like Chuck, they always have a ministry.) Chuck laid much of the concrete for our church and for many other churches and ministries without pay. For him, laying foundations was a delight. He did his best work on his knees!

My father recognized Chuck's benevolent spirit and his inability to say no. He took him aside and said, "You have to get a regular job that pays real money. You can use your contracting skills on the side, but you really need something that will put food on the table."

Chuck followed my father's advice and applied for a fireman position, which would give him three days off a week and still allow him to do cement work. He passed the exam with a top-ten-percent score and served for twenty-seven years, eventually becoming a fire inspector. But his first love was always cement finishing, something he continued to do throughout his life. (He finally laid down his trowels at the age of 86.)

∽∽

As we learned about missions in Bible school, both of us desired to be world Christians and to reach people near and far away with God's love. We decided that although we might not be able to physically go to the mission field, we could always give.

When I was younger, my mother taught me the importance of tithing. She'd often say, "You cannot out-give God." So, even as poor as Chuck and I were when we started our married life together, we set aside a tithe for God's work. We still practice that discipline.

We also kept a little box on a shelf in our kitchen that we called "God's box." Over the years, any extra money we had went there. If we were tempted to make an unnecessary purchase, we put the funds in God's box instead. That money was above and beyond our tithe, and we used it for missionary gifts and special needs related to God's work.

One day in 1961, twelve years after we married, I read a blurb in our church bulletin about a missionary pastor who worked with the Zapotec people in a remote area of Mexico, where Wycliffe Bible translators had been. Pastor Nehrenz's ministry with this indigenous group in the southern state of Oaxaca intrigued me.

Curious to know more, and wanting to support the missionary, I took all the money we had in God's box—$10—and stuck it in an envelope with a note. I asked a few questions and assured the missionary of our prayers. Then I sent it to him in care of Pastor Harold Moench, a pastor who served in San Antonio, Texas.

After several weeks, we received a response that came through the San Antonio pastor. The first paragraph said, "Thank you for your $10 donation." I smiled, pleased that it had been received.

The second paragraph—a long one—was typical of many missionary letters, which give updates on the highs and lows of their ministry. It reported the heart-wrenching story of a teenaged girl who was unwed and soon to be a mother. She faced terrific shame and rejection from her people. Pastor Nehrenz had shared with her about the transforming power of God's love, and she prayed—just as I had years earlier—to receive Christ as her personal Savior. That's great news, I thought.

The pastor and this young lady had also been praying that God would provide a Christian home for her baby. I made a mental note to add that situation to my prayer list.

Then I got to the third paragraph, which wasn't so typical. It said, "We were led to write you . . ."

I wasn't familiar with that particular expression at the time, and it gave me a strange feeling. The words that followed greatly increased the strange feeling. "Would you consider adopting her baby?"

Certain I had misread it, I looked at it again, this time more carefully. "Would you consider adopting her baby?"

Nope. I had it right the first time.

As the words sunk in, the pastor's crazy question triggered a flood of rapidly flowing thoughts, which changed mid-stream to a full-fledged verbal rant. It didn't matter that no one was home to hear it. "Seriously?" I said. "I mailed him $10 and now he wants to send me a free sample? What was he thinking?" I shook my head in disbelief.

"He must be nuts. He doesn't know anything about us! He doesn't know our family or our circumstances. Besides that, I don't know a thing about Oaxaca. I don't even know how to pronounce it! And they want me to adopt a child—a newborn baby—from there?"

As soon as Chuck got home from work that day, I handed him the letter and said, "You have to sit down before you read this. You're never going to believe it."

Chuck sat at the kitchen table, read the letter, and contemplated it for a minute. He said softly, "Well, maybe we should pray about it."

I wasn't ready to hear that. I was a wife and mother who had just gone through twelve long, wearing years. We had three school-aged children and a nephew we were caring for. I had plans, and a baby was not on that list!

I pulled out all the ammunition I could find. Of course, that meant using Chuck's proper name. "Charles, I don't need to pray about it. You know I've signed up to take the Bethel series. I'm going to deliver tapes to the shut-ins at church. I'm teaching Sunday school." I gave him a long list of things I planned to do, and in a higher-than-normal-decibel voice I said, "I want to do great things for God! How can I do that with a baby?"

"All he's asking you to do is pray about it."

I tried another approach this time—the financial one. "Half of our income goes to Laurel Hall School for tuition." Then I pointed dramatically toward the kitchen floor. "And look at this linoleum! Do you see how worn out it is and how it's taped down so people won't stumble over it? Our washing machine is on the fritz. We're already trying to feed four children, and we have one with special needs. Our house is too small." All good reasons, right?

Chuck stayed calm the entire time. He listened to my long-winded discourse and said, "Why don't you talk to Pastor Wold about it?"

I gave in and showed the letter to our pastor the next day. He told me he knew Pastor Nehrenz, the missionary, and was familiar with his ministry in Mexico. Then he asked, "Have you prayed about it?"

"I don't need to pray about it! I'm not interested in a baby!"

After several days of wrestling with questions and dealing with inner turmoil, I answered the missionary's query. I listed every possible excuse—along with explanations—for why I was the wrong person to adopt this child. He should see that clearly as he reads my letter, I thought.

A week or two later, I received a message from a member of the San Antonio pastor's congregation. Mrs. Shawd "felt led" to write me and asked that I prayerfully consider taking the baby. Other people, including some of my dearest friends, "felt led" on my behalf as well.

Why did everyone else but me feel led about my personal business? I wondered.

Eventually, I got to a position where I questioned how this matter fit into God's will. I needed to talk with someone who was wise and discerning, someone I could trust to help me work out my deep concerns. So, I met up with Marge, my pastor's wife. I spilled out everything that was on my heart.

She looked me directly in the eyes and asked a series of significant questions. I could sense the care in her voice. "Charla, you've been born again, haven't you?" I had no doubt what it meant to be born again, and I nodded. "Okay, if you've been born again, you're a child of the King of kings, the Lord of lords. Do you believe that nothing can come into your life that doesn't first come by the throne of grace?"

I thought about that for a while. And I remembered the sign that hung in my mother's kitchen for years. It said,

"God is love." I *knew* God's love. I had *experienced* God's love. Suddenly, several important truths came to mind. The first was that if I'm a child of God, then He's personally concerned about every intimate detail of my life. The second truth was that God allows things to come into our lives—and allows us to go through things—for our ultimate good. It's not always an easy concept to grasp.

So, I went home, and although I was still struggling, knelt by the couch and prayed. "Well, God, I don't understand about this little baby and the mountains of Oaxaca and the Zapotecs. I really don't. But, to the best of my ability I can say, 'Thy will be done on earth as it is in heaven.' I can trust that You want only good for me. I can trust You."

I got up from my knees and felt as if a knapsack of rocks had been taken off my back. Then I did everything in my power to find another home for that baby!

I really thought I had done my part by saying, "Thy will be done," and God would just send the child to someone else.

Finally, I halfheartedly acquiesced and wrote Pastor Moench a note. "If you try every possible avenue and absolutely cannot find anyone else to take the baby, I guess we'll do it."

Still believing God would provide another family, I felt at peace about the circumstances.

That peace dwindled on November 9, 1961, when at about 6 p.m. I received a phone call from Pastor Moench. "Mrs. Pereau," he said, "your new baby boy has been born."

I thought I was going to die.

The pastor told me how the very pregnant Zapotec girl had taken many buses to get to San Antonio from Oaxaca. She was staying at his home and delivered her baby there with the help of a doctor.

I was so shaken by everything I learned that I could hardly think straight. However, I had an important Sunday school teachers' meeting at the church within the hour, and I needed to turn my attention to that.

I went to the church, longing to erase the memories of what had just happened. At that particular moment, attending a meeting was the last thing I wanted to do. But when I walked into the room, I got the shock of my life. It was a baby shower—for me! My friend Ruth Marshall had an inner knowing that God was going to send that little baby to our family, and she planned the shower to help us get ready. What Ruth didn't know is that he had been born just a few hours earlier.

Probably about a hundred women were in the room, as well as everything a baby could need—a crib, a stroller, diapers, clothes, bottles. On top of that, a new washing machine would be delivered to our home! The shower hostesses presented me with a small purse with $178 inside. Someone had taken up a collection from all of the Sunday school children I had taught over the years. It was enough money to cover round trip airfare to San Antonio.

The next morning, I booked a flight to Texas. The plan was to meet up with Pastor Moench the following day at the San Antonio airport. He would give the infant to me, and I would take the return flight to LAX. But due to poor weather conditions, the plan didn't work. He ended up driving me to his home.

Mrs. Shawd was there and came into the living room holding a tiny baby boy bundled in a pink blanket. I'd never seen an indigenous baby before, and this one had a full head of thick black hair. He looked nothing like our children.

I thought about his name. If he were raised in Mexico, he might have been called Lucio or Manuel or something similar. Instead, the little one I gazed at would become the namesake of the 31st vice president of the United States—Charles Curtis, a leader with significant Native American ancestry. (Our history-buff son, Dana, suggested the name, and the whole family agreed it was perfect.) And he would carry the last name of Pereau.

As I listened to his quiet breathing, observed his baby-sized movements, and counted his itty-bitty fingers and toes, reality hit that he would be going home with me.

"Would you consider meeting his mother?" Pastor Moench asked. "Seeing you would remove her fears and give her peace of mind that she's done the right thing."

I understood the reasoning and hesitantly agreed. Within a few minutes, a beautiful, dark-haired teen, with almond-shaped eyes and brownish skin, entered the room. She was a petite thing—not even five feet tall—and she exhibited far more self-confidence and grace than I.

The young lady looked at me, and with the help of a translator said, "Mrs. Pereau, are you happy with your son?" I smiled and nodded my approval. "Then I leave you accountable only to God for his care."

My father told Chuck he needed to get a regular job that pays real money, so he became a fireman. Here he is in his uniform.

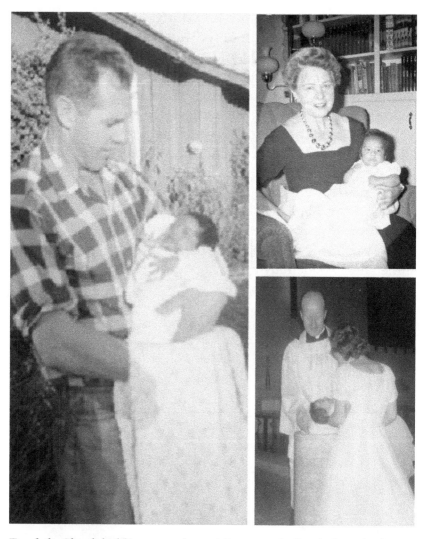

Top left: Chuck holding our adopted Oaxacan Indian baby, Charles Curtis

Top right: My mother, Olive Davis Thayer, with Charles Curtis

Bottom right: Pastor Erling Wold baptized Charles Curtis. His big sister, Colleen Andrea, is holding him.

Never the Same

When I left Texas, I had a newborn baby in my arms. I didn't know what God had planned for his life or ours. I didn't know how our extended family, church friends, acquaintances, or people on the street would receive him. All I knew was that I would be returning to California and starting over with middle-of-the-night feedings, diaper changes, and everything else baby-related.

Chuck met me at LAX. (In those days, you could meet passengers at the gate.) He took the little bundle into his arms and turned back the pink covering. As he gazed at Curtis's face and gently stroked his soft cheek, I could see the wonder in his eyes. He turned toward me and said, "Oh, he is so beautiful!" It's a moment I'll never forget. Chuck has repeated that statement many times since then.

We drove to our home in North Hollywood, where family and friends were awaiting the new arrival. The date was November 11—11/11—Armistice Day. Now, every year as veterans are honored with the holiday, I think about the spiritual significance of the day I brought Curtis home. It was a new beginning for us, a transition into an amazing plan that God had in store.

Our children immediately fell in love with Charles Curtis. The people at church welcomed him with open arms. In fact, they gave him his acting debut at six weeks old when he played the first-ever infant Jesus in the manger at the big "Night in Bethlehem" production.

Reactions from people outside the family and church varied, but my favorite was our mail carrier's. One day, he came to the door while I was holding a bundled-up Charles Curtis. Surprised at seeing a baby, he said, "I didn't even know you were expecting."

I turned Curtis toward him as a way of introduction, and the shocked look on the mailman's face was priceless. He had noticed his dark eyes, hair, and skin tone, and said, "How will you understand him?" After that encounter, I wondered how our mail ever got delivered.

Social workers frowned on interracial adoptions in the sixties, and we went through a difficult and complicated adoption process. But through it all, these things were certain—he was heaven sent, he was our son, he belonged to our family, and the deep love that grew in our hearts for him was unwavering.

The more our love grew, the more we paid attention to news events and reports of conditions south of the border. Concern for our Mexican neighbors began to develop.

"Lord, why did You move Charles Curtis thousands of miles away from his people? Why did You spare his life? Why did You entrust him with us?" I had so many questions for God, and even though I didn't understand everything, I was thankful. Oh, so thankful.

Because of the way he came to us, we couldn't help but sense God had something special planned. I often prayed, "Lord, what do You have in mind?" I spent a lot of time pondering the future.

Perhaps Charles Curtis will one day go to Oaxaca and become a mighty evangelist to his people. Maybe he'll go into remote mountain regions and reach the lost. I was fixed on those thoughts, so we consistently fed him the Word. We invested in his spiritual training. We taught him everything he needed to know in preparation for becoming a great missionary.

But God was at work on another plan.

I read a *Newsweek* article about the plight of abandoned children in Mexico. More than a million children trying to survive on their own. More than a million children living in squalor, digging through garbage for food, and sleeping in streets, sewers, and dumps. More than a million children with bronze-colored skin, dark eyes, and black hair—just like our precious Charles Curtis.

How does a person with a beating heart respond to something like that? All I could do was cry out to God. "Why, God, why? Why is this happening? It doesn't make any sense! Please show me what I can do to help!"

Then God gave us our own up-front-and-personal glimpse of Mexico in 1965. A local Lutheran Bible institute had taken on a mission project to gather clothing, blankets, and supplies for an orphanage in Tijuana. Knowing Chuck had a servant's heart and that he had extra time off because he was a fireman, they asked him to take the load of donations across the border. I decided to join him on the trip. We were excited about the opportunity to visit Tijuana for our first time.

With our pickup truck piled high, we made the trek to Tijuana; and once we crossed over from California, we noticed a significant change in our surroundings. Filthy, barefoot children with rags for clothes reached toward passersby. They were as young as 4 or 5 years old and pleading for pesos. Little boys with shoeshine boxes offered their services to anyone within earshot. We observed open prostitution and pimping. The sight overwhelmed us.

Finally, we found our way to the orphanage at the top of a hill and unloaded the "gifts." When I entered the big, two-story building, I saw a sea of raven-haired children who were warehoused there. Of course, they looked just like my little guy at home. It was a terrible place—a squalid environment, with no beauty whatsoever—and it lacked any evidence that Jesus lived there.

My heart ached. "God, where are You in this mess? You are the God who promises to be a Father to the fatherless. How is it possible that children could live in these conditions?"

Chuck instinctively volunteered to help the director dig a well. He was soon thirty feet down in a hole, shoveling away and watching for water to appear. I went outside and started to walk the premises. I hadn't even gone a block before realizing the orphanage was on the brink of a garbage dump. Since that day, nothing has been able to shake the nightmarish scene from my mind.

I stood before a huge expanse where rubbish smoldered twenty-four hours a day, and I watched as malnourished children and adults foraged for salvageable remnants of food. If they found a tortilla fragment or a sliver of non-spoiled meat, they'd put it in a dirty pouch or discarded baggie to eat or share later.

Some of the dump dwellers rummaged through the refuse with a stick, trying to find trinkets they could sell for a peso on the streets. When garbage trucks came in to deposit their "fresh" goods, waste pickers swarmed the area hoping to be the first to discover buried treasures.

An overpowering stench permeated the atmosphere. I couldn't get the repulsive smell out of my nostrils, yet men, women, and children lived there among the mounds of debris. Multiple stray dogs with matted coats meandered among them, and rats scurried from pile to pile.

My observations shook me to the core of my being. I thought I knew poverty. I had grown up in a large family in the heart of the Great Depression, and during the first years of our marriage, Chuck and I suffered extreme hardship. But nothing compared to what I faced that day. Nothing. These were the poorest of the poor. They acquired all their food, clothing, and possessions—including the cardboard boxes and scraps of metal that housed them—from the dump.

As I lifted my eyes and looked beyond the scene in front of me, I could see the skyline of San Diego with all its affluence. What a jolting contrast! Everything within me tried to understand this generational curse of abject poverty.

Grieving deeply for the people, I again looked to God for answers. "How can this be, God? How can this be? What can I do to make a difference in their lives? What can I do to help break this cycle?"

That day, I left Tijuana never to be the same.

After our initial trip to Mexico, I visited other orphanages in Tijuana and Ensenada and noticed they had a lot of things in common. They were poorly run, understaffed, and lacked organization and order. Storage shelves held an overabundance of mismatched clothes, inadequately labeled medical supplies, and a jumbled mess of food products, much of it out of date.

Most concerning to me, though, is that the homes just seemed like a holding place for children until they were released back into society at about the age of 14. They didn't offer vocational training or biblical training.

How would the children survive in the real world if they had no practical life skills? How would they learn about the transformational, unconditional love of God if they aren't taught?

The children needed caring people to invest in them, to champion them, to teach them that God has a purpose and plan for their lives.

If they didn't have the right upbringing, they'd end up back on the streets or in the dumps, in trouble, and with their hands out thinking everyone else owed them a living.

That realization didn't set well with me. The more I thought about it, the more troubled I became. Bottom line? Somebody needed to do something about the sad situation and soon.

This precious child was in the Tijuana garbage dump. From the dump, I could see the skyline of San Diego and the city's affluence. The experience left a lasting impression on me, and I was never the same.

A Life-Changing Vision

A few months after our unsettling trip to Tijuana, I read a fascinating feature article in the *Van Nuys Valley News and Green Sheet* about a man who took an adventure on the Baja Peninsula. He set out to visit the ruins of old Spanish mission sites, which had been established by Jesuit, Franciscan, and Dominican priests centuries earlier.

While he was in the area of the Santo Domingo mission in Colonia Vicente Guerrero, he stumbled upon the Hamilton Ranch, a popular fly-in guest ranch for the Hollywood elite during the 1920s and 30s. He found the guestbook, and the newspaper article shared some stories about the people who had stayed there. He also discovered a few abandoned buildings nearby—a casino-cantina, a motel-brothel, and an unfinished motion picture theater.

As a history enthusiast, I was intrigued by the information about the Hamilton Ranch, the deserted buildings, and the old missions. And that triggered an idea. With Chuck's October 2 birthday approaching, I suggested a possible outing.

"Wouldn't it be fun to do a little exploring south of the border?" I said and mentioned a few of the interesting points I had read in the article. "There's a dude ranch where Will Rogers and other rich-and-famous people vacationed, as well as several old mission sites along the way."

We lived about 150 miles from the border. With another 178 miles on top of that, it would be a 328-mile trip each way. "We'd need to leave pretty early in the morning, but it should make a nice excursion for us."

Chuck enjoyed driving and was all for it. We invited Roy and Nell, our good friends from prayer group, to go along with us. They were celebrating an anniversary at the same time and agreed that it would be a delightful way to spend the day.

Before dawn on the morning of Chuck's birthday, the four of us settled comfortably into our new yellow Chevy Impala station wagon, and we headed to the Baja Peninsula, excited about the day's potential. We left our children with a babysitter and told her we'd return late that evening.

But, as a familiar quote reminds us, the best-laid plans often go awry.

We failed to take into consideration the horrible road conditions, the steep mountain drop-offs, the absence of guard rails, the lack of gas stations, the unending miles of barrenness, the safety risks, the language barrier, and so many other things. By evening, what we hoped would be a day of fun had turned into hours of stressful, scary lostness.

We were in the middle of nowhere in Mexican desert land and hadn't seen signs of life in a long while. Without house lights or street lights perforating the darkness, the atmosphere was as black as could be. Our gas gauge registered empty. And we had no way to contact our babysitter or anyone else—all the makings for a desperate situation. We grappled with thoughts that we'd never see our homes or children again.

Then God sent an angel—a man standing alongside the road.

Using the Spanish-English dictionary stashed in the glove compartment, we attempted to communicate to him that we were lost and out of gas. Frustrated because we couldn't understand each other, he got into the car with us and pointed out directions as Chuck drove. About a mile east of there, we came to a group of buildings. The man went to the door of one, spoke to a woman who responded to his knocking after a few minutes, and motioned for us to go inside. That was the last we saw of him.

Grateful the woman could understand us, we explained our plight. "Do you know where we can purchase gas?" We also asked where we could find a place to stay.

"I have a 30-gallon barrel," she said in heavily-accented English. "You can fill up in the morning." She offered to let us spend the night there and pulled out a mattress for us to use.

After a sleepless night, I got up at dawn and ambled around the old adobe building. Because it was so dark when we arrived, I hadn't noticed the extent of its deterioration or the rest of our surroundings. Then I wandered the grounds, wondering where God had brought us. As I walked and prayed about our troubles, a strange peace overcame me.

I noticed the different structures and realized we were in the exact place I had read about in the *Van Nuys Valley News and Green Sheet*! I saw the old theater and the L-shaped motel-brothel. We had spent the night in what used to be a casino and cantina. A smaller, wood-framed building with a flat roof was on the property as well.

Especially curious about the motel and the many stories it held within its walls, I turned in that direction and went over to take a look. I thought about the celebrities who had come to the nearby Hamilton Ranch to play cowboy on weekends and who also patronized the businesses on this land. The history of it all captivated me.

The long-abandoned adobe building had seen better days. With broken-out windows, weatherworn doors barely hanging on their rusty hinges, and Baja sand and tumbleweeds drifting into rooms, it reminded me in some ways of an old western movie setting.

As I stood there and meditated on the interesting details, I heard the sound of children's voices. Laughing voices. That's odd, I thought. I hadn't seen any children that morning.

I stepped inside and looked around. I went back outside and looked to my right and to the left. And I looked over my shoulder, but I couldn't find anyone.

Again, I heard the unmistakable sound of children playing and laughing, so I walked to the backside of the motel. Still, I found no one. *This is strange. I wonder what it means.* Nothing like that had ever happened to me.

Then I looked outward, and instead of an expanse of desert flora and rocky, sandy soil, I saw a golden field of waving grain. Immediately, words from the Bible filled my mind: "The harvest is plentiful, but the laborers are few." Although I didn't know what was going on, God certainly had my attention.

I thought of the children living in garbage dumps in Tijuana and Ensenada, and those on the streets—the ones who looked like my little boy at home. *Maybe these abandoned buildings could be adapted into a safe haven for them. Maybe this could be a refuge for children in need.*

I thought of the physical and spiritual needs of the Mexican people. *Maybe someday there will be a revival here.*

I thought of what my favorite Bible school teacher, Reverend Rieke, had taught me about missions and how he cried while singing "Lord, Lay Some Soul Upon My Heart." Each time he sang it, I could sense his longing for the Lord to work through him to love those precious souls. As I stood there, I could almost hear his voice as the words floated through my mind. *Maybe someday there will be a Bible school here like the one where Jesus became Lord of my life.*

That sacred moment in time touched my heart in a powerful, life-changing way. I quickly returned to the old casino building and told Chuck, Roy, and Nell about my experience. They requested a tour of the property, so we walked the land and prayed, dedicating it all to God and His purposes.

Our long, dreaded drive back home gave us time to ponder many questions. How did we get so far without gas the night before? Who was the man standing beside the road in the dark of night? Where did he go when he disappeared? Why did God bring us to that particular location? What did the sound of children's voices and the vision of waving grain mean? Who would fulfill the work God had planned? How did all of this relate to us?

The one thing we didn't question was God's permeating presence in that place. My spirit sensed He had something significant in store for the property. I just didn't know it involved me.

Later, we learned some backstory.

In 1963, a retired minister, Alexander Brody, stumbled upon this same parcel of land with the abandoned buildings. He was so moved by God that he knelt down and prayed that the buildings and land would become part of the Lord's ministry. Included in his vision was a home for children and a Bible school.

He did what he could, including constructing a small building that served as a chapel (the flat-roofed building I had seen), but he was too old, too tired, and had too many setbacks, so he left the job to others. That didn't work well. Although technically considered an orphanage, only a few homeless children lived there. The place was in shambles, those who served as directors in his place had failed in many ways, and it was rife with problems. It had been a huge disappointment.

Little did that pastor know God would give a similar vision to someone else just three years later. God was now at work in setting His plan in motion.

This is an aerial view of what Chuck and I saw when we first visited the property, which in time became the mission. The inset photo shows the front view of the old theater. Over the years, it has served multiple purposes at the mission.

1. Mission Church
2. Bible Institute
3. Staff Housing
4. Home for Children
5. School and Day Care
6. Disabled Children's Learning Center

7. Outreach
8. Workshops
9. Warehouse
10. Angel Ministry

Baja Mission

An updated aerial view of the Baja mission

Evolution
of a Vision

Lessons in Trust

After our trip to Colonia Vicente Guerrero, Chuck and I couldn't shake the questions that continued to nag us. What did the vision mean? While we were there, we had also witnessed a supernatural occurrence in the chapel with a small group of children. What's the explanation for that? we wondered.

Everything we experienced there left an indelible impression on our minds, and we felt an urgency to return and see if God would reveal more details. Upon reflection, I acknowledge the Holy Spirit's hand in drawing us back.

It seemed crazy to subject ourselves to that traveling trauma again—a 15-hour drive, including one hundred miles of dirt road and washboard surfaces where we could only travel five miles an hour. But when God is involved, you just sometimes do crazy things without understanding why. We returned to the site in November and again in December.

We became engaged with the children. We acquainted ourselves with the area. We did what we could to make a difference.

In the spring, the property went up for sale.

I was convinced God had a plan for the land and felt strongly that it should be a home for children—and much more—so I determined to find a buyer for the property. I called on Bob Pierce at the World Vision headquarters in Pasadena and Rev. Donn Moomaw at Bel Air Presbyterian Church; and I visited with the leaders of several mission organizations. I couldn't understand their lack of response to such a huge opportunity for ministry.

Then I went to see Mother Mitchell, an old pioneer missionary who founded a missionary-sending organization called the Go Ye Fellowship. She offered me these wise words: "Charla, if God gives you a vision, trust Him to equip you. God uses very ordinary people to do an extraordinary work because they're dependent on Him."

A pastor I talked with gave me similar advice. "No one has the vision that you have, Charla. If God gives you the vision, He will give you the implementation."

The task seemed insurmountable for an ordinary homemaker like me, but I decided that if a children's home was meant to be, and if I were to be an active participant, God would bring the implementation.

Chuck and I met with our Friday night prayer group and encouraged them to pray specifically for God's will for us. (At the time of this writing, our group still meets every week. The numbers have varied, and people have come and gone, but the members all have a passion to reach the world for Christ.)

These faithful prayer warriors were already supporters of our involvement with the orphans and had been asking God to bring about the manifestation of my vision. That night we all agreed to fast and pray for God's direction and meet again on Sunday afternoon.

When we reconvened, we gave each person a chance to share what God had spoken to them. One pregnant young mother with two small children said, "Charla, if we do this, it's going to cost us something. It may cost our lives, but can we give less for the Lord Jesus?"

Another said, "You know, those old buildings down there were used for the devil's purposes—a gambling hall and a brothel—and if we go into an area where Christ has not been proclaimed to raise up a cross, we'll have a battle with the enemy."

The more we shared and discussed and continued to seek God for answers, the more our group overwhelmingly sensed His nudge to purchase the property. Now we faced the looming questions: How will we do it? How will we come up with the money?

I have a handwritten note in the back of my Bible that says, "Don't pray for a task equal to your ability or power. Pray for power equal to your tasks." And that's what we did.

We were given a three-week option to come up with a deposit of $5,000 toward the purchase price of $15,000. As young married couples with families, none of us had a surplus of money, so it was an opportunity for us to trust God for His provision and timing. We all consented to refrain from soliciting the funds.

Praise God, without our begging for help, and without our publicizing the need, God brought us the exact amount required in remarkable ways. And we had it on the due date! It was confirmation that we were in the center of His will.

Unfortunately, I couldn't get to Ensenada to make the transaction until the next day. When I arrived at the property owner's home, his wife said, "He's at his attorney's office on Calle Ruiz."

I panicked. *What's going on? Why is he at his attorney's office?* Señora Gomez must have seen the concern on my face because she scribbled the address on a scrap of paper and pointed out the direction to go. I hurried away.

After what seemed like an eternity to find a parking place, I entered the office, went straight to the receptionist's desk, and introduced myself. "Is Señor Refugio Gomez here talking with his attorney?" I asked. "If he is, I'd like to speak with him."

"Yes, they are meeting right now," she said. She wrote down my name and delivered my message. A minute later, she invited me back to speak with him.

Señor Gomez greeted me. I told him I had the money to make the transaction, and he said, "You're a day late. I've already accepted a better offer."

The news devastated me. As I walked to the lobby crying, I had a little heart-to-heart talk with God. "Lord, what's going on? Why did You bring me all these miles to face this disappointment? Why did You provide the funds if the deal's not going to go through? Now I have to return all the money to the people who donated it. Do You know how much work that is?" I had so many questions, so many things about the situation I didn't understand.

A man sitting in the reception area saw my tears. He wasn't American, but he spoke English well. "Why are you crying?" he asked.

I just wanted to say, "none of your business" and go home. My mother taught me better, though, so I said, "Well, I came here to buy some land, but another person beat me to it." As I walked toward the door, he kept asking questions.

"Where is this land?" I told him it was about 110 miles south of there. "Why do you want property in Mexico?"

"It's not that I want it, but I believe God wants me to establish a home for children on the property." I started to describe the area. "There's an old gambling casino and motel, as well as a couple of other buildings . . ." He motioned for me to sit in the chair next to him.

I went on to explain the sequence of events that brought us to the point of purchasing the land. "Our prayer group prayed for God's provision and timing. We trusted Him, and He gave us exactly what we asked for. Now it appears we're too late." When I met his gaze, I could see compassion in his eyes.

"You know, that sounds like the land I just put an offer on. I planned to use it for a resort and hunting lodge." What he said next turned my feelings of defeat to hallelujahs. "I'm going to withdraw my offer. I want to help you with your endeavor."

The man's name was Al Vela, a San Quintín businessman and owner of the Old Mill Inn. He assisted us in making the transaction and then set up a nonprofit corporation in Mexico so our land could be secure. He also became an avid supporter of our ministry over the years and served on our Mexican board.

God had the big picture and knew just what we needed.

For me, that day in the attorney's office in Ensenada was what I call a Proverbs 3:5–6 moment. I like the way the Amplified Bible puts it: "Trust in *and* rely confidently on the LORD with all your heart and do not rely on your own insight *or* understanding. In all your ways know *and* acknowledge *and* recognize Him, and He will make your paths straight *and* smooth [removing obstacles that block your way]."

Since then, we've headed down many unknown—often scary—paths, and we've faced countless obstacles. We've come up against impossible situations and closed doors. At times we've struggled to answer the "Why?" questions and are left feeling frustrated and confused. But the verses in Proverbs remind us that our job is not to understand everything we experience; it's to trust God with all our hearts and acknowledge Him in all our ways. When we do that, He fulfills His promises.

I've learned that trusting God isn't always easy, but it's something He always rewards.

At the time we gained ownership, the area was sparsely populated, which made it possible to see the old Hamilton Ranch, the red rock, and the mountains. Our property held three dilapidated buildings: what used to be a casino, the motel-brothel, and the unfinished theater. We also had the chapel that Pastor Brody built. The place had an eerie beauty about it, but the offshore wind often stirred up the powdery beige sand, creating a blinding dustbowl.

For years we dealt with unpaved roads. We were without electrical power and used kerosene lamps for light. Knott's Berry Farm donated an old generator, which we ran from 6 to 8 p.m., if we had enough money to purchase the gas. Everything from pumping water to cutting hair was done during those brief hours.

Until we acquired laundry equipment, we washed clothes and linens by hand on cement washboards. Telephone lines weren't installed until 1991. We prayed earnestly for our daily bread.

Through all the inconveniences and lack of modern luxuries, our goal always remained the same: to bring the home to a standard where we could minister effectively to the physical, emotional, spiritual, and academic needs of those entrusted to us.

In the beginning, we made plenty of mistakes and gained a PhD from going through the "school of hard knocks." But God didn't waste anything. Our ups and downs taught us important lessons in trusting Him, and He continued to reveal His character and power to us.

Early on, we set up an operating committee and a board of directors; some of those positions overlapped. Many of the members came from our Friday night prayer group. Although rarely acknowledged, they bonded together to serve, assist, and bless the endeavors of our missionaries on the field.

For thirty-seven years, the kitchen table in our North Hollywood home doubled as my desk, and the back bedroom as the corporate office. We held board meetings in the living room, and visitors coming or going to Mexico constantly filled the guest bedroom.

With the goal of keeping US administrative costs to a bare minimum, we lived amid what seemed like a three-ring circus. We had mailmen greeting us at the front door, UPS delivering at the side, and furniture, food, and medical supplies coming in at the rear. Bells, phones, and the fax machine rang from 7 a.m. to 11 p.m. and sometimes later.

Our two-car garage never saw a car for decades because it served as a depot for donated supplies. And did we ever have the stuff—just about anything you could imagine! It was in the garage, in the backyard, and everywhere! Volunteers came in weekly, but they couldn't keep up with the flow of goods.

One time, a caring friend left a thousand pounds of freshly-picked apples on our patio. Good apples are a rare treat in Mexico, so I was grateful for such a special gift. But I had a dilemma on my hands. Our truck was broken down, we had no cold storage, and we were experiencing a heat wave. *What are we going to do with this mountain of beautiful apples? We can't let them rot in the sun!*

At a prayer meeting that night, I asked for prayer for the situation.

Just as He had done countless times before, God answered in a marvelous way. For two days straight, from 8 o'clock in the morning until 10 at night, God sent His choicest friends to help with the task. A continuous stream of men and women dropped in, almost as if on scheduled shifts. In fact, more men than women came—some who had never before peeled an apple! What a blessing and a delight to see God provide the laborers.

And God always thinks of everything. The very morning that we were peeling apples, a thoughtful friend "just happened to" stop by with gallons of lemon juice. It was exactly what we needed to keep them from turning brown.

At the end of two days, we had stacks of bagged, frozen apples. Another dear brother came by and was able to take all the remaining apples to the mission. We didn't lose a single one of them.

In addition to volunteers who helped with our supplies and special projects such as saving apples, God gave us an excellent office crew. We started each day with devotions, prayer, and the study of *My Utmost for His Highest* by Oswald Chambers. These exceptional servants assisted with the newsletter and general office duties, and they worked through piles of pink envelopes that held monetary donations—sorting, opening, and processing them while thanking the Lord for our generous, faithful supporters.

When the need for a full-time staff member became apparent, we prayed that God would provide the perfect person for the job. We put the word out, and days went by without receiving an application. A bit discouraged, we wondered where we'd find someone willing to work long hours with minimal pay. Yet we remained convinced of God's faithfulness and trusted His timing.

Then one day we received a large manila envelope in the mail. Somehow it came to us, though it was addressed to High Adventure, a local Christian ministry. We opened it before we realized the mistake, and the contents caught our attention. It was an application for office work from someone by the name of Lorraine Barter. She had all the qualifications we desired. This must be the Lord's handiwork, we thought.

Right away we phoned Lorraine. We explained about the mail mix up and asked, "Would you be interested in interviewing with Foundation for His Ministry?" She said yes.

After meeting with her, we knew she was heaven-sent. Within the week, she started working as our FFHM bookkeeper. We marveled again at how the Lord provided for our needs in above-and-beyond ways.

No one could have filled that position like Lorraine. Not only did she become a precious friend to everyone in the office, but she also served as a talented hostess for board meeting luncheons and Friday night prayer meetings. She housesat when needed, ran errands, helped with hospitality, cut hair, sorted clothing and apples, and did anything asked of her in support of His Ministry. Lorraine was a one-of-a-kind gift from God.

I could tell of similar occurrences again and again. As we've presented our needs to our heavenly Father, He provides the gifts, resources, and people to make things happen. From the beginning, we've abided by Hudson Taylor's spiritual secret: "God's work done in God's way will never lack God's supply."

Because God is creative, the help doesn't always come in the manner I'd expect. But that way He makes sure I have plenty of fun and fabulous stories to share with others. And I love to tell the stories!

During the first few decades of our ministry, I did a lot of traveling to Canada, the Pacific Northwest, the Midwest—and wherever I was asked—to speak at churches and raise support for the mission. I'd tell the stories, as mentioned above, starting with Curtis's adoption, and I'd report how God was at work in Mexico. People responded. In addition to monetary offerings, churches sent work groups and supplies.

Christian Renewal Center at Silver Falls State Park in Oregon helped us reach even more people by paying for the creation of a professional 37-minute video, called *The Harvest*. We made that available for groups to watch so they could learn about our home for children and our other ministries.

Our supporters come from many denominations, locations, and interests, and they are all united in the common bond of caring for Mexico's poor and needy. We're grateful for each person, because without them we wouldn't be able to fulfill our three-fold mission of rescuing children, reaching the lost, and restoring the broken.

We've come a long way from where we started. What began as a little orphanage with a staff of three has become a multifaceted mission on the Baja Peninsula and mainland of Mexico that has the ear and favor of government officials. We also now operate from a lovely office in San Clemente, California, which is closer to the border. It's all a testimony of God's provision, faithfulness, and grace—and proof that He can be trusted.

Top: The front yard of our home in North Hollywood

Bottom: The back yard always overflowed with donations for the children's home.

Top: Juan and Elisa Carrillo and I hosted a birthday party for Lorraine Barter. She worked as our mission's bookkeeper for twenty-seven years and greatly blessed us in many other ways.

Bottom: After his workday as an engineer was over, Fred Sass came to our home office and taught our first secretary how to use a computer.

Hogar Para Niños

When we took over as administrators of the orphanage, just a handful of children lived in the 1920s-built former casino—a dark and dank adobe dwelling with a mold problem. The children shared their home with rodents that skittered across the floors and ran up and down its decaying walls. On rainy days, the structure leaked in numerous places. Although conditions were less than perfect at the time, that facility ended up serving as a sanctuary to hundreds of children until we were able to start a building program years later.

As our little family grew and our home became more established, God brought the funds, resources, and supplies to build—most of which came through our generous supporters and volunteers. But we never had enough at one time to let us forget our provider. The ministry's growth and expansion brought us to a new level of living by faith.

Over the years, FFHM has learned to operate on God's schedule, and we've been careful to never go in debt. Although waiting on God's timing hasn't always been comfortable for us, He's used those experiences to teach us valuable truths and show us His amazing ways. And they have been many!

Months before our new building was ready for the children to move in, we went through the rainy season, which brought us a reminder that our new facilities couldn't be ready too soon.

In Baja, persistent torrential downpours can turn arid land into raging rivers that sweep away everything in their paths. In early 1980, rain-ravaged waters threatened the buildings at Rancho Los Chilpayates, an orphanage about a mile and a half from our property. Thirty-seven children lived there at the time.

A Christian woman named Cora Mendez had moved her family into the vacant buildings a few years prior, along with six abandoned children from Mexico City, where she had run a day care center. She planted trees on the property and raised chickens and other livestock to support her blended family. And she took in children with needs from the area.

When we were beyond capacity at Hogar Para Niños, Kay and Bill Lawrence (our directors at the time) would tell people who wanted to drop off children, "We're all out of room, but there's a lady over by the river who has a heart as big as Mexico. Why don't you go see Cora Mendez?" Before long, that incredibly compassionate woman's buildings had run out of space as well.

After Cora died from a massive heart attack in July of 1979, her son David and his wife, Isabel, left their studies at La Puente Bible Institute in California and took over her ministry. At just 21 years old, and with the desire to be a pastor, David felt ill-equipped and inadequate to run an orphanage. He did the best he could with the lack of support and funding available to him.

Then, in mid-February of 1980, only a few months later, the turbulent waters came and deposited about thirty acres of their property into the Pacific Ocean.

During that same period of time, Chuck and his fireman friend from Oregon, Rex Morningstar, were at our children's home. They had just delivered a load of supplies before the storm hit. The brute force of the winds and rain blew out the front windows of the old casino building where we housed our children, and while they were at work securing them, soldiers from the small, local military base showed up with an urgent appeal.

"The orphanage . . . the one down by the river . . ." The spokesman's words came out quickly as he gestured frantically in the direction of Chilpayates. "The river has changed its course. The bridge is out and many niños are there." His desperate plea continued. "Someone needs to take a bus and get them out of there immediately! The place is being washed away."

Chuck, Rex, and a small group of men loaded the bus and flew into action as soon as they arrived on the scene. Dodging floating chickens and uprooted trees, they carried each of the thirty-seven children through waist-deep water to safety. The rescuers brought the frightened young ones—and anything that could be salvaged—back to Hogar Para Niños.

Because we didn't have room to integrate them with our more than eighty children in their overflowing quarters—and our new facility was still under construction—our crew created a makeshift dormitory in the little flat-roofed building that served as our chapel. Staff members gathered up old army bunk beds, cots, used mats, and blankets that we had stored in the warehouse and helped get the children settled in. It was a chaotic time!

Chuck and Rex needed to get back to work in the states and couldn't make the trip due to the washed-out bridge, so we arranged for a small plane to fly into the Hamilton Ranch airstrip to transport them. As soon as he arrived home in Southern California, Chuck said to me, "You need to get down there right away because something is happening with those children. They have sores all over their bodies and are in bad shape."

I could tell by the serious tone of his voice that I shouldn't waste time. I packed my bag, then headed off to Colonia Vicente Guerrero in my Volkswagen Beetle.

I was appalled at what I saw when I got there—thirty-seven children with sores that looked similar to impetigo or ring worm. Yes, all thirty-seven of them. They had lice, too, and appeared to be malnourished. These suffering children reminded me of those living in the garbage dump. My heart broke for them.

I knew how to deal with lice. I knew how to give baths. I knew how to clean wounds and apply ointments. So, after a quick trip to the local pharmacy to purchase medication and supplies, I got right to work. But their sores didn't respond to my treatment, and I didn't know anything about nursing. I faced a situation that was well beyond my ability.

What have I gotten myself into? It's a question I've pondered many times over the years.

Although I felt incompetent in my own strength, I knew how to pray, and God intervened in a most wonderful way.

As I was attending to the children, an attractive Spanish-looking woman poked her head inside the door. She was tall and slender and appeared to be in her fifties. When she saw us, she came in. A handsome man with graying hair accompanied her. Everything about this couple—the way they carried themselves, their classiness, their dignity—made it obvious they weren't locals.

"Hello," the woman said. "We were just walking by and heard voices, so we decided to see what was going on."

I greeted them and introduced myself. From our conversation, I learned that they had read some old articles about the historic Hamilton Ranch and had flown down from Orange County, California, to visit it.

"We were so disappointed to discover that it was in ruins," she said. "We didn't have anything to do there, so we decided to take a walk, in hopes of finding a town and lodging. That's what led us here." She talked about how she had taken a few days off work and mentioned that she was a nurse at a hospital in Brea, California.

I couldn't believe my ears!

I filled her in about the flood and the sorry plight of these children. "I came immediately after my husband told me about their condition, and I've been doing what I can to help them," I said. "But nothing I've done has made a difference. Their sores aren't responding to normal topical treatment, and I don't know what to do."

She nodded her head in a way that showed she understood my frustration. "Let me take a look," she said before inspecting a few of the children.

As she examined them, she seemed puzzled. "This doesn't appear to be a normal infection." She stood quietly for a moment, as if deep in thought, and then the light in her eyes brightened. "I have a culture kit on the plane," she said. "I'll get a few samples and take them to the hospital where I work." She went on to tell about a South American doctor there who specializes in tropical diseases. "I'll show them to him and get his advice."

At that point I was in awe. *She just happens to have a culture kit with her? What are the chances of that?*

The kind woman did what she said she would do—and much more. In four or five days, she returned with the specialist and a team of medical professionals. They had a variety of medications with them and upon their arrival started treating the children for staphylococcus and e-coli. And both she and the doctor could speak Spanish! What a gift that was.

Within a few days, the once raw, infectious sores had become light pink scars.

We never saw the woman or the specialist again. But I'll never forget their tender care for those little ones. I'll also never forget God's perfect timing, His attention to detail, or His miraculous ways.

When our new facilities were ready for habitation not long afterward, we were able to integrate the children with our other children without fear of spreading disease. God is good!

In hindsight, we've been able to see God's fingerprints all over that period of time. Shortly after the rescue operation, our FFHM board agreed to permanently merge the Chilpayates orphanage with our children's home. Their small staff took on a variety of responsibilities at Hogar Para Niños that included being house parents for the children, teaching Sunday school, helping as needed in the kitchen, and many other things.

We gained a pastor for our chapel who also served in the community through Bible studies and outreach. We experienced such great growth during his ministry with us that we had to move services to the old theater building. Within a few years, we needed to expand again and started a building program for a new church that can seat a thousand. Many times, we had standing-room-only crowds during his tenure. He also was instrumental in starting seven satellite churches and mentored several of our Bible school students who became missionaries in Oaxaca.

Although the rains dealt a devasting blow to the Chilpayates property and disrupted many lives, God—the author and finisher of the creative process—brought order and beauty from that chaotic situation and used it to further His plans.

God works in mysterious ways. He works in wonderful ways. To Him be all glory for the great things He has done.

Top: This is the sign that greets our guests at Hogar Para Niños today.

Bottom: Our big truck made regular trips to deliver supplies. Here it is at the border.

Children at Hogar
Para Niños

Precious Jewels

In 1979, Jesus appeared to me in a dream. A Man in shining white garments held out two vessels in His hands—one of seeming gold, the other a clay pot, typical of the black pottery made by the Oaxacan people. "Which one would you choose?" He asked.

I found myself in a quandary. After pondering His question for a while, I responded with, "The gold one."

Sadly, the Lord answered, "Child, how long will you choose by the outward appearance? Why don't you ask what is inside?"

Then He poured out the contents of the two vessels. The one that appeared to be gold was filled with sand. The primitive black clay vessel held precious jewels. Immediately, God reminded me of the words from 1 Samuel 16:7: "Man looks at the outward appearance, but the LORD looks at the heart" (NASB).

The Lord also brought to mind the promise He gave King Cyrus in Isaiah 45:3. "I will give you treasures hidden in the darkness—secret riches. I will do this so you may know that I am the LORD, the God of Israel, the one who calls you by name" (NASB).

I believed that dream had, and continues to have, prophetic significance. Little by little God has revealed its meaning to me as I've experienced the unfolding of His amazing plan.

The clay pot in my dream represents the indigenous people from the state of Oaxaca, Mexico. That's where our Charles Curtis's roots are.

I'm in awe when I reflect on how God brought that special child into our lives. Back then I questioned God's purposes and struggled with trying to understand it all. Again, the truth of Proverbs 3:5–6 was at work. He wanted me to trust Him without the need to understand. As I did that, He promised to show me His ways. And He has.

Because of Charles Curtis, God gave me a deep love for the people of Mexico. I have a heart connection with them— a mother's heart.

During the initial trip Chuck and I took to Colonia Vicente Guerrero in 1966, God entrusted to me a two-fold vision: build a home for children in need and reap a field ripe unto harvest. With God's guidance, the help of countless volunteers, and the provision of widows' mites, we successfully established the first stage of the vision. Our faithful God has done a great work at Hogar Para Niños.

As our ministry expanded and grew, we became what is technically referred to as a mission and outreach while still operating our original home for children. The expansion and growth happened because of an unexpected call of God, and within that unexpected call we have uncovered many precious jewels and treasures hidden in a field ripe unto harvest.

Here's how it came about.

In 1976, scientists discovered that the region was extremely fertile and that an underground river had created its pure water supply. Word quickly spread that the valleys near Colonia Vicente Guerrero held miles and miles of rich farmland.

Before long, major United States corporations started making arrangements with Mexican growers along the Baja desert's coastal plains to supply them with ever-increasing amounts of tomatoes, strawberries, cucumbers, Brussels sprouts, and other fresh produce. The growers had a problem, though. They needed thousands of laborers to till and harvest the new fields, but the area was sparsely populated. If they hired Mexican workers at the accepted standard wage, prices for the produce would be too high.

So, they started looking for laborers, and for a reason known perhaps only to God, they went to the southern-most state in Mexico—Oaxaca, from where God had sent us a little Zapotec baby years before.

Oaxacans are noted for their continuous hard work. They are simple people who will labor until they're told to stop. Recruited with deceptive promises of jobs and pros-perity, they packed up their families (sometimes of up to forty people) and boarded the back of stake bed trucks that transported them two thousand miles to the Baja Penin-sula. News of work in Baja also spread rapidly through the hundreds of migrant camps in Sinaloa.

What the recruits weren't told is that they wouldn't have housing. They wouldn't have water. They wouldn't have sanitation. Their high hopes for a better life quickly came crashing down.

At that time, indigenous men earned about $3.50 per day, and the women earned even less. The dismal pay for their ten-hour-plus days hasn't increased significantly in the years since. The Mexican laws governing minimum wage are widely ignored in their case. In addition to the pittance they receive, the tens of thousands of indigenous workers are often met with harassment and abuse.

They arrived in Baja from the high mountains and val-leys completely unprepared for their new environment, where mild, sunny, winter days dropped to freezing at night. Because housing facilities at the camps were for the most part nonexistent, families huddled together in tiny huts—maybe eight feet square—that they cobbled together from cardboard, tar paper, or rolls of plastic tied to frames fashioned from broken tree limbs. Bursts of wind wreak havoc, and heavy rains flood the dirt floors, causing their makeshift homes at times to collapse.

The workers are given "company store" credit, which, due to the inflated price of goods, keeps them in constant debt to their employers and living as indentured servants. It limits their ability to leave the ranches. They can't afford even the simplest things we take for granted, like food and toiletries. And most families are large! Their wretched conditions, along with a lack of nourishment and necessities, lead to a wide range of health problems. It's heartbreaking.

As the migrant camps became established in the San Quintín Valley, people started lining up at our door and asking for food and other handouts—sometimes seventy of them at a time. They had so many needs. How could we turn them away?

When I was a child in the days of the Great Depression and thought my family was poor, I observed my mother reach out and help others. She was generous to a fault! Mama instilled in me the truth found in James 2:15–16, which says, "Suppose a brother or sister is without clothes and daily food. If one of you says to them, 'Go in peace; keep warm and well fed,' but does nothing about their physical needs, what good is it?" (NIV).

I cannot bear to see people in need of food, clothing, and medical help and not at least try to do something about it. I just can't! God gave me a burden for these dear, hurting people. So, after a discussion with our FFHM board, we moved forward with an outreach program. It was yet another opportunity to trust God for direction and provision.

One of the commissions Jesus has made clear to us at FFHM is that we are to "bring good news to the poor." Of course, the best news is found in John 3:16, where it talks about God's great love for us, but good news also comes in the way of beans, blankets, tarps, shoes, clothing, lice removal, medical assistance, education, and so many other avenues. As we serve our neighbors first with practical helps, doors open for us to share the good news of Jesus Christ.

In their natural environment, the indigenous people are often resistant to the gospel because of the cultural, political, and religious pressures they face. But when they are in Baja, they're free from the pressures and are more receptive to the message of truth and life. Through our mercy ministry and outreach efforts, many thousands have received salvation and been discipled. We've started numerous satellite churches as well.

God's ways never cease to amaze me. He brought these beautiful people to us in the early 1980s. A few years later, we opened a Bible institute to train the indigenous people so they could go back to their mainland and reach their own people with the gospel of Christ. Some have been martyred for their faith, but churches are being established in remote areas where God is softening hearts and revealing Himself in supernatural ways.

I praise Him for giving us this mission field. He has used us to "mine" His precious jewels—treasures redeemed from darkness and brought into His glorious light.

∞

My mother loved spending time at the mission and serving the indigenous people in Baja. I found the following insightful thoughts in her Bible years after she wrote them.

It is a Saturday morning, October 1, 1983, and I am sitting here in my friend's home with my cup of coffee, looking out over the great Pacific Ocean, and it is raining. Such a peaceful sight watching the big raindrops make ripples in the swimming pool. The reflections of the yuccas and timberline cypress make dark pictures in the pool against a backdrop of heavy, dark, threatening clouds. A beautiful picture.

But as I sit here comfortable and warm, my thoughts turn to the cardboard huts a few hundred miles from here, but an eternity away in reality. I can see brown-eyed children cuddling up to a frustrated mother who is wondering how much more rain the cardboard roof can withstand before it collapses, and there is no defense against the savage elements.

But for the grace of God it could be one of my grandchildren in those huts—cold, wet, and hungry. *Thank You, God.*

Yet I do feel guilty sitting here with a microwave and a Mr. Coffee at my fingertips, with hot cinnamon toast, a bowl full of fruit, and a vase of yellow mums on the table beside me.

God, forgive me for being so comfortable when my brothers and sisters in Mexico are in misery, and beautiful little brown-eyed babies are cold and hungry.

Nearby I hear a foghorn sounding a warning to a passing ship. "Beware of the rocks." We must also be aware—God is speaking.

Mother's words are a reminder that sometimes we become too comfortable in our own surroundings, and we forget how blessed we are compared to so many others. A good dose of perspective can jar us from our complacency. Yes, the needs are great, and the workers are few. We have an important job to do while on this earth, whether it be in Mexico or somewhere else. I wonder what would happen if we all were willing to answer His call.

These pictures show the poverty and living conditions at the migrant camps.

As part of our outreach to the migrant camps, we give children a cup of milk and a spoonful of peanut butter.

Bearing Fruit
in the Desert

Harry and Betty Sherda, board members who were very involved with Camps Farthest Out (an inter-denominational, Christ-centered organization), invited Chuck and me for a week-long camp in Big Bear, California. We got assigned to a small group with John and Ginny Moore from Santa María, California, as our leaders. They were school teachers ready to retire.

John was a well-respected, world-class agronomist who had published many articles on the topic of agronomy. He encouraged us to visit his home and the backyard plot he called "God's little acre."

"You'll see that I especially love experimenting with sub-tropical plants," he said.

When we took him up on his offer, we saw what looked like an extensive agricultural test site. The orchard on his land flourished with four hundred kinds of fruits, nuts, and berries—all protected from the Pacific Ocean's strong winds by a self-designed wall of army-surplus window panes and lath work. Many varieties grew together on the same tree due to his ambitious grafting program. He had one tree that produced six types of citrus fruit, including oranges, tangerines, an orange-tangerine cross, two varieties of blood oranges, and pummelos.

His extraordinary giftedness and the things he had accomplished through his trial-and-error ways amazed us.

At about the same time, Inez Sorenson, one of our staff members in Baja, was talking to John about the mission.

She had taught in the same school district with him for many years, and they were good friends. After she retired, she went to Baja to teach our missionary children, and whenever she returned home, she made a point to visit him.

The more reports John heard, the more intrigued he became with our ministry in Mexico. "I'd like to see what we could grow there in the desert," he said. "Maybe we could turn a profit to help support the mission."

He shared his ideas and giant-sized vision with us, and we welcomed him to come. "We have almost two acres next to our little chapel you can use for research and development. Go for it!"

So, in 1980, he made his initial trip to Colonia Vicente Guerrero.

His first order of business was to analyze the soil, our weather conditions, and needs. He got the best trees for the area and installed an easy-to-maintain drip irrigation system.

One of his concerns was how to create a windbreak to protect the young saplings. While on a trip to Hawaii, he conferred with a specialist who had been doing research on natural windbreaks for similar needs on the Islands. He came back with the seeds of the giant koa tree to try. That caused the University of Hawaii and the US Department of Agriculture to show interest in the progress of his experiment.

As he traveled with Camps Farthest Out to places such as Korea and Israel, he collected small branches and brought them home to use for grafting purposes. He tried every new thing in the field.

In just over two years, the experimental orchard had more than five hundred trees with a variety of fruits and nuts from all over the world. That included seventeen varieties of apples, thirty types of figs, fifteen types of peaches and nectarines, apricots, kiwis, grapevines, blackberries and raspberries, persimmons, and more. We also had walnut, pecan, and macadamia trees.

John's special interest in rare fruits was evident by the tropical guava, passion fruit vines, cherimoya, and carambola. His most unusual specimen is what he called the "condominium tree"—a fig tree that was already growing there to which he grafted fourteen other varieties of figs.

He was working on developing a particular avocado tree, trying to increase the fruit's shelf life to beyond the norm of fourteen days. To his amazement, he noticed the macadamia tree right next to it had long, gorgeous blossoms and clusters of nuts. The tree was thriving in the desert with drip irrigation! After doing extensive research and keeping detailed weather and rainfall records, he came to the board with his thoughts.

"I believe we can grow macadamia trees," he said and shared what he had discovered. "I think we have a drought-resistant macadamia nut." He asked if he could use ten acres on the periphery of the property to start a project. His idea was to build a little greenhouse and then begin to sprout nuts in Styrofoam cups to plant when the time was right. The board agreed to his request.

John built his greenhouse, and pretty soon he had a jungle of macadamia shoots sprouting inside. He ran out of room and had no other choice than to plant the young trees in the field. It's not exactly the way to start a commercial venture, but it's what happened.

Because it was an experiment and the board didn't want to use mission funds to support it, John financed everything out of his own pocket. However, the drip irrigation system required wells and pumps and electric motors—an extraordinary expense. To help with the cost, I wrote an article for the newsletter, offering a tree to be planted in someone's honor for just $15.

Money started coming in from all across the country in memory of Aunt Martha, Uncle Joe, or another special person. Our donors adopted hundreds of seedlings. It seemed like a win-win situation.

But . . .

We had three below-freezing nights in January. I came down to the mission and went out right away to walk the rows and inspect the trees. From my perspective, after snapping some of their tiny branches, they were all dead.

I'm thankful Mother wasn't on the trip with me. Whenever she was at the mission, she was either in the soup kitchen or walking through the orchard praying over every tree. She believed the macadamias would be a blessing to the ministry.

Of course, my mind went to all the people I'd need to write. "Aunt Martha just died in a killer frost." And I felt the responsibility of everyone who'd donated money to purchase a tree—a tree in an orchard that had been saturated in prayer. I just knew they'd all be wondering what kind of research this was.

I went to town to call John at his home in Santa María. (He made the sixteen-hundred-mile pilgrimages to the mission every two months and stayed two weeks at a time.) "John, we've had three below-freezing nights," I said. "The trees are all dead."

He arrived as soon as he could, and we immediately walked the rows together. My thoughts agonized me while John carefully examined the branches and leaves. He didn't say much, other than an occasional "hmmm," but when we got to a certain spot in the middle of the orchard, he jumped straight up and down like a crazy man and started praising God.

"I don't see anything to praise God for, John," I said. "I've got a thousand letters to write."

"But twenty percent have survived!" he said.

"Yeah, big deal. That means eighty percent are dead. D-e-a-d. DEAD." I had a hard time understanding his excitement.

He went on to explain. "We'll take the wood from the survivors, graft it onto the rootstock of the other trees, and we will have developed a frost-tolerant, drought-tolerant macadamia nut."

And that's what we have today.

Mama was right to believe the orchard would be a blessing. Through a travesty, God fulfilled John Moore's original vision of a cash crop. Because of John's diligence and many years of faithful service, we now have natural resources on our site that subsidize the work of the ministry. Our two-acre diversified garden supplies our kitchen. The experimental orchard continues to be a botanical wonder. And thousands of macadamia trees are thriving.

But agricultural fruit isn't the only fruit thriving in the desert. Here's another story that shows God's master plan at work.

Juan Merino is one of the precious jewels I mentioned in the previous chapter. He worked in our orchard for fifteen years.

As what happens with many migrant workers, Juan and his wife, María, along with their large family (seven daughters and two of their four boys), left their home in Copala, Oaxaca, with the promise of paying jobs and a better life. They followed the crops, starting with pineapples in Vera Cruz and then on to tomatoes in Sinaloa. Enticed by rumors of good jobs in Baja, they arrived there in 1981, only to discover the bitter reality of hard work, horrible living conditions, and little pay.

Because he didn't have the money to return home with his family, Juan silently accepted what he couldn't change—with the help of alcohol. The stress of poverty and a 3-year-old daughter who couldn't walk due to multiple birth defects, together with the need for their two oldest daughters to labor with them in the fields, led to more alcohol consumption, drunkenness, and increased fighting between Juan and María. The daily despair they carried was common among their migrant neighbors.

Shortly after arriving in Baja, their grown son Felix visited them from Tijuana. His demeanor had changed noticeably since they last saw him, and he spoke with passion about God and His Son, Jesus. He said to his parents, "Jesus can give you hope and new life through His power," and then explained how Jesus had made a difference to him personally.

But Juan and María were staunch Catholics steeped in Mexican tradition—which often combines ancestor worship and witchcraft—and María didn't want anything to do with what Felix had to say. When Juan expressed a desire to at least listen to Felix, María stated emphatically, "Felix is Christian. We are not Christians!"

"It wouldn't hurt us to learn more, María. Look at how he's changed. Maybe what he's talking about could help us." Although he struggled with the thought of offending the Virgin Mary and Guadalupe, Juan couldn't deny what he saw in his son.

The next time Felix came to visit, he said, "Papa, I want to pray for Dominga."

Juan hesitated at the request. He had already prayed to numerous spirits and tried all the healing rituals practiced in Oaxacan culture on behalf of his 3-year-old daughter. He and María had given up hope that she'd ever walk.

But Felix persisted with his parents. "Jesus can heal her," he said, and then he prayed confidently to Jehovah Rapha, the Lord who heals.

The following day, Dominga began to walk for the first time. God had healed her!

Seeing his daughter's miracle transformed Juan's life. He realized that maybe God *was* real, and he prayed, "God, if You exist, help me leave everything bad." He also prayed that God would change his heart. At about the same time, our mission's pastor was doing outreach at the camp and invited the family to attend church, where Juan heard more powerful truths and surrendered his life to Christ.

Soon afterward, Juan experienced God's answer to his prayer. He lost his desire to drink. He quit smoking. He left his bad companions. He gave up the paraphernalia related to Oaxacan rituals and superstitions. He released his fears. He and María fell in love again. And their family got involved in the ministry of the church.

People couldn't help but notice Juan's transformation and his humble, sweet spirit. He served the Lord faithfully—fasting, praying, and sharing the good news with others. Although he didn't have much, he was grateful.

After three years of back-breaking labor in the Baja fields and living in the squalid conditions at the camp, Juan received an offer from a man named José, who oversaw the mission's orchard. He said, "Would you like a job? I have work and need someone to help."

Juan readily accepted the opportunity. In addition to the job, he was also given a small plot of land along the river bed at Chilpayates, where he could build a house for his family.

But there's something he and others didn't know because John Moore had sworn us to secrecy.

John had come to one of our board meetings and said, "We have long lines of people waiting at the outreach window to get clothes and shoes for their families. They rely on handouts. Isn't it better to give them work? We could use some help."

However, we had a few people on our board who didn't have John's vision for the orchard and didn't believe it would pay off. They couldn't get behind investing mission funds in the project. So, John then made an impassioned appeal. "I will personally hire six men to work in the orchard." And he did. He supported all of them with his own money until he died.

Juan enjoyed his work in the experimental orchard, the macadamia orchard, and the diversified garden, and didn't miss a single day. He planted, pulled weeds, and prayed over it all. "This is Yours, Lord. Thank You, Lord," he said as he lovingly attended to his duties.

When he walked through the rows of macadamia trees, he carried on a running conversation with God and discovered his calling as an intercessor. He named each tree after someone he knew and diligently interceded on their behalf.

At around the time Juan started working for the mission, Marie Yeager de Morales, one of our staff members, requested permission from our board to use a room in the back of the chapel to teach literacy to a select group of Oaxacan children from the local community and nearby work camps. None of the children had any formal education but were eager to learn and to be "in school." Marie taught them for several months before the Mexican government shut down the program. By then, however, all but a few of her twenty students could read and write and were able to enter the local school.

Juan's son Antonio was one of her pupils. A boy of about 7 or 8 years old, he had a head start among others in his community because of the classes. Not only that, but Marie taught him important lessons about the Lord and greatly influenced his spiritual path.

What Marie had hoped for her students came true in Antonio's life. He learned how to read the Bible on his own, gained a passion for ministry, and wanted to pursue an education. When he was old enough, he studied at our Bible institute. After graduating, he received an invitation to stay and help in the orchard under John Moore's tutelage, which he oversaw once John retired.

Antonio desired to help the mission as much as possible and started studying on his own. He learned a lot about technical production and how to do different applications in grafting. In total, he spent about fifteen years working the orchard, until he was sent out as a spiritual leader ministering to the people.

God has done a mighty work in and through Juan Merino's family. Here's something else that happened.

As a new Christian, Juan struggled to understand his Spanish Bible. He asked Marie if she could find another

Triqui Christian to help him in his own language. She contacted Wycliffe Bible Translators and soon had a response from Barbara Hollenbach, a missionary with New Tribes Mission. Since the time they first connected, Barbara and Juan have worked together to bring the Triqui New Testament to completion.

In 1995, Barbara brought a crew from the United States to record a Triqui version of the *Jesus* film, using the voices of the Merino family. Because a written Triqui language had only recently been developed, most of the Triqui people could not read their own language, so Juan and his family were also involved in recording the entire New Testament. The tapes are copied and distributed through Gospel Recordings.

Today, all of Juan's eleven children are professionals who serve the Lord in various ways. The curse of poverty was broken in one generation!

Even though Juan is well past retirement age, he and his wife, María, still fervently pray for the sick and share the love of Jesus. They also disciple Triqui Christians in surrounding towns.

Juan's story is just one example of how God planted a seed through the work of our mission and caused it to grow into an abundant harvest. God continues to bear fruit in the desert that will last throughout eternity.

⁂

When my mother was 96 years old, she was in a nursing home due to suffering several physically disabling strokes. On my daily visits, she asked about things like family, friends, the children's finances, and whether the mission supply truck got across the border. But of most interest to her was the macadamia orchard.

From the time they were first planted, Mama walked up and down the long rows, praying for the trees and often stopping to read the names on the tags affixed to each one.

The names represented the FFHM friends someone wanted to honor or memorialize.

I enjoyed keeping her updated on the orchard news, such as the latest candy confections created in the Nut House and the health of our current crop. She oohed and aahed and expressed her pleasure at God's continual goodness. But the more we talked, the more I could see in her eyes the longing to be there. Her heartbreaking plea to me on numerous occasions was, "I so want to see the nut orchard."

My reply to her request was always the same. "Uh-huh." But I started to get a nagging feeling of conviction in my spirit. To say yes, when I knew it was impossible for her to make the 16-hour round trip by car, was wrong.

Then God made a way when there seemed to be no way. I talked with Pilot Paul Evans, who had once served on our board, and said, "Do you think Mama could make the trip? She weighs only eighty-five pounds and could easily be lifted into the plane, couldn't she?" I knew Mario, our mission administrator, would be willing to meet us at the air strip with a van and wheelchair.

It all worked out, and Mama's heart desire to see "her" orchard was granted. She enjoyed every minute of her first flight in a small plane—the vistas, and especially the landings. Paul made sure she had the VIP tour.

When we took her back to the nursing home, she seemed somewhat mournful as she said, "They will never believe that I flew down and had lunch in Mexico today!" But we gave her an 8 x 10 color print that captured her experience, and placed it by her bed for all to see. It served as a wonderful remembrance of that special day.

And God gave me a precious memory of Mama and the macadamia nut orchard that will stay in my heart forever.

Top: John Moore was our agronomist for many years. Here he is with his wife, Ginny.

Bottom left: John at work in the macadamia orchard

Bottom right: A package of premium macadamia nuts sold at our mission's coffee shop

Juan Merino was a faithful worker who constantly prayed for the orchard.

In the bottom photo, I'm with Juan and his son Antonio.

My mother, Olive, loved the macadamia orchard and spent a lot of time there. At the age of 96, she longed to see it one last time. God made it possible.

A Touch of Class
at the Mission

A diverse group of people with a variety of backgrounds and denominations makes up our Friday night prayer group. Our love for the Lord and the passion we have for missions around the world is what bonds us together.

One of our earliest members was Pat Durkin. As soon as I found out she'd grown up in a Catholic orphanage, I had a soft spot in my heart for her, and I wanted to learn all about her childhood experiences. The connection we had grew into a close friendship, and she eventually became secretary of our FFHM board. She typed like the wind, could spell, took shorthand, and had marvelous clerical skills—something I greatly appreciated and admired. (Those were the days before computers.) For decades, her family has offered strong support and help to the mission, and her son Keith served there for several years intermittently.

Through Pat, I met her dear friend Corrine Ehrick and invited her to join our group. Corrine was a doll—a tiny, dark-haired lady who oozed charm, beauty, and class. Although she appeared to have so much going for her and displayed a sunny disposition, her life had been full of challenges and heartache—including an abusive childhood and a failed marriage—and at one time she contemplated ending it all. Corrine had attended a special church-sponsored prayer meeting with Pat, which resulted in her having a life-changing encounter with the Holy Spirit.

After Corrine started coming to our home-based prayer group, she volunteered on Saturdays to help sort, size, and box the mountains of clothing and other goods that we warehoused in our garage. As I got to know her, I noticed her unique traits and realized how gifted she was. I also knew she was ready for a fresh start after her devastating divorce.

"Corrine," I said, "I have a wonderful plan for your life." I brought up the idea of her going to the mission and volunteering as hostess, a role that had recently opened up.

At first, she poo-pooed the opportunity and presented a number of excuses for why she couldn't do it. "I can't. I'm still working at the bank in Glendale." "I'll think about it when I'm retired." "I'm not qualified." "I've never been to Bible school."

But then God started working on her and kindled a desire for her to go. One day, she told me she had decided to quit her executive position at the bank and to give up her lovely apartment and all her beautiful furnishings. "I'm going to Mexico," she said.

The information surprised and delighted me.

In July of 1985, Corrine moved to Colonia Vicente Guerrero, intending to fill the hostess position and work with visiting teams. However, the hostess had changed her mind about leaving, so Corrine was assigned the job of bookkeeper and bilingual secretary. Not exactly thrilled with the new arrangement, she vowed to give it three months.

But God had bigger plans for her amazing talent and benevolent spirit, and she forgot to go home.

If ever there was a "jewel of the mission," it was Corrine. By the time she became administrator after only four years, she had already served as bookkeeper, secretary, hostess, discipler, minister of mercy, outreach coordinator, and assistant administrator. She had the admiration of local business leaders and brought the element of respectability to the mission.

After nine years, Corrine took a break to care for her ailing mother and then returned—acting as communications liaison, counselor-at-large, and helping with whatever else was needed.

My spunky and elegant friend was as comfortable in high heels as she was in work boots. I watched in awe at how she could charm guests at a luncheon with the governor's wife and hobnob with the most illustrious people. Yet she was okay with cleaning the toilets at Hogar Para Niños.

Her dedication to the desperate and lost in the San Quintín Valley showed in the way she joyfully ministered to the poorest of the poor. She met a 79-year-old blind man named Cleofas while doing outreach. Her first visit with him was after a rainstorm in his dilapidated, chicken-coop home. His roof amounted to a tarp filled with ridges of rainwater, and his place was so filthy she couldn't find a spot to sit.

Due to his blindness, he couldn't see what he was consuming, and Corrine noticed he drank from a jug green with mold. He didn't have a family to care for him, so from that day on she made sure he was bathed, shaved, and had laundered clothes, as well as fresh food and a clean living space.

Corrine's unique blend of fearless determination and grace enabled her to touch the hardest of hearts, including a rancher who had a thousand laborers in his camp. Back then, conditions in the camp were horrible—cardboard shanties, no water, and no electricity. Corrine was the catalyst that led the rancher to tear down the unstable shelters his workers lived in and to provide them with block homes.

Because of her resolve, dramatic improvements were made in many of the camps. Those in charge learned she was a force. She had a way about her that made it impossible to say no.

I learned that as well.

As Corrine served in outreach, she realized that many young children were left alone to care for themselves while their parents worked in the fields. One experience in particular affected her greatly. She saw a 5-year-old girl taking care of a 3-year-old boy and an 8-month-old baby. There was a pile of slop on the ground. Naturally, Corrine thought it was the dog's food, but then the children began to eat it.

She came to me and said, "I think we should start a day care center to help these single mothers."

"That would be impossible," I said. "There are thousands of children in the camps."

"But we could make a difference for thirty." Referencing our Hogar Para Niños facility, she said, "Look at this fabulous building we have here. Why can't we use it?"

She made a convincing argument. How could I say no?

Because of Corrine's vision and insistence, we started a day care program that serves thirty preschool-aged children of migrant workers with great need (children who would otherwise be left unattended). We provide a bath, food, education, transportation five days a week, and peace of mind for their mothers. The best part of all is that the children carry home with them the gospel of Christ and the lessons they've learned.

Since that time, we've opened another day care program in a different area as part of our outreach ministry. It's one of the practical ways we can bless our neighbors and have an eternal impact on their lives.

I'm thankful for Corrine's vision and especially grateful to God for how He worked in her life to bring her to Baja. She was a shining example of God's love to all of us, and her legacy continues.

∞

When she first came to the mission, Corrine lived in a 10 x 10 space without a bathroom or running water. Her inconvenience became a burden for me, so I asked the heavenly Father for better housing for my beloved friend.

Who would have guessed that an auto accident would produce an answer?

While I was driving the stretch between Tijuana and Ensenada, a spare tire flew off the truck in front of me. I swerved and missed hitting it by inches. As my passengers and I thanked God for our narrow escape, I suddenly realized that the vehicles behind us had not been so fortunate.

A truck towing a first-class trailer swerved. The car behind them hit the tire, spun, and hit the trailer, which in turn broke loose from the truck. When the screeching and smashing ceased, we all prayed while one of my passengers used a crow bar to pry the couple out of the overturned truck.

Dr. Ratzlaff from Red Deer, Alberta, another passenger in the car with me, administered emergency medical care until the ambulance arrived to take the injured woman to the hospital. We stayed with her husband and helped him gather up their valuables, which had been thrown all over the road upon impact.

After the tow truck and police came, we continued south to Colonia Vicente Guerrero. I couldn't help but keep thinking of that beautiful trailer.

A few days later, I returned to the US and phoned the couple involved in the accident to check up on them. The man told me the amazing story of how a Mexican policeman had stayed five hours, helping him with his truck, trailer, and wife.

"Whatever happened to your trailer?" I asked.

"Well, it's kind of strange," he said. "They pulled the trailer out of Mexico, and right now it's at a salvage yard near the border, east of San Diego. The insurance company totaled it."

"Totaled it? The only thing wrong with it was a bend in the front!" I was shocked. "That was a gorgeous trailer!"

"Yeah, I have the papers. The insurance company is paying me off and then the salvage company will put it up for auction." As our conversation ended, he gave me the address where I'd find it. He also said he had the option to buy it back, if I was interested.

Yes, of course, I was interested! Visions of the trailer had been floating through my mind for days. But how would I get it?

The sixth chapter of Matthew talks about praying to your Father in secret, and the Father who sees in secret will reward you openly. That's what I did. And here's how He answered—

That night I spoke to a small prayer group at Magnolia Park Methodist Church in Burbank. After the service, the pastor gave me a check for $1,274. Maybe you can guess the rest, knowing God's sweet grace. The salvage price of the 30-foot Holiday Rambler was $1,250 plus $24 for the storage fees (six days at $4 per day).

Hallelujah! God provided. But now that I had the money to purchase the huge trailer, how would I transport it two hundred miles south with a broken axle?

I immediately thought of Rod Johnson, a man from Santa Rosa who had a vehicle equipped for that type of work, but try as I might there was no reaching him. "Lord, what do I do?"

Then I received a call from Mojave, California. Who else but Rod Johnson, traveling back from Nevada and wanting to stop by in his fully-equipped truck. "Hurry," I said, "because I have a wonderful plan for your life."

Three days later, he delivered Corrine's home. Bob Southard and Art Egger, both excellent craftsmen, happened to be on hand to repair the outside of the trailer while their wives cleaned the inside.

God's wonderful answer to specific prayer inspired others to participate. A stranger provided the gas money. Someone else paid for the trailer hitch repair. Our Friday night prayer group provided carpet and furnishings. New dishes, utensils, and linens came from a family in China Lake, California.

Our heavenly Father showed up in above-and-beyond ways. As Corrine and I cared for the needs of others, He cared for us.

My dear friend Corrine Ehrick was comfortable in high heels or work boots.

Bottom left: Corrine is with Eva Schiaffino Quick, who also served at the mission. At one time, they were lovingly referred to as "the generals."

Bottom right: This is Cleofas, a 79-year-old man Corrine met while doing outreach. Because he was blind and had no one to care for him, she made sure his needs were met.

Top: Corrine and me

Bottom: Jack and Pat Durkin were with us from the beginning. Pat has been an intercessor every step of the way and was consistently present at the Friday night prayer meetings for FFHM. She also served as a valuable secretary. She's the one who introduced us to Corrine.

The Birth of a Medical Center

In the early-to-mid 1980s, I visited one of the mission's staff who was a patient at Hospital el Buen Pastor in San Quintín. As I headed toward the door to leave, a petite Mexican woman rapidly waved her arms to get my attention. She was in a big room, where at that time parents or loved ones stayed with their hospitalized children and took care of their needs.

The woman rattled off what seemed to be an urgent message, but she spoke in Spanish so fast I couldn't understand. "No hablo español," I said, and tried to get her to slow down.

She continued speaking and gestured to help me grasp the meaning of her words. Finally, I understood that the newborn baby she pointed to in the Isolette across the room had been abandoned by his mother and had been there for two days without being fed.

I'm not sure why she brought me into the circumstances. Maybe she saw that I was an American and she thought that Americans could get things done. I don't know. But she wouldn't let me go until I did something about it.

I found a nurse who, thankfully, spoke English and told her what the lady had said. "Why isn't this baby being fed?" I asked.

"He is too weak to suck, and we don't have a needle small enough to feed him intravenously."

Seriously?

"You can't let a baby die because you don't have a needle! What's keeping you from getting one?" The passion building in my voice was noticeable.

"The closest source is Ensenada, and our vehicle is broken down."

The whole situation infuriated me, and the nurse became somewhat defensive as I stated emphatically, "You cannot let this baby die here for lack of a vehicle."

"You take him!" she said. "The only place he can get help is in Ensenada. We can send a letter along with you explaining that the baby was abandoned, the mother is unknown, and we don't have the ability to care for him."

She's got to be kidding me, right?

Within a few minutes the nurse placed the weak, tiny bundle with beautiful black hair in my arms and gave me a bulb syringe. "You'll probably need to suction his nose to keep his passageways clear."

This was crazy! I visit a friend at the hospital, and I come out with a dying baby. They handed a complete stranger a dying baby! Nobody in the states would believe such a thing.

Lord, how do I always get myself into these weird predicaments?

I placed the infant on the front seat of my car and headed north. On my way, I remembered that Chuck was due to arrive at the mission with the weekly load of supplies. *He drives faster than I do. He's a trained paramedic. He loves children.* My thoughts led me to the conclusion that it would be best to transfer the responsibility to him. Ensenada is about 130 miles from the mission. In those days, with bad roads and all the mountains, the trip took several hours each way.

I got to the mission at the exact time Sam and Nell Greenburg pulled in. They were from Osborne Neighborhood Church in Arleta, California. I had been inviting them to the mission for years because they were passionate soul winners, and it was their first time to visit. Nell just happened to be a registered nurse.

Before she had a chance to put her feet on the ground, I blurted out, "Nell, I've got a dying baby here, and I'm going to ask Chuck to take him to Ensenada. He needs suctioning. Could you ride with Chuck and take care of the baby on the way?"

Nell looked at me as if I were nuts. "I just got here," she said, "and it was a stressful drive on those terrible roads!" But she took one peek at the baby and—even though she was tired after many hours of traveling—got in the car with Chuck and went with him to Ensenada.

Once they arrived at the hospital, they encountered problems with check-in. "We won't admit the baby unless you give us $700," the hospital representative said.

That took Chuck by surprise. "I don't have $700."

"Well, we can't take the baby because we don't know that you'll come back."

"What if I leave my badge here—my fire department badge? It will be my guarantee that I'll return and pay whatever the baby's bill is." As a matter of principle, firemen and policemen never surrender their badges. It's a big risk. But Chuck offered to part with his to help save the little one's life.

The hospital rep agreed to the compromise, and Chuck and Nell returned to the mission. The next morning at Sala (the meeting place where morning devotions are held every day), the staff and visitors covered it in prayer. They took up an offering and collected enough to settle the debt.

Fred Zavala, our mission administrator at the time, followed Chuck to the Ensenada hospital, planning to bring the baby back with him to keep in our care. Sadly, the little one had died. Fred returned with the lifeless infant in his trunk and buried him in an unmarked grave.

The experience greatly impacted Nell. "That baby should never have died," she said. With that, and observing the poor conditions at the nearby labor camps, Nell realized something needed to be done to help our migrant neighbors.

She told her husband, "I can make a difference here." So, they decided to relocate to the mission. She attended to basic medical needs and educated people about healthcare. He pitched in by doing maintenance work.

With the board's approval, Nell converted four Sunday school rooms at the back of our chapel into a clinic—our first medical center. Word quickly got out to the camps, and Nell faced long lines of people every day.

Before long, she met a Oaxacan doctor who had moved to Colonia Vicente Guerrero from the mainland. Dr. Naftali Mendoza was trying to establish a practice in town, but struggled because of the prejudice Mexican people had against indigenous people. Nell asked if he would consider helping at the mission and in the labor camps. He readily agreed.

What a gift Dr. Mendoza was for us! He became our first doctor and volunteered his services two days a week. He was also on call for emergencies. In the meantime, we offered him our support and helped him grow his practice in town. It was a win-win situation. The number of people he treated highlighted the community's great need for free medical care.

Over the years, our little clinic in the back of the chapel evolved into a beautiful, high-tech medical center built on our premises. Blessed with countless contributions from our supporters, miraculous provisions from God, and the help of excellent medical professionals, we've been able to extend hope and a healing touch, as well as form many redemptive relationships with our neighbors. The vital work continues to this day.

⁓∞⁓

The importance of the clinic became even more clear to me while I was at the Baja mission in the fall of 1985. A knock on my door awakened me in the wee hours of the night. I climbed out of bed, swung open the door, and in the dim porch light I faced a worried and distraught Oaxacan man.

The young-adult Oaxacan had ridden his bicycle from one of the nearby migrant worker camps and was breathing heavily as a stream of words flowed from his mouth. I couldn't understand what he was saying, but I could sense the desperation in his voice. I promptly sought out Corrine Ehrick to translate for me.

"Hermana, my wife is in hard labor, but the baby doesn't come. Please help!" he said. "She's been in labor for two days and there isn't a midwife or anyone who can help."

I threw on some clothes, and with Corrine sprang into action. We notified Dr. Mendoza about the situation and helped get the struggling woman settled in at our little medical clinic.

The young mother, Monica, was in excruciating pain, but all we had to offer was compassion, prayer, and aspirin. Our clinic, though clean, was primitive. We had no delivery table, and the single cot being used was too low, too soft, and made the contractions more difficult. Soon after we arrived, the lights went out. Power outages were common, but this one couldn't have come at a more inconvenient time.

A piece of plywood served as a door on a bathroom stall. "Perhaps we could lay this on the saggy bed," I said, and Corrine and I got to work. She held a flashlight as I used a teaspoon to remove the screws from the hinges. That provided a firmer base, but because of the bed height, Dr. Mendoza had to work from his knees.

Excitement and apprehension filled the next six and a half hours. When the baby girl's wet head full of thick black hair finally emerged, we could understand the reason for the delayed delivery. The umbilical cord was wrapped around her body and neck.

After capably handling the problem, Dr. Mendoza cleaned the little one and wrapped her in a blanket. Then, with a big bright smile, he introduced her to her mother, who named her Esther.

What a joy and privilege to observe this miracle of birth! The story would have had a different—and probably tragic— ending if it hadn't been for nurse Nell's vision to start a clinic and Dr. Mendoza's dedication. (Esther went on to attend our Bible institute years later. It's just one of the wonderful ways God works.)

On each subsequent trip to the mission, I visited the family at their nearby labor camp and brought them a care package. They lived in one of the hundreds of cardboard hovels there. On one such visit, Monica shared her concern about her babies. One of them was covered with ringworm, and little Esther had open, weeping sores that looked like impetigo.

A group of men, on their first visit from a church in South Barrington, Illinois, accompanied me and joined me in prayer for the children. Before leaving, I assured Monica that we would return later in the day with medication.

When we pulled up a few hours later, Monica ran out to meet us. She lifted baby Esther's clothing to show us that she had been completely healed. Instead of raw sores, pink new skin covered the area. It was a supernatural blessing from God!

A couple of decades later, on a trip to the mission, I saw Monica, Esther (who was now 27), and Esther's young son, Jesus, in the waiting room of our new medical center. I hadn't seen them in years. After introductions and embraces, Monica asked, "Do you remember the day Esther was healed of the skin disease?"

How could I forget? I'll also never forget the day she was born or how far we've come since then.

Top: Nell Greenberg inspired the birth of the medical center.

Bottom: Dr. Naftali Mendoza, our first mission doctor, with his family

Investing in
Our Neighbors

My mother and I were at the mission and asleep in Noah's Ark (a mobile home named after Noah Davis, the first president of our board). At 10:30 p.m., we heard a knock. It got louder and more urgent.

I opened the door to a slightly-built Oaxacan man with a terrified look on his face. When he saw me, a rush of words in his native dialect spilled from his lips. I couldn't understand him, but in my heart I knew he was pleading for help.

He gestured for me to go with him to his camp up the road. All I could discern were the words "accidente" and "tragedia." And I could feel the anguish in his cry.

"You're not going out in the night, are you?" my mother asked.

"I have to go with this man, Mother," I said. "He needs me."

We walked in the darkness about a mile up the road near the Hamilton Ranch. The frightened man tried to communicate with me, but I understood very little. We continued up a hill toward an open-sided packing shed.

What I saw at our destination required no translation. It was horrific and devastating beyond anything I'd ever experienced.

Forty-two migrant farm laborers had been packed in a stake bed truck and riding home from the fields. The northbound truck mismanaged a curve and dip in the road and rolled over. Twenty-one lifeless bodies lay in front of me. Twenty-one young men with wives and children.

There was no wailing, no weeping. Just a multitude of women standing or sitting on plastic buckets with children at their sides. Their heads moved up and down, but they remained silent as they processed unimaginable grief. The deafening stillness of death filled the air.

If I ever doubted God's existence, it was then. Overcome with agony, my heart cried out. *God, where are You in this mess?*

Then, for the first time in my life, I heard God's audible voice. "I am with you always." It was so powerful, I actually turned to look over my shoulder.

Today, I think of the many times in the past that God sent promises of His presence to give comfort, courage, and strength to those who needed it. They're preserved in the pages of His Word to encourage us from day to day.

Here's a beautiful one He gave in Isaiah 41:10: "So do not fear, for I am with you; do not be dismayed, for I am your God. I will strengthen you and help you; I will uphold you with my righteous right hand" (NIV).

When Joshua faced a terrifying situation in Joshua 1:9, God said, "Be strong and courageous. Do not be afraid; do not be discouraged, for the LORD your God will be with you wherever you go" (NIV).

And in Exodus 3, when Moses questioned God about a job he didn't think he could handle, God replied, "I will be with you."

That night, as I stood among those who suffered so deeply, feeling helpless and without answers, God used a similar message to calm my aching spirit and to offer comfort for the grieving families. None of us knew what God had planned for their futures, and we certainly didn't understand the purpose, but we had these words of assurance to cling to: "I will be with you always." It's a promise that brought a measure of peace.

I knew some of what the women would face in the days ahead. Without husbands, they would have no provision, no benefits from the owner of the farm or the Mexican government. There would be no caskets for the twenty-one men who died. Instead, their bodies would be moved to the local cemetery and placed in an open trench.

The situation was well beyond my comprehension.

I did the only thing I knew to do—placed my hands on the women and prayed. But I had another conversation happening simultaneously in my mind. *God, how could You have allowed this?*

The camp closed after the tragedy, and the women and children resettled in another location—on the road to Don Diego's Restaurant. Because Corrine Ehrick had invested time in the camps, she knew the women were artisans from Oaxaca and had the ability to weave beautiful tapestries. She helped them set up their looms and readied them for business. To support the women and their families, we brought groups of visitors and work teams to them to purchase their woven placemats, table runners, and other handcrafted items.

I'm grateful we were able to assist the women in getting established.

But this story is only one small example of the countless opportunities we've been given to help our neighbors and invest in their lives. As I ponder the magnitude of their needs and the disadvantages they face, I'm overwhelmed.

When the tens of thousands of Oaxacan people migrated to our area, they brought with them their culture, their poverty, their impact on local social structures, their numerous native languages, and their illiteracy rate of about ninety percent.

The Lord has taught our FFHM team many things as we've ministered to them over the years. We began by giving them food, clothing, and medical care. Then we introduced them to the risen Savior who gave them eternal life and hope. But because the Bible is so central to the Christian faith, these people were crippled in their walk without the ability to read the Word of God.

They didn't have the advantage as we do of picking up a Bible and reading God's many promises, such as "I will be with you" and "I have not forgotten you." They're unable to mine the treasures that remind them of the future and hope God has in store for them. Interpreting the message of how much God loves them was impossible.

Not only did their reading detriment create an obstacle to feeding on God's Word, but it also caused tribulation, persecution, and shame.

One time we hung a big sign on the back door of the medical clinic. It said in Spanish, "The doctor is not here today." During the day, I walked by the clinic on my way to the day care center and saw a long line of people waiting. When I came back about four hours later, the line was still there. I said to one of the men, "The doctor is no aquí este día" and pointed to the sign.

He said, "Hermana, we can't read."

They had come to the clinic and waited for hours because they couldn't read!

As someone who personally knows the challenges and pain of illiteracy from my childhood, I was not okay with that. And as Mexican society continues to become more literate, I couldn't bear the thought that our migrant neighbors would always be considered second-class citizens in the eyes of the Mexican people.

The FFHM board discussed the issue and decided to start an adult literacy program. We knew that teaching the Oaxacan people to read would be an ambitious undertaking. With 157 languages or dialects, totally unlike Spanish, we also knew that it would be a slow process. And it would require the right person to take on the task.

God, in His perfect timing, sent us Diana McLaughlin. I met her at Christian Renewal Center in Silverton, Oregon, where I was teaching at a retreat. When I learned that she spoke Spanish, was trained by Wycliffe Bible Translators, had a linguistics degree, and specialized in teaching adults to read, I said, "Diana, I have a wonderful plan for your life."

Diana visited the camps and got to know the people and their needs. She prepared the teaching materials and began with an initial target group of Spanish-speaking Oaxacans who had come to know the Lord through our outreach ministry.

As they learned to read and write, they gained confidence and self-respect. Teaching literacy is an investment on our part that has been well worth the effort and has led to lasting change.

We want our migrant neighbors to live with purpose and dignity, and most of all, we want to shine light into their darkness. Through our three-fold initiative of rescuing children, reaching the lost, and restoring the broken, we have a multitude of ways to do that. There is much yet to be done.

Top: Dr. Patrick Murphy and his family

Bottom: Dr. Murphy was gone for the day. He had posted a sign on the door that said the clinic was closed, but a long line of people formed and stayed for hours because they couldn't read. That was the beginning of our literacy program.

"This is my commandment:
Love each other in the same
way I have loved you."
(John 15:12, NLT)

A Bible Institute

In October 1986, I visited my good friends Pastor Allan and Eunice Hansen at the Christian Renewal Center in Silverton, Oregon, a ministry they founded in 1970. While we were catching up on each other's lives, Allan asked me a couple of questions. "Charla, what two things do you have in your heart? What are two desires that haven't been fulfilled?"

Because of the rapid expansion of our mission—and I had just returned from the longest fund-raising trip I'd ever made—I said, "Well . . . first of all, I can't keep up the pace with so many long trips on the road, going from little church to little church." I had been away from home for twenty-one days and spoke twenty-seven times. During that period, I received less than $200 in offerings. "A video that we could send to churches, rather than my needing to be there in person, would be nice."

With that suggestion, the Hansens and their ministry in Silverton blessed us with a professional, first-class video called *The Harvest.* We made it available for churches throughout North America, and it was a great help in gaining new support for the mission and freeing me up for other things.

The video was something I'd had on my heart for a while. But the second desire I mentioned had been tucked away inside of me since that early October morning in 1966—the day God gave me His vision for the property in Colonia Vicente Guerrero. "I'd love to have a Bible institute where we could train nationals to do the work of the ministry and to take the

121

gospel to unreached people groups. I'd love to have a Bible institute like the one where Jesus became Lord of my life."

As I finished talking, I saw Allan look over at his son-in-law, Terry Yarbrough. His eyes glanced back at me and then returned to Terry. I could tell by their body language and the little nods they gave each other that God was up to something big. My spirit quickened within me, and I knew that this was the birth of a Bible institute.

He said, "We will help you do whatever it takes to get it established. After four years, FFHM will have full responsibility for the institute. By then it should be self-supporting."

In March 1988, a team began remodeling the chapel to be used as part of the Bible institute facilities. Then the ownership of Rancho Los Chilpayates was transferred to us. The old buildings on that property had been ravaged by the flood in 1981 and needed a lot of renovation. The plan was to use that site, which was only a mile and a half from the mission, for housing our institute staff and students.

Our loyal supporters prayed. Work groups supplied the labor. God faithfully provided the resources and help we needed.

Terry raised additional money by getting pledges from sponsors for a bicycle ride. He, along with Keith Durkin (one of the quiet heroes who helped make our Bible institute a reality) and a few other men, pedaled 1,524 miles from Silverton, Oregon, to Colonia Vicente Guerrero and collected more than $13,000.

Our Bible institute (Instituto Biblico Cristo Por Su Mundo) officially opened on January 2, 1989, with twelve enthusiastic students—nine men and three women—including seven from Oaxaca, one from Guatemala, and the rest from various places in Mexico. On Sunday, December 10, 1989, eight of them marched up the aisle of the mission church to the tune of "Onward Christian Soldiers" for graduation. (We've since developed a three-year curriculum that includes practical ministry service hours.)

After each graduate received a diploma from director Max Christian, the teachers, pastors, and members of the Bible institute committee seated on the platform greeted them. The students then honored Terry Yarbrough for his vision and guidance with a special diploma they had all signed.

In a scene not to be forgotten, a group of raggedy, wide-eyed Oaxacan children excitedly observed the ceremony from the front row of the crowded church. I couldn't help but wonder if perhaps a seed of hope was planted in their hearts that they too could someday follow in the students' footsteps.

Severiano Flores, one of our graduates that day, was a 23-year-old married man with two children. He came from the Copala District of Juxtlahuaca, Oaxaca. A Christian for seven years, he initially heard the gospel in Mexico City and then began a relationship with Christ through the ministry of our mission church.

During his year of Bible school, Severiano learned to speak, read, and write Spanish, and then he learned to read and write Triqui, his native language. (We're grateful for the help of Wycliffe Bible Translator Barbara Hollenbeck, who specialized in many of the Oaxacan dialects.) This young man became the main narrator for Campus Crusade's production of the *Jesus* film in the Triqui language and went on to serve as a church planter among his people in Copala, Oaxaca. Sadly, Severiano faced persecution and was martyred because of his faith, but not before reaching many with the good news of Christ.

Since its inception, the Bible institute's goal has been to make disciples and raise up ambassadors who carry the gospel to those who need hope. We have commissioned many of our graduates to return to Oaxaca and minister to their own people on the mainland. They're able to go into remote areas—often primitive and dangerous places—that would otherwise be impossible for us to reach. Some of our students have become full-time pastors. Others are serving in mercy ministries, evangelism to adults and children, and outreach among their people in the camps.

Not long after we got the Bible institute running, Max Christian, the dean, decided to move classes from the Hogar Para Niños campus and to make it a separate entity. So, a crew from Silverton, Oregon, began construction on two new classrooms at the Rancho Los Chilpayates site where we already had the recently renovated housing units.

From the very beginning of our Bible institute discussions, Chuck had said, "Do. Not. Build. By. The. River." He still had vivid memories of the flood years earlier when he and a small group of other men carried the thirty-seven frightened orphans from there to safety at our home for children.

Because of his insistence and uneasiness, we sought out the help of an engineer from Southern California, who suggested we install gabions (Reno mattresses) on the riverbank to protect the property from erosion. Chuck purchased the large chain-link, cage-type things from a supplier in Sacramento, and a team put them in place. All summer long, while classroom construction progressed, volunteer work groups filled the cages with rocks and boulders to create a retaining wall along the river.

Finally, in March of 1992, after two years of students' going back and forth from the mission chapel, the Bible institute had its own classrooms on its own property. We were able to take extra students in the fall because of the additional space and generous contributions from our supporters.

Things were progressing well, and then, in early January 1993, we experienced a surprise turn of events.

I had visited a hospital in California and saw that they had a fabulous, almost-new Hobart dishwasher for sale. I looked at the specs, saw what it was capable of doing, and fell in love. My immediate reaction was, *I want that dishwasher for Hogar Para Niños! That's exactly what we need!*

But as I longed for the appliance and imagined how sanitary our home for children's kitchen could be with that particular model, reality reminded me that I'd have a hard time selling our board on replacing the existing dishwasher. We had just purchased it—and it was a good one—but our facility didn't have the required water pressure for it to sterilize the dishes effectively.

Then I had an idea. I sent a fax from our home office in North Hollywood to Bill Brabham at the mission. (Bill was one of our gifted volunteers who did so much for us.) I said, "Bill, would you please go to Chilpayates and see if we have enough pressure to operate a commercial dishwasher over there? It's really important to me." My hope was that we could move the dishwasher from Hogar Para Niños to the Bible institute and purchase the Hobart for the children's home. It would be a win-win situation.

Bill's reply came quickly. "Pressure?" he wrote. "The kitchen and dining room have just been washed away. Torrential rains . . . floods . . . shift in the river."

As I kept reading, I learned that the Bible institute was almost gone—the assistant director's house, the kitchen, the laundry room, and the trees had all been washed away—and the foundations of the dorms were being eroded. A complete evacuation was in progress.

A strange combination of frontal rain and unusual atmospheric warming over the distant snow-capped mountains had turned the usually docile Santo Domingo River north of the mission into a raging monster. The deluge tore up roads, washed out bridges, isolated communities, and stranded many up and down the Baja Peninsula.

Throughout the day, I continued to correspond with Bill. He asked, "Do we tear down the classrooms to salvage the roofing material and windows? We won't do that without your direction."

I gave the go-ahead to save as much building material as possible. Thanks to the outstanding leadership of Bob Bond from Cottage Grove, Oregon, all available hands pitched in to carefully dismantle everything that was nailed down. Even as they raced against time, not a window was broken!

Another fax with questions came. "Do we send the Bible school students home? We don't have any room for them to stay here at the mission."

"Keep the students," I replied. "Surely we can find a place for them to stay."

I can't begin to describe my pain and heartbreak due to the day's devastating news. The weight of the circumstances pressed upon me, and by nighttime I couldn't hold back my tears. I cried out to God, "All our efforts, Lord. All our efforts. I don't understand You. I really don't. In one day, it's all washed away. Everything the men from Silverton built. Everything our volunteers have done. The Bible school that You established. All our efforts gone."

In the midst of releasing my pent-up thoughts and emotions, I sensed the gentle voice of my heavenly Father. "The Bible institute hasn't washed away, Child. Only the buildings have. The Bible institute was birthed of Me. It will survive." I took that as a word from the Lord, and I felt an urgency to deliver that message to the students and staff south of the border.

After receiving God's comfort that night, I allowed myself to dream a bit. I envisioned what a new facility might look like if I could build it myself. As the picture became clear in my mind, I described it to Chuck, and he sketched it on paper. I tucked his drawing away for later.

We had a three-month supply of food in our warehouse, and I knew that our migrant communities and neighbors would be in need of blankets, food, and so many other things. If the bridges were washed out, it could be a long time without relief. So, I followed my heart to Mexico, riding down in the big truck with Ken Gustafson.

The rain continued to come in torrents, and the first load of provisions had to be dropped off at one of our satellite churches on the north side of the river due to a washed-out bridge. Realizing the danger, and because of apprehension about the bridges to the north, Ken turned around and headed immediately back to Southern California. I stayed behind and slept on a pew in the church.

Determined to deliver God's important message to the intended recipients—our Bible institute students and staff— I followed five men (pastors from the satellite churches) into the river. Holding a rope, we crossed against a strong current in muddy water that at times was waist deep. The weight of the sand in our shoes made lifting our feet almost impossible.

Using my left hand, I held a waterproof office mailbag— with $10,000 inside—on my head. I needed to get that money to the mission for its survival. My right hand grasped the rope tightly. One of the pastors kept saying, "Hermana Charla, don't look at the water. Just keep your eyes on the other side." Praise the Lord, we all made it across safely, but not without a few scares.

Once we arrived and I had the opportunity to speak to the students in the prayer chapel, only five of the original twenty-seven remained—Glenn, Raúl, Lilia, Galia, and María. The others had returned to their homes. The five who stayed had no place to go. Yes, I was disappointed, but I was confident God had a plan. "We're going to rebuild," I promised, and encouraged each of them to hang in there with us.

Although I didn't know the future, I knew something about the body of Christ and that God worked in mysterious ways. I wanted to assure our discouraged students that God could cause good to come from this challenge. "The finest hours of the church have been in times of tribulation," I said. "We will rally, and we will rebuild—but this time on higher ground. And we will be stronger for it." I invited the students to speak to me privately if they had questions or concerns. Glenn needed more assurance and lingered behind.

Shortly after that, we enlisted the help of Peter Bianchini, a Chicago building contractor, who also served for years as chairman of our board of directors. He designed a beautiful structure for us. The blueprint was almost exactly like what I had envisioned that January night, including the arches, and looked amazingly similar to the sketch Chuck drew. The only difference was a missing palm tree. And Peter hadn't even seen the picture, which just proved that God's fingerprints were all over it.

In the fall of 1993, we held a groundbreaking ceremony on the mission property, and in April of 1995, we dedicated the new building. Each of the five students who stayed with us has become a vital part of the mission's far-reaching ministry today.

I still don't understand why things happened the way they did. And it's sometimes hard for me to admit that Chuck was right about building by the river. (He hasn't let me forget it.) But I'm grateful to God for fulfilling His promise to me and for doing bigger and better things with—and through—the Bible institute than I could have ever imagined.

A flood in 1993 washed away our newly built Bible school.

Top: Pastor Severiano Flores was one of the first graduates from our Bible school. He was later martyred in Oaxaca.

Bottom: After the flood, only five students remained—Glenn, Raúl, María, Galia, and Lilia.

Our Servant-Leader
and His Gift of Grace

When I think of the strange way God brought Mario Cordoba to us, I'm reminded of Abraham's story. Genesis 12:1 says, "The LORD had said to Abram, "Go from your country, your people and your father's household to the land I will show you" (NIV).

In November 1988, God took Mario out of his land.

He didn't know God in a personal way at the time. In fact, the idea of a God who had allowed the excruciating pain and turmoil in his life enraged him and caused him to question God's existence. But on November 12, he awoke with a strong sensation in his spirit that he needed to leave his home in Pachuca to seek a peaceful environment for his three young daughters.

He didn't understand the feeling of urgency, and he thought it would go away, but it only intensified.

A well-learned man and a single father, Mario had a successful career in the Department of Education. His mother's side of the family provided good help with his children, so he didn't have a cause to leave, nor did he have a place to go.

As he discussed his internal struggle with a co-worker, he remembered something his friend's wife had previously mentioned about a place in the north that helped people. He asked for more information.

Thanks to their assistance, by that evening Mario held a crumpled-up envelope with these words written on it: Hogar Para Niños, Colonia Vicente Guerrero. His co-worker's wife hadn't been there for a long time and wasn't even sure whether it still existed.

Things didn't make sense, but Mario, compelled by that inner voice, took his three greatest treasures—his daughters—to the public bus station the next morning and left all he had ever known behind.

He had specific instructions about which buses to take from Pachuca to Mexico City and then on to Mexicali, which is near the California border. From there they'd travel south to Ensenada, where they would board another bus headed toward a tiny place called Vicente Guerrero. They would ride more than two thousand miles.

His notes said, "When you arrive, you will see a bank on the other side of the street. At the bank there will be a sign. That sign will tell you where to go."

After three days of traveling, their bus stopped in Colonia Vicente Guerrero. As the instructions advised, Mario went to the bank across the street and looked for the sign. A taxi driver came along, got out of the cab, and helped them load their luggage in the trunk. "Get in," he said. "I'll take you where you're going."

"How do you know where I'm going?" Mario asked. The driver didn't respond, but he delivered the tired travelers to the parking lot at Hogar Para Niños and drove away.

So, there they stood in the dark at 8 p.m. on Friday, November 18—cold, hungry, weary. A 30-something-year-old man holding his 9-year-old daughter with cerebral palsy, and with a 7-year-old and 6-year-old at his side, he was a man without a job. His family had no home. They were in an unknown land for an unknown reason and carrying only a few small suitcases.

Mario knocked on a door of a nearby building, and the house father who answered connected him with Max Christian, the mission administrator. Max wouldn't have been there at the time because of a meeting in North Hollywood, but he realized he had forgotten something and returned to get it.

Max provided hospitality that evening. His wife, Alicia, prepared a bed for Mario's daughters and offered the family a good meal. Into the wee hours of the night Mario answered Max's many questions. "What are you doing here?" "Where are you coming from?" "Where is your wife?" "Where is your family?" "What do you believe?" "Where do you work?" "What do you do?" Finally, after the long grilling, Mario went to sleep on the sofa.

Max left early the next morning, promising to discuss Mario's situation at the meeting and whether his daughters would be able to stay. That day, Alicia took them to a tiny, one-bedroom trailer and got them set up there temporarily. They didn't leave the trailer at all on Saturday or Sunday.

Insisting they show up for the morning meal on Monday, Alicia said, "Breakfast is at 7 a.m. in the dining hall, and you must be there. You can sit at my table." Mario made sure they were there on time. When promptly at seven o'clock someone stood up to pray, Mario had a revelation. The people who surrounded him were Christians. He wasn't happy.

After the meal, they went back to the trailer and Mario told his girls, "Pack your bags. We're leaving." Thankfully, God intervened and that didn't happen.

Over the weekend, while at the North Hollywood board meeting with Max, I heard about the new arrivals. My immediate response was, "We cannot care for a severely handicapped child. It takes three people full time to care for one." But governed by sympathy—and even empathy—rather than reason, I drove from North Hollywood to the mission, a 10-hour drive. When I met Mario and his three little ones, I knew it would be a criminal act to separate him from his children. His daughter Sandra was helplessly dependent on him; he had to feed her and care for her every need.

A strange thought came to my mind as I talked with our mysterious surprise guest. *One day this tall, handsome man, filled with compassion, will be the administrator of the mission.* Another thought followed, and I knew it was from God. *Touch not His anointed.*

I asked Max if we had any open staff positions. He hesitated. "Just one," he said. "A pig keeper. And it pays only $50 a month plus room and board."

Max was almost too embarrassed to bring it up, but he talked with Mario after that and extended the offer. "You're welcome to stay here with your little girls," he said, "but the only job we have available is one that involves caring for the pigs and pulling weeds in the orchard."

Although he was unfamiliar with that type of labor and had previously worked in a supervisory role, Mario humbled himself and accepted the position. He learned about animal husbandry and agriculture and worked harder physically than he ever had before. The many blisters on his hands proved it. He also attended the mandatory morning devotions for staff members, but tuned out the singing and messages that talked about God.

He did a lot of on-the-job training with Juan Merino, who tutored him in orchard and gardening work. As he observed Juan's gentle, Christ-like manner, he noticed his unusual habits. Mario had assumed the bag hanging across Juan's body held his lunch, but he didn't know what to think when Juan reached into the bag and pulled out a big black Bible with large letters. During his breaks, Juan sat under a tree pouring over its words. Then he'd spend time praying before returning to work. Mario had never seen anything like that. The more he watched Juan, the more of an effect Juan had on his life.

The mission provided a good environment for the girls, and the staff lovingly cared for them. God ministered to their needs in above-and-beyond ways. For example, not long after they arrived that November night, one of our staff

members found an old wheelchair for little 9-year-old Sandra. But because she was totally dependent, she couldn't sit
up on her own and just tumbled out of the chair.

In God's perfect timing, He sent Carol Knott of Roystone,
B.C., Canada, to visit the mission. As a therapist, Carol had
been trained in rebuilding wheelchairs. She and Ramon
Aguilar (our outreach supervisor) worked several nights
until 3 a.m. taking the chair apart and remaking it to fit
and hold Sandra in a sitting position. For the first time in
Sandra's life, she was able to sit up and share in the surrounding activities.

God gave her the gift of hope—a hope that will never dis-
appoint. He was actively in process behind the scenes of
doing that for the entire family.

Although the girls were adapting well to their environment, Mario's acceptance of the circumstances didn't come
easily. He performed hard labor. He didn't have the resources
he once had. He was dependent on others and had to follow
their rules. He was surrounded by constant reminders of
God—a God he considered a myth. For about six months,
Mario fought a raging inner battle.

Then one afternoon after work, through the encouragement of a co-worker, he went to Sala (the meeting room
where morning devotions are held). Corrine had called for
a period of prayer and fasting for all the staff, and everyone
had already been gathered for most of the day. Mario didn't
want to be rude and resist, so he agreed to go. He quietly
entered and sat in the back of the room on a sofa.

Jon Cowpersmith, a Bible institute teacher and the mission's spiritual advisor, was leading the meeting that day.
As he talked, he turned his head and looked straight at
Mario. Suddenly, he started walking toward the back of the
room, weaving his way between the couches. He grabbed
Mario's arm, and in a Holy-Spirit-led moment asked, "Do
you want to receive Jesus as your Savior?" Mario said yes
and followed him to the front.

That was the beginning of a dramatic experience with the Lord and a turning point in Mario's life.

Not long afterward, Max and two other overseers called Mario to the office. "Benjamin, the experimental orchard supervisor, needs to return to the mainland," Max said. "He's leaving us, and we'd like you to be the new supervisor."

Mario thought they were crazy. "This doesn't make sense. Benjamin is an agricultural engineer—an agronomist. I'm not."

As if on cue, one of the men opened his Bible to James 1:5 and read out loud, "If any of you lacks wisdom, you should ask God, who gives generously to all without finding fault, and it will be given to you" (NIV).

Mario followed the advice from God's Word, and God granted him wisdom in all he did.

After a few years serving in the role of orchard supervisor, he was promoted to mission administrator. The mission was much smaller back then. It included the home for children, the outreach program, the Bible institute, and the church. But under his leadership, the ministry grew. We added new programs, and our reach expanded into new areas on the mainland, including Sinaloa, Morelia, and Oaxaca.

At the time of this writing, Mario is the pastor of our mission's church and the legal representative of the ministry in Mexico.

I never walk by the old pig barn without thinking of Mario's humble beginnings. We've traveled together on incredible journeys of joys and sorrows. We've seen countless miracles of changed lives through the proclamation of the gospel in word and deed. Demonstrating his deep love for God and people, his life is an example of a living sacrifice, aptly described in Romans 12:1 as holy and pleasing to God—an act of true and proper worship. I have tremendous respect for him.

∽∞∾

What I wrote above represents only a tiny part of Mario's story. Here's more.

When Graciela Vasquez was a girl, she always wanted to work in a children's home. It's something she and her cousin Alicia frequently talked about. Years went by and they both grew up. Alicia came to work at Hogar Para Niños and ended up marrying Max Christian, who also worked at the home. Eventually, Max and Alicia became the administrators.

In February 1988, Max and Alicia visited Graciela at her home. "We're here because we need a substitute house-mother," her cousin said. "Would you like to work with us?" They talked to her about the responsibilities of a houseparent and gave her a quick rundown of the mission's ministry.

Graciela wasted no time in responding. "Yes, yes, yes! Give me a couple weeks to quit my job and to get ready. I'll go." She arrived at Hogar Para Niños on March 2, 1988, and after a few days of instruction started serving children as a housemother—a job she loved.

Two years passed, and Corrine said, "You are an evangelist and shouldn't be a housemother. You need to be in outreach." They moved her to outreach, where she visited with people in the migrant camps, discipled them, helped with their practical needs, and prayed with them. She devoted her evenings to the child evangelism program. It was hard but rewarding work and suited her well.

Although he was a quiet, shy man, Mario felt comfortable around Graciela and occasionally sought her advice when issues arose with his girls. He wasn't interested in a relationship and had no desire for marriage. His last experience with marriage hadn't ended well. It put his three daughters in danger, his house burned to the ground, he lost all his possessions, and his wife was admitted to a sanitorium.

Graciela had little time to think of romance because of her busy schedule, but whenever she prayed about marriage, she had specific requests. At the top of her list was her desire to marry a pastor and to be a pastor's helper. She also asked for opportunities to serve God with her husband and to bless others through her marriage. Her plans certainly did not involve a man like Mario—a divorced, single father of three children, who at the time worked in the orchard.

But something happened. Although at first there was a lot of resistance on both parts, God drew them together. He had the bigger picture.

An opportunity of a lifetime presented itself after Barry Wineroth had a dream. (He was from the YWAM base in Chico, California, and often brought groups of young people to the mission.) He shared his dream with Keith Durkin, then they shared it with me. "We'd like to take a group of children to the Summer Olympics in Barcelona to minister through street evangelism and mimes. But it would require birth certificates, passports or visas, and money to make it happen."

To a lot of people, that might sound like an idea beyond the realm of possibility. Yet I know how God works. I said, "God specializes in things thought impossible. Go for it!"

They spent many hours trying to get the necessary documents for fourteen children, and the funding came in at the last minute. Barry asked Graciela to accompany them as a chaperone. The group participated in the opening and closing ceremonies and through their ministry led many to the Lord. What a special memory for all of them!

But Graciela has another special memory from her Summer Olympics trip. Mario had arranged for her to receive a beautiful bouquet of red roses in Spain on her July 14 birthday. It came along with a marriage proposal! For a quiet, shy guy who wanted nothing to do with marriage, he sure turned out to be a romantic. They were married on December 12, 1992, and spent their honeymoon at Silver Falls Renewal Center in Oregon.

In January 1993, he became the mission administrator. As a couple, they are a mighty team. During Mario's first seven years in administration, Graciela filled in wherever needed. When an administrator was needed at the TJ house, she filled that role. When the center in Morelia needed an administrator, she filled that role. When we didn't have a director of the home, she filled that role. When we didn't have a director of the Bible institute, she filled that role.

After seven years, they went to Oaxaca to establish the mission there. Five years later, they returned to administration in Baja. As I mentioned earlier, Mario is now the pastor of the mission's church.

God gave Graciela the desire of her heart. Together she and Mario continue to serve God in unimaginable ways. And it took a while, but in God's timing she got her number one request—a pastor-husband.

God gave Mario a beautiful gift in Graciela. She has been a faithful, indispensable helpmate for him and a loving mother for his three daughters.

Their story has God's fingerprints all over it.

Here's one more of His fingerprints. Much to their surprise, Mario and Graciela learned years later that they were both on the same bus the day he arrived in Colonia Vicente Guerrero. She had been in Tijuana to celebrate her brother's birthday and was on her way back to the home. The taxi driver just assumed Mario and his girls were going to Hogar Para Niños because he had delivered Graciela there several times in the past.

I smile when I think of God's ways.

Even before Mario knew God, and even without it making sense, he listened to that strong "call" in his spirit and followed it. His actions required extraordinary courage and great sacrifice. At the time, Mario didn't realize God had a purpose and a plan for his life—a plan that would bless countless people throughout Mexico. All of us at FFHM are grateful he stepped out, and we're delighted that God's plan for him included Graciela.

Top: As a single father with three young girls (one with cerebral palsy), Mario Cordoba made a challenging trip to the mission. He has proven to be a faithful servant and wise leader.

Right: Mario's daughter received excellent care at the mission.

Bottom: Max Christian served as the mission's administrator for ten years. His wife, Alicia, served wherever needed. They helped Mario get established at the mission.

Top: Along the way, Mario married Graciela Vasquez, a precious helpmate.

In a more recent picture at the bottom, Mario and Graciela are with Juan Merino. Juan was an inspiration, role model, and mentor to Mario in his early years at the mission. Mario claims that Juan's Christian testimony lived out taught him more than words could.

Summer Olympics 1992
Barcelona, Spain

Barry Wineroth (pictured at top) and Keith Durkin organized
and sponsored mission children to go to Barcelona, Spain, for the
Olympics. The children marched, representing Mexico. They also
participated in street evangelism. Graciela accompanied them on
the trip. It was during that time when she received Mario's marriage
proposal.

God's Doctors

Because the health needs in our sphere of influence are so great, we spend a lot of time discussing the matter with God in prayer. He has been good to provide us with highly skilled physicians and medical staff who humbly serve those who could never pay a fee. And His methods of bringing them to us showcase how amazing He is.

I mentioned Dr. Naftali Mendoza in an earlier chapter. He volunteered part time for about five years, treating a variety of ailments related to poverty, such as skin disease, dysentery, and tuberculosis. Under his care, we were also able to offer mothers a clean and safe place to have their babies, which reduced the childbirth death rate substantially.

We appreciated his help and supported him as much as we could. Over time he became like family to us. In fact, he named his first daughter Charla, after me.

Little by little, as his medical practice in town grew, Naftali had to cut back his hours at the mission. He carried the huge responsibility of providing for his poor family back in Oaxaca, and we understood his need to generate a real income—something other than a bag of tomatoes, a few eggs, or just a grateful smile.

As our FFHM board kept the search for a long-term replacement in prayer, I spoke at a church in Milwaukee, Wisconsin, through the invitation of my dear friend Linda Strom. At the end of the event, a couple by the last name of Schmidt came up to me. They said, "Our daughter and son-in-law have been trying to go to Africa to serve for a year as medical missionaries, but they're unable to get a visa."

I knew it was a divine appointment and enthusiastically shared my plan for their lives. "We're desperate for a doctor," I said. And that's how Dr. Patrick and Anna Murphy came to us from Wisconsin.

The Murphys were a wonderful couple, filled with the Spirit of God, and true servants. Never once did I see them express an egotistical concern. They had a cute-as-a-button, towheaded little daughter, who ran all over the place and caused everyone to smile. I was heartbroken when a year was up and they had to leave. I truly believed God would keep them with us longer.

"Lord," I prayed, "there are lots of doctors in Wisconsin to care for the poor. We need the Murphys here." But God had other plans for them and for us.

His provision of our next physician came through the unlikely channel of my new fax machine. First, I must say that electronic objects and I don't get along—I can more easily handle a flood, poverty, or disease—so imagine my apprehension when I faced it down for the first time. I was in our FFHM office (the back bedroom of our house in North Hollywood) alone, when Keith Durkin called from the Baja mission with an important request.

"Charla, we need the instructions for installing the new walk-in refrigerator," he said. "We don't know where to begin." I explained my ineptitude with the fax machine, and Keith promised to give me step-by-step directions.

Back then, outgoing faxes had to be handfed one sheet at a time. As I stood at the machine and began my fumbling attempt at feeding the first of sixteen pages, an incoming transmission interrupted the process. Foot after foot of shiny paper emerged from the contraption in front of me, fell to the floor, and curled up at my feet. It was some kind of an application for service to the mission, written in French.

I couldn't let that disrupt my focus, though. Keith needed those walk-in refrigerator instructions, and I had to make it happen!

With more questions for Keith, and his continued coaching, I made at least five more attempts to transmit the refrigerator instructions to Mexico, but they never arrived. In the meantime, I received another incoming feed. Another long roll of slick thermal paper with words written in French fell to my feet.

My fax experience turned into a real fiasco. From a phone call later in the day, I learned that all the faxes intended for Keith in Mexico had gone to Calgary, Canada. Rev. John Lucas, one of our board members, said, "Charla, I have enough faxes from you to cover my living room walls!" And after our phone bill came later in the month, I noticed a charge for a call to India from the same day.

The whole situation was a mess—a memorable one. And the most memorable part of all was that incoming French fax. When I had the opportunity to look at it more closely, I realized it was an application from a doctor. His name was Luc Chaussé.

Dr. Gary Johnson from Mt. Vernon, Washington, was a medical advisor to our board, and I knew that he had studied French in college, so I sent the application to him. Not only did Gary interpret the information, but he also followed up with all the references listed. He inquired with the college in Ottawa where Luc had studied and did research on his medical practice.

Before long, I received a call from Gary. "This is your man!" he said. "I've checked his school records. The guy is a genius! He had a rural practice in a remote area of Quebec, and he's well loved. He's your man, Charla!"

I said, "Yeah, that's just what we need—a French-speaking doctor. We haven't got enough languages already in the mix, so we need French too." I wasn't too crazy about a new, French-speaking doctor because I was still convinced Patrick Murphy was supposed to stay.

"Charla, trust me. He's the one."

I gave in to Dr. Johnson's recommendation, and after a couple of telephone interviews, he contacted Dr. Luc to see if he'd be able to come right away. Dr. Luc and his family arrived just two days before the Murphys departed. God's timing was incredible.

Here's what God was doing on Luc's side of things to bring it all about—

Luc grew up in a good Roman Catholic family in Quebec, but as a teen started questioning his beliefs. His time in medical school—and intimate contact with death, sickness, and human affliction—only caused his questioning to intensify. He anguished over things like the existence of God, the purpose for life, and the reason for suffering and injustice.

After years of searching for truth in philosophy and other religions, he read a book called *The Sermon on the Mount* and had an aha moment when he came across the words from John 14:6: "I am the way and the truth and the life. No one comes to the Father except through me" (NIV). That passage resonated with his spirit, and he was convinced Jesus was the answer he was looking for.

His thirst for God's Word grew, and he started talking with God in a personal way, although he didn't attend church. He was shy about his faith and was afraid to speak openly about it. For a long time, he didn't even tell his wife that he had been reading the Bible.

He served seven years at a position in Quebec, working in all fields of medicine. But during that time, he grew spiritually restless. He prayed for God's help to come out of his shell and to be able to share with others the things God showed him. He also asked God to help him do more than just prolong life for his patients. He wanted to give them some kind of hope. Luc promised to follow God wherever He wanted him to go, if He would just guide him.

That prayer led to Luc's decision to take a one-year sabbatical from the hospital to travel with his family from Canada to the tip of South America in a converted bus. But their journey was cut short by a God-arranged appointment with

Dick and Weezy Bundy, a retired couple from the United States they met while camping on a Mexican beach.

Dick and Weezy talked about their volunteer work for a mission in Colonia Vicente Guerrero and explained that the doctor who practiced there would be leaving soon. They also gave Dr. Luc a copy of *Charla's Children* to read. The idea of working at a children's home/mission intrigued Luc and his wife, Lise, and they agreed to write a letter offering their services.

Without knowing what to expect, Luc prayed for God's will in the situation. And God's will brought them to us.

To be honest, I had mixed feelings the first time I met them. Luc wasn't at all like other doctors I've known. He had a full head of dark, curly hair with an accompanying beard and mustache, and he spoke in heavily accented English. His wife spoke no English, and the way she dressed reminded me of the hippies from the sixties and seventies. I didn't know anything about their spiritual background, which concerned me.

I had a little chat with God after that. I said, "God, I don't believe You. We needed a doctor, and You sent us some hippies?" My opinion changed quickly, though. By the time Dr. Luc left five years later, he ended up being the most humble, servant-hearted, extraordinarily real, and closest-to-Jesus man I'd ever met.

Lise was an enormous help to Luc and the mission. She was a teacher, artist, and avid reader. She assisted with minor surgeries, helped with baby deliveries, attended to dying children, did secretarial work, and a variety of other things. They also both loved working in the migrant camps and somehow identified with the people there.

As Dr. Luc's faith continued to grow while he served at the mission, Lise struggled with his spiritual enthusiasm, thinking it was overly exaggerated. She believed in God, but didn't believe God intervened in human lives. Then one day God opened her eyes to His wonder-working power and changed the way she thought.

She had been caring for a severely malnourished 18-month-old girl that someone from the outreach team found on the dirt floor of one of the camp shacks. Near death, with a skin-and-bones body, the child had the appearance of a 6-month-old baby. Lise tried to feed little Teresa with a dropper, but she refused to drink because she was too weak.

A short time after they started caring for her, Luc and Lise left the dining room with Teresa in a stroller. I stopped to greet them and, as is a natural gesture for me, I placed my hand on the child's head and prayed, "Lord, heal this little girl." Then I went on my way.

As soon as they returned to their trailer, Lise again attempted to feed Teresa. But something had changed. This time the child drank milk in gulps—the start of a healing. The miracle was Lise's turning point. She knew in that moment God was real, present, and eager to respond to our needs. It was the beginning of her personal relationship with Jesus and sparked a spiritual excitement in her.

The more Luc and Lise saw God work, the more prayer for every patient became the cornerstone of their ministry—even for those who seemed beyond hope. One day Dr. Luc asked me, "Charla, is it okay to pray for people with cancer?" After I assured him that it was, he invited me to join him on a return visit to a makeshift hovel where a skeleton-thin young man—in his final stages of cancer—lay on filthy blankets. I stood quietly by as Dr. Luc tried to make him more comfortable and then asked Jesus to heal him. His humble, childlike faith touched my heart.

On my next trip to the mission two months later, Luc rushed up to me and said, "You have to come with me!" He couldn't wait for me to see the man again. And what a joyful occasion it was! The man had gained thirty pounds and was back to working in the fields.

During their tenure in Baja, Dr. Luc and Lise learned to believe, pray, and live as if God really was bigger than their own limitations. And in early 1996, I gave them a project that caused them to stretch their faith even more and wrestle with feelings of inadequacy.

Although our FFHM board had no money or plans in the budget for it, I said to the couple, "I want you to design the medical center of your dreams—the one you would build if money weren't an obstacle." We already had many people praying for a larger, more adequate facility, but Luc was surprised by the assignment. He wasn't convinced a new building was necessary, especially since the converted rooms in the small chapel had worked fine for our medical, dental, and obstetrical clinic.

Now charged with an enormous task, he asked God about the reasoning behind it and how he, as a doctor, would do the work of an architect. God reminded him that His thoughts were not Luc's thoughts, nor were Luc's ways His ways. He also taught Luc that he had to build the structure and the ministry not with his hands, but with his knees. Luc committed himself to God's will and prayed through the entire process.

As he and Lise dreamed and brainstormed, they started to sketch out the ideas that came to them: a spacious waiting room where sick people could sit comfortably while watching Christian videos; a play area for children; examining rooms with topnotch equipment; a delivery room furnished to safely handle risky births; a maternity room for mothers and newborn babies; extra beds—clean ones—for seriously ill patients who needed to stay overnight; an x-ray room; storage for medications and supplies; a laundry room for hospital gowns and linens. On and on they went, giving their imaginations full rein.

Weeks later, they put their completed plans away and wondered again about the purpose of their wishful fantasy. God didn't wait long to show them. Almost immediately, an envelope arrived with a one-time gift from an anonymous donor. With the gift came specific instructions. "Use this to build a medical center." The check was for $100,000!

God clearly made His will known, but Luc then started to wonder how he would handle an entire medical center by himself. So, the Lord put it in his heart to pray for doctors who would really love God and the poor. He guided Luc to pray that no doctors would ever change our love-giving and Christ-centered ministry into a humanitarian and pride-building work or a hospital only concerned with making money, which so often happens in Canada and the United States.

Again, God provided. As the building was taking form, the Lord sent a great pediatrician and man of God, Dr. Arnie Gorske. Then Dr. Gerardo Caballero came to visit with great vision for the surgical part of the ministry. George Wakeling, from Circle of Concern, furnished the beginnings of an operating room.

In the meantime, Luc felt God calling him back to the mission field of Quebec. He continued to pray for doctors who could meet all the criteria needed and for his replacement.

In June of 1996, the mission joyfully dedicated the new—and fabulous—medical center but sadly bid farewell to our beloved Dr. Luc and his family. In their five years with us, the Chaussés ministered to thousands of God's children and left a lasting legacy.

God faithfully answered Luc's prayers for replacement doctors. He connected him with two highly-skilled physicians who loved God, had pastors' hearts, and loved the poor—Dr. Marco Angulo and Dr. Ramon Avitia. Their involvement at the time made it look impossible for them to join us at the mission, but prayer is powerful when it's in God's will!

From the platform built for the dedication ceremony of La Clinica del Señor, Dr. Luc pointed to a man in the crowd and told me, "Do you see that man? He will be the one who takes my place." He knew in his spirit that God would arrange for Dr. Angulo to come. And not long afterward, Dr. Avitia joined him. Dr. Cammack from Alaska also came to become part of the team.

God has blessed us with many mighty men and women of medicine who have served His precious people of Baja in our medical center since the 1980s. I could fill the pages of several books with stories about the countless lives touched and miraculous healings as a result of their gifted hands and humble prayers. We can't begin to adequately thank them for their devotion and loving care, but God knows each one of them by name and has a special reward for them in heaven.

Top: God provided a series of dedicated doctors and a dentist for the medical center.

Bottom: Dr. Luc Chaussé is one of the doctors God provided in a miraculous way. He's pictured with his wife, Lise, a mother, and a Oaxacan baby born with a cleft lip and palate.

The first baby Dr. Luc delivered at our mission had a cleft lip and palate. When Luc practiced medicine in Quebec, he had never experienced a delivery with these deformities, and now he was coming across many cases in Oaxacan infants. After doing extensive research, he found the cause to be a deficiency in folic acid.

During their time with us, Dr. Luc and Lise arranged for forty-three children to have cleft-lip-and-palate-repair surgery in the United States. We helped with immigration papers and lined up off-duty flight attendants to transport the infants to Wisconsin. Jan Holter, one of our faithful volunteers, arranged for foster care.

The Sound of Music

About a year and a half after Dr. Luc came to the mission, he approached me with a concern. Even though it was clear the children in the home were receiving superb care in a loving family environment, ample food and clothing, education, spiritual training, and the finest medical services, he sensed that something was missing.

"These children need music," he said.

We already had too much going on, and I didn't want the burden of adding one more thing, so my response was less than positive. "That's just what we need, Luc—another program."

But Luc had a musical background. He had studied piano since the age of 6, took guitar lessons in high school, and played the flute and saxophone as an adult. He was well aware of the benefits of music and the beauty it brought to life, so he pushed past my resistance and started building his case.

"Music is healing, Charla. It's therapy. These children have been abused and abandoned, and they need music. It would be valuable in so many ways." He went on to explain how music could also help them develop a discipline that would carry over into other areas of life.

Then he made an offer I couldn't refuse. "If you can get me forty recorders, I will teach the children to play."

Trusting his wisdom, I began the search for the plastic, flute-like instruments. I discovered a fabulous sale, and we were able to purchase them for less than $4 each. Michelle Cumberland, one of our board members, provided the funds.

With the recorders on hand and the good doctor ready to roll, the mission's music program was born. Dr. Luc put aside one day each week from his busy schedule at the medical center to give music lessons to the children.

Before long, continuous melodies of "Mary Had a Little Lamb" and "Twinkle, Twinkle, Little Star" could be heard coming from Luc and Lise's home in the old motel. The children were playing, and it was amazing!

As they became more and more proficient on the recorders, they started praying for band instruments. What an encouragement for them to see donations of saxophones, trumpets, clarinets, trombones, baritones, concert flutes, and many others streaming in from all over the United States.

Dr. Luc nurtured the budding musicians. After a few months, they formed a band and started performing dramatic productions. The enthusiastic reception and applause from their audiences caused the children's self-esteem to grow. Often teased by schoolmates for living in a children's home, they were finally able to hold their heads high. As the only musicians performing concerts in the whole San Quintín Valley, they had accomplished something unique and wonderful.

At first, the children practiced at Dr. Luc's and Lise's home, turning it into a music conservatory. Eventually, Lise transformed the balcony of the old theater into practice rooms. She became the overseer of the music program and made sure the children rehearsed their lessons.

Lise was incredibly creative and used her giftedness to bring their presentations to another level. She'd write plays, design scenery and costumes, and choreograph everything around a recital. So, instead of a long, boring stretch of children performing a rehearsed song one by one, she wove their music into a story. She incorporated lighting effects and used different settings. Her brilliant work showcased her passion for the program.

For one particular event, more than three hundred people gathered at the community center. Forty of our children performed a great diversity of music, and forty of our staff members participated in the organization, preparation, and cleanup.

A flute and piano duet of "Sentimental" brought a standing ovation. Many in the audience wept as Floriberta, an orphaned indigenous girl, played a piano solo of "What a Friend We Have in Jesus." Listeners responded with delight to the trombone-saxophone-flute-clarinet-trumpet quintet that played "Yankee Doodle" and "Rock O' My Soul."

But the finale topped it all. Each of the forty instrumentalists simultaneously played their own rendition of "Onward Christian Soldiers," creating chaotic and jarring results. Then Servando, one of our house fathers who served as the master of ceremonies, said, "Our lives were filled with discord and were without direction until we made Jesus Christ Lord and chose to follow Him."

Dr. Luc came to the stage after that and directed a stirring rendition of the well-known hymn. It was a powerful and memorable experience!

Following the event, Dr. Luc told me how several of our timider students had tried to get out of the concert. "They gave me plenty of made-up reasons why they shouldn't play," he said and chuckled. "The most rebellious of them—one of our boys who had spent little time in practice—announced he wouldn't participate. But he did! After the concert, he thanked me again and again." The boy's response to his concert experience touched Luc in a big way. "That made it worth it all."

Thinking back to my original conversation with Luc, when he said, "These children need music, Charla," I can see how right he was. Their self-confidence increased, and their feelings of accomplishment made a difference in their lives. I'm grateful he convinced me that we should give it a try.

As the music program grew, the children had many opportunities. They played their instruments for dignitaries in Ensenada and for the participants in a track and field competition. They marched in parades and performed concerts at the mission and in town. A good number of them participated in the worship team at church.

An even greater opportunity arose from an obviously God-inspired idea that took root and grew in Dr. Luc's heart. "Lise and I would like to lead a team of students on a musical evangelistic outreach to Quebec," he said, and explained that fewer than one percent of the people there had a personal relationship with Jesus Christ. "The children could put on concerts in various public places and share their testimonies." He had thought out all the details, including how friends there could provide transportation and hospitality.

We presented his vision to our supporters, and money to cover the cost of airfare to Quebec and donations of winter clothing poured in. So, in late December 1994 to early January 1995, Luc's dream became a reality.

Fifteen of our young musicians from the advanced ensemble—along with Dr. Luc, Lise, Anita Steinberg (accompanist), and Minerva Trujillo—went on tour, performing and sharing their testimonies in thirteen different locations. The venues ranged from churches and nursing homes to even a Burger King on Christmas day. They also had the privilege of performing at the prestigious cathedral in Montreal, where the famous Italian opera singer Luciano Pavarotti gave annual concerts.

Numerous people in their audiences responded to the gospel message by giving their hearts to Jesus Christ. What a joy for the children to see how God answered their prayers!

During the lead-up to the trip and while they were on tour, the team experienced a number of trials, but they experienced many miracles as well. God used that special adventure to teach them valuable lessons and to grow their faith. It's something they'll never forget.

By the time Luc and Lise left our mission in mid-1996 to minister full-time back home in Quebec, fifty music students had received instruction from five staff teachers. A children's choir was launched, and strings were added to the band. Musical drama presentations of the gospel were given in the United States, Ensenada, and in our community and churches. Music also became a part of our day care program.

I praise God for the gift of music and the insight of Dr. Luc and Lise.

∽∾

In the 1970s, Chuck and I were guests of our dear friends Jack and Pat Durkin at the Saint Patrick's Day dance at Holy Rosary Catholic Church in Sun Valley, California. Hans and Nancy Benning, a couple from Los Angeles, sat at the same table with us.

As we chatted, we learned about the Bennings' fascinating history. They own Benning Violins in Studio City, California, and carry on a four-generation family tradition of crafting and repairing stringed instruments, some of which are used by the world's finest musicians.

We had the opportunity to tell them about our ministry in Mexico. To my surprise, Hans and Nancy visited the mission nine months later. Since then, they've contributed innumerable hours to the work of FFHM.

Both of them have servant hearts and considerable talent. Hans was involved with the Navajo nation in Arizona and New Mexico, and over a period of ten years built fourteen churches for them. When Glenn Almeraz, one of our Bible institute graduates, was ready to build a rehab facility in Zapata, Hans brought a group of Navajo believers to the Baja Peninsula to help build it. He's also played a significant role in the construction and overseeing of Rancho de Cristo, a men's residential rehab ministry we started later.

Nancy's love for music and her belief, like Dr. Luc's, that music changes lives, spurred her on to get involved in Dr. Luc's instrumental program. She said, "We need strings. Why have just a band when we could have an orchestra?"

With that, she introduced strings to the mix and began offering lessons in 1994. Twice a month, she made the 800-mile round trip to work with the children who expressed a desire to learn. (For the next twenty years, she taught violin at the mission, and a number of her students have continued playing, teaching, and sharing the gift of music.)

The Bennings' shop on Ventura Boulevard provided the violins for practice and for use, and the agreement was that students could keep their instrument as long as they played. Whether the students decided to continue, Nancy's goal was that they would at least have a good understanding of music. She used a classic teaching method that focused on theory and instruction.

Nancy had one criteria for accepting students into her program—they had to be at least 10 years old. But we had a special 8-year-old boy, the son of a staff member, who badly wanted to take lessons. He approached Nancy and asked, "Hermana Nancy, could you teach me to play the violin?"

"I'm sorry," she said, "but you're too young right now." He cried big tears.

I pleaded with her. "Can't you please reconsider and give the little fellow a lesson or two? He's so cute." Thankfully, she gave in.

Little Tito Quiroz practiced diligently and exhibited extraordinary talent. Right away, he became her best and most enthusiastic student. He went on to become a virtuoso, eventually even playing for the president of Mexico and other government officials.

Tito's family had to move when his father took a position in Ensenada with DIF, a social services organization, but Nancy continued to give him lessons on her bi-monthly trips to Colonia Vicente Guerrero.

After Tito's father died of cancer, his mother opened up a dress-making shop, and Tito used the other portion of the shop to give violin lessons. The number of students continued to increase, which led to the need for larger facilities and additional instructors. So, in 2011, he founded a music school in Ensenada and named it the Benning Academia de Música to honor Nancy and Hans, his special mentors.

Their prominence in the classical music scene helped Tito make numerous important connections that in turn expanded his reach. Since then, he's opened another academy on the mainland in Cuernavaca, Morelos. It's located in a beautifully renovated train station. He has a third academy in Emiliano Zapata, a city just outside of Cuernavaca.

Tito also convinced the Mexican prison system to allow him to offer music lessons to hardened young inmates at an Ensenada jail. He received permission to build a studio inside the facility—with Hans's help—for the incarcerated musicians. Although thought crazy by some at first, the music program there has been a resounding success, reducing recidivism by huge amounts. Other prisons in Mexico have taken note.

Because of Tito's faithfulness, love, and dedication to serving the Lord through music and evangelistic conferences throughout Mexico, countless lives have been touched. Only God knows the impact.

It all started because a doctor at a children's home in Colonia Vicente Guerrero believed the children needed music. I'm amazed at what happens when God is involved.

Dr. Luc said, "Charla, these children need music." Above, the children are marching in a parade in Ensenada, playing their recorders. The band was invited to play at a cathedral and other places in Montreal, Quebec, Canada.

Top: Nancy Benning said, "We must have an orchestra." Here she is with a violin student.

Middle: Hans Benning established Rancho de Cristo, the men's rehab ministry, and is still involved in leadership. Several years ago, he and some of the brothers from the Rancho built a music room inside the juvenile prison in Ensenada. Pictured are the prisoners (whose faces cannot be shown) with Tito Quiroz, their music teacher and originator of the music program within prison walls. Tito grew up at the mission with his parents, who were on staff at the children's home for a number of years.

Bottom: Hans and Nancy Benning

A Gangbanger Reformed

One day I received a phone call from my good friend Harald Bredesen, a founding board member of the Christian Broadcasting Network. I first met him in 1961 when he and Dr. William Standish Reed prayed with me at a conference to receive "more of Jesus." After he moved to California, our families grew close. We had a lot of common bonds, including our adopted children, and he offered great support to our ministry in Mexico.

He said, "Charla, I've got a young man who wants to go to Bible school. He doesn't have money. He doesn't have family. How much do you charge?"

"We don't charge anybody for anything," I said.

"Then you'll accept my recommendation?"

"He'll need to fill out an application first," I said and explained how to do that. As we chatted, Harald enlightened me on Glenn Almeraz's background.

Glenn was born in Tijuana, but grew up in San Diego. When he was 11, his mother died of cancer, and that set off a downhill series of events. He transformed into an angry and rebellious youth who blamed God for taking his mother's life.

His father drowned his grief in alcohol and became abusive toward him. In a fit of rage one day, he said, "Get out of my sight and don't ever return!" He kicked Glenn out of the house and slammed the door behind him.

Still a child, Glenn found his "home" in the streets, and his life spiraled out of control. He hung out with the guys in the neighborhood and little by little started using drugs with them. By the age of 14, he had become a heroin addict.

He claimed that being high helped ease his pain and made him forget about his past, his mom, and his family.

Glenn's gangbanging, drug-addicted lifestyle turned into a continuous cycle of incarcerations and paroles. He served time in several correctional facilities within the California prison system, including Chino, Donovan, Jamestown, and Corcoran, among others. During his stint at Corcoran, his natural leadership abilities came into play, and he soon controlled his yard.

As I got to know Glenn in a personal way later on, he shared some of his story with me. He said, "I used to fight and steal and hurt people. I stabbed a lot of my own friends, the ones I grew up with. It's all I knew."

He told me that he would get mad at God and ask Him why he was even created. "I wished God wouldn't have made me. Every day was a reminder that nobody cared for me. Nobody loved me. I didn't have anything to live for, and I didn't want to live."

Glenn fully expected to die on the streets from a heroin overdose, a gang fight, or some other way behind bars. He didn't foresee anything ever changing in his empty life.

But it did.

A terrifying dream and a divine appointment with a stranger—who talked to him about Jesus and asked him if he wanted to change—led to an invitation of help. "I know a pastor who runs a rehab center. I can take you there."

After hearing the offer, Glenn became skeptical. "What do they do there?"

"They read the Bible."

He burst into laughter. "How can I go to a place where they read the Bible? Can't you see how I am?" The man assured Glenn that there were many people just like him in the rehab center and that God had changed their lives.

To end the discussion, Glenn said he'd think about it and walked away.

The next day, he needed a fix and found one of his buddies so they could shoot up together. A couple walked by, and Glenn's friend started shouting crude remarks their way. Within seconds, fists were flying and the knives came out. The violence escalated to the point where Glenn blacked out.

When he came back to consciousness, he found himself on top of a body oozing blood from dozens of stab wounds. The knife in Glenn's hand was still imbedded in the man's shoulder, and sounds of screams and sirens saturated the atmosphere around him. Before the ambulance arrived on the scene, he pulled his knife out and hurriedly escaped down the alley.

After a restless night, he woke up with a feeling he'd never had. Guilt. He could hardly bear the heavy weight upon him and acknowledged it as the hand of God.

He thought about the stranger he had met a couple days earlier. With an overwhelming desire to find him—and not knowing who, or where, he was—he headed to their original connection point. And in the midst of thousands of cars coming and going in downtown traffic, Glenn's "angel" reappeared.

The kind man took Glenn to the El Shaddai Rehabilitation Center (which was only three doors down from his heroin supplier). Two days later, Glenn responded to the chaplain's altar call and surrendered to Almighty God. That's the day he points to as changing his life completely.

He developed a hunger for God's Word and, though reading was difficult for him, began to devour its pages. Six weeks later, he preached his first message. Within three months, he sensed God's calling to Bible school. But that seemed like a hopeless dream for him, especially since he lacked a basic education and could barely read or write. Then there was the money issue on top of that. He questioned whether he had heard God correctly.

God was at work behind the scenes, however, and Glenn's anointing for the Lord's work was obvious to everyone at the center. His leadership skills helped him rise rapidly to the position of director.

Each week, he and twenty of the other men attended a Bible study at Pastor Harald Bredesen's home near Escondido, California. (Harald founded the rehab center.) After the study, the men earned money by doing various jobs on the grounds. One day, Harald took Glenn aside and said, "What do you really want to do, Glenn?"

"I want to preach the gospel," he said.

That confirmed something Harald had known in his spirit for a long time, but he had waited until the right timing to talk with Glenn about it. "You're going to be a good pastor."

Two months later, Harald asked him again, "What do you want to do, Glenn?"

"I want to go to Bible school."

"Good, because God has already spoken to me about it, and He wants you to go to Mexico."

"Mexico?" The disdain in Glenn's voice was apparent.

"Yes, Mexico. I know a woman named Charla who has a Bible institute in a little place called Colonia Vicente Guerrero. It's in the Baja Peninsula, and we're going to send you there."

At the time, Glenn had zero interest for anything related to Mexico. He wrestled with God in prayer about the situation and, after several days, the Holy Spirit grabbed his attention with a simple message. "My will, Glenn. Not yours."

Weeping, he got down on his knees and yielded his life once again. "Lord, I'll go wherever You want me to go, as long as You go with me."

Things fell into place quickly after that. About a month later, Max Christian, the administrator of the Bible school at the time, went to North Hollywood to purchase some books. On his way back, he picked up Glenn from the El Shaddai

Rehabilitation Center in Chula Vista and took him to his new home south of the border.

The big flood came and destroyed our Bible institute three months after Glenn arrived. It was devastating to everyone, but seemed even more so for him. After I faced the discouraged students in the prayer chapel and made a promise that the Bible institute would not close, I invited them to speak to me afterward if they had questions.

Glenn approached me and said, "Hermana Charla, are you for real? Did you really mean that?" His voice had an urgency to it.

"I certainly did," I assured him.

"How will you do it?"

With more calmness than I felt, I said, "I don't know, but God will show us."

As I peered into his dark, pleading eyes that were so full of concern because he had nowhere else to go, and saw the numerous tattoos on his exposed skin, I realized I was talking with the young man Harald Bredesen had told me about. He was the only one of the remaining students I hadn't met.

I recognized some of his markings as symbols of the Mexican Mafia. "Let me ask you a question now."

"Okay," he said.

"You've done hard time, haven't you?"

"Yeah."

"Where did you serve?"

He started naming off prisons and then mentioned Donovan and Jamestown. At that point a little bell started going "ding, ding, ding" in my head. I knew something about those two places. Jamestown was up in the gold country of Northern California, and Donovan was near the southern border. They were about sixteen hours apart.

"When you went from Donovan to Jamestown, did you ever run across a guy named Craig Pereau?"

He gave me a funny look. "Yeah. I caught the chain with him." (Most prisoners in the state of California are transferred every six months unless they've done capital crimes. They're chained together when bussed from place to place.)

I was shocked. I said, "Glenn, that's my son."

Something happened within me in that moment that's hard to explain. I thought about the years of pain Glenn had endured. I thought about my own son who had experienced hardship as well. And God filled my heart to overflowing with a deep love and compassion for him. We had an immediate bond that remains to this day.

Shortly after Glenn and I had that encounter, I wrote to my son in prison. I said, "Craig, you will never believe this, but Glenn Almeraz is in our Bible institute."

He wrote back and insisted I was mistaken. "No, Mother, that's impossible. He's the head of the Mexican Mafia." He went on to give me some of the insider scoop he knew about Glenn. It took a while, but I was finally able to convince Craig that Glenn was indeed with us at the mission.

I'm still in awe that—out of the thousands and thousands of prisoners within the state of California—Glenn and Craig were on the same bus together. Amazing!

Although Glenn worked hard at school, learning didn't come easily for him. He struggled to overcome his weaknesses and at times drove poor Minnie, one of his teachers, to exasperation. (Our board drafted Minerva Trujillo out of the mission office after the flood and put her in the recently vacated position of Bible school administrator. She also taught classes for us. Minnie is an experienced teacher who came to us from Mexico City and has served the mission in many ways over the years. We're grateful for her dedication and flexibility.)

One day Minnie gave Glenn an assignment to rewrite a composition and to add punctuation and capital letters. He did exactly as she asked. He rewrote the paper in the same way but added a row of punctuation marks, followed by a row of capital letters, at the end. His note to Minnie said,

"Dear Teacher, please put these where they belong. If you have any left over, let me know."

Many doubters questioned whether he'd be able to complete his courses, but Corrine Ehrick and I both saw God's hand on Glenn's life, and we believed in his calling. We became his biggest cheerleaders as we supported him, prayed for him, and mothered him throughout the process. He persevered and finished Bible school in the spring of 1995.

Getting to graduation day was a huge accomplishment for Glenn. He said, "It's the first time I've completed anything—other than a prison sentence—in my life." What a day of rejoicing that was!

∽∝∾

While he was a student at the institute, Glenn helped out as a youth leader at one of our satellite churches. That's where he met Rosa, a native from La Mixteca (a region in the western half of Oaxaca). She also graduated from our Bible institute and had a ministry to her people in the area.

Rosa was the answer to a specific prayer he had lifted to God for three years. Glenn wanted a girl who would be with him in good times and bad—one who would pray for him, encourage him, and speak the truth to him. He also asked God for a wife who could preach and teach.

After he graduated, he accepted a position with our outreach department and began his married life.

Glenn and Rosa purchased an acre of land in the village of Zapata, a few miles north of the mission, with the $1,000 wedding gift Harald and Gen Bredesen gave them. They lived in an old converted bus on the property.

The newlyweds deeded the land to the mission and worked together building a rehab center there. What first started out as a pegboard shanty became a block building that could house twelve to eighteen men. Hans Benning and a Navajo group of believers helped construct it.

The Almeraz's ministry grew quickly. Glenn initiated Bible studies, which were so popular with the surrounding villagers that a church had to be built. He found some old wooden framed windows in the mission's warehouse, put them together, and built what they lovingly referred to as their crystal cathedral. That makeshift building was eventually replaced with a much bigger church that still serves Glenn's thriving congregation of predominantly indigenous people.

As I think of how God has used—and continues to use—Glenn for His glory, these words from the Old Testament book of Joel come to mind: "I will repay you for the years the locusts have eaten." It was a promise given to another people at another time, but it also rings true for Glenn in a big way today.

Top: Pastor Harald Bredesen and his wife, Gen, were supporters and encouragers of FFHM from the very beginning. He made it possible for Glenn Almeraz to attend our Bible institute.

Bottom: Getting to graduation day was a huge accomplishment for Glenn. Chuck, Glenn, and I are all smiles.

Top: Glenn, an anointed preacher of the Word, held open air meetings at the rehab center in Zapata. After seeing stacks of old windows outside the warehouse at the Baja mission, he asked Chuck Mills, our construction supervisor, if he could have them to "build a church." It was affectionately known as the "Crystal Cathedral."

Bottom right: Glenn and Rosa purchased an acre of land in Zapata, a few miles north of the mission, with the $1,000 wedding gift Harald and Gen Bredesen gave them. They lived in an old bus on the property, and Glenn built his first building ever—a men's rehab center for four men. Here we are at the dedication in 1994.

The Healing Power
of Redemption

Chuck and I had a standing invitation to join the Sherda family for Christmas brunch every year. Harry served our board as treasurer, and his wife, Betty, was our board's Spanish translator.

As per tradition, we gathered together on Christmas Eve day in 1993, but it was a solemn occasion. We tried to make merry, but our son was back on drugs after being paroled.

When we returned home, we discovered that our television and the gifts under our Christmas tree were gone. We knew Craig had stolen them to support his addiction.

"This is the worst Christmas I've ever spent," I said. While I had promised myself that I would allow Craig to make his own choices and mistakes, my heart broke nonetheless.

At three o'clock the next morning, we received a call from Craig's landlord. "There's something going on in the North Hollywood apartment," he said. "You'd better get over here."

Craig had dashed our hopes that he would change. "There's nothing we can do," I told the landlord. It hurt me to respond that way, but it was the sad truth.

At 5 a.m., we got another call. "I think there is someone dead in that apartment. You'd better come before I call the police."

Because Chuck couldn't cope with the pain of seeing his son in that condition, I called my dear friend Lorraine and asked her to go with me to Craig's apartment. When we arrived, the apartment door was open. We found Craig stretched out on the couch—unresponsive.

I knelt by his lifeless body and held his wrist. I tried to find a pulse, but there wasn't one. Anguished, I cried out, "Oh, God, is this the way his life should end?"

In that moment, God, the Holy Spirit, brought back a memory of when our little black-and-white dog, Elizabeth, had been poisoned. Craig ran into the house saying, "Mother, come quickly and pray for her!"

We went to the patio where the dog's lifeless body lay. Chuck, who understood medical things because he rode rescue with the LA Fire Department, shook his head and said, "That dog is gone."

I looked at Craig, who had tears streaming down his face. "Let's pray," I said, and we knelt together to talk with God.

When we finished, Chuck muttered under his breath, "If that dog lives, I'll believe anything!" Just then, the three of us watched in awe as the dog's tail began to wiggle. Twenty minutes later, Elizabeth was fully alive!

As I remembered that scene while at the side of my unresponsive son, I said to God, "You are far more concerned about this boy than You were about a little black-and-white dog."

Suddenly, I felt a faint pulse on Craig's wrist. He was breathing again!

Fearful that calling 911 or the police would send Craig back to prison on a parole violation for drugs, we searched for other answers. After making several calls, we found Victory Outreach, a rehab facility in North Hollywood, that agreed to take him. Lorraine and I somehow carried Craig's limp body to the car and drove him to the facility, where a handsome, young, black man welcomed us.

"My son is in the car," I said. "He may be dying from an overdose. Please help me!" And he did.

Unfortunately, Craig left Victory Outreach after only a few weeks, and the cruel hold of drugs and alcohol on his life grew. He was rearrested, spent more time in prison, and the cycle continued for years. As parents, we had a long, heart-wrenching walk on the trail of tears.

But God didn't waste that experience. He showed us once again the valuable truth found in Romans 8:28: He is able to bring about good from the not-so-good parts of our lives.

Craig had received Christ as his Lord and Savior when he was a young boy, but for most of his life he listened to the lies of the enemy and rejected the truth of God's Word. He didn't think he could measure up to expectations and had a hard time believing that he was worthy of the heavenly Father's devotion and care.

Holy Spirit had plenty of time to work on Craig's heart while he was in prison. As his relationship with God grew and his faith deepened, Craig developed a longing for God's Word and was finally able to grasp the life-changing reality of the Father's love and forgiveness.

While he was incarcerated, a kind prison guard gave him access to the library and other resources. He took advantage of the opportunity to study and learn, and eventually earned a master's degree in theology from Andersonville Theological Seminary in Georgia. He discipled several inmates and ministered to many others. After he was released, he faithfully taught a Bible study at a rehab center in San Clemente.

During his stay at Chino State Prison, Craig wrote a story called *The Little Lost Pup*. I added a mother's viewpoint and more details to it, and after Craig died of lung cancer in November 2014, FFHM published a small book with the same title in his memory. Craig's compelling account— one that showcases God's redemptive grace—is now being given away in prisons throughout North America.

Because of my experiences from childhood and as a parent, I have an extra special spot in my heart for the work our mission does with its rehab and prison ministries. I'm thankful for our devoted staff and volunteers who bring the love of Christ to each person in need of hope and help.

In 2015, Chuck and I, along with the rest of the family, had the delight of dedicating a new prayer chapel at Rancho de Cristo in Craig's memory. God's presence was clearly there. My granddaughter Melissa wrote about the event, and we included her remembrance at the end of *The Little Lost Pup*. Here's part of what she said:

> Yesterday at Rancho de Cristo, the drug and alcohol rehabilitation center, a beautiful new prayer chapel was dedicated to my Uncle Craig. Stepping into the chapel, I felt overwhelmed, not by grief, but by the presence of God.
>
> Across the room, a picture of my Uncle Craig playing the guitar caught my eye. Looking at the image, I didn't see a man broken by a lifetime of drug use and incarceration. Instead, I saw a boy who wore a red cowboy hat and brought home wounded animals to comfort. I saw a Bible scholar, a gifted musician, a master chess player, a loving father, and a surfer, effortlessly one with the waves. In that picture, I saw a man of quiet kindness who loved Jesus with all his heart. I saw a man redeemed.

Melissa went on to say that she felt the healing power of Jesus in that chapel. Many others have said the same thing. We're grateful to God that Craig's life testified of that power.

༺∞༻

God caused good to come out of Craig's troubled years in yet another way. Because of Craig's time at Victory Outreach after he overdosed, we developed a relationship with the people there.

Victory Outreach's call is similar to ours. They evangelize, disciple, and give a hand up to those who are hurting and broken. They minister to men who struggle with substance abuse and have a variety of problems.

Knowing that many of their residents lacked an education, and realizing the ability to read would improve their chance to find jobs and learn skills, we began a literacy class in the den of our North Hollywood home for eleven or twelve men. We met for an hour in an afternoon once a week for six months.

Using *Charla's Children* as their text book, Marilyn Jones, our accountant, taught them basic reading skills. In the meantime, they learned about FFHM's ministry in Mexico.

As the weeks passed, we discovered that several of the men needed glasses. I contacted Dr. Creech, an optometrist and faithful supporter of our ministry. He said he'd be happy to help, so I loaded a group of six men into my van with the intention of taking them to my doctor-friend's office in Santa María, about 140 miles north of the San Fernando Valley.

Call it a state of cluelessness—or perhaps it was a temporary mental lapse—but in that moment I had no idea that transporting them out of Los Angeles County without permission would cause them to violate their parole. After the California Highway Patrol stopped me, I explained the situation and asked to continue our important mission. Praise God, with the Lord's intervention, we were allowed to go on. I prayed the entire way back for grace to get home without complications.

I'm grateful we were able to accomplish what we set out to do. God provided glasses and prevented yet another of my precarious predicaments from turning into a greater problem.

Whether it be caring for Craig in prison, or touching others' lives because of Craig's story, or even saving us from our silly mistakes, God has proven again and again that He is worthy of our hallelujahs. Great is His faithfulness!

THE LITTLE LOST PUP

By Craig Pereau
Written in Chino State Prison
Illustrations by Elberta Knowlton

Top: Eleanor Cowpersmith loved my son Craig. Here they are together. Over a period of time, they exchanged a volume of letters. She served as administrative assistant at the mission for many years.

Bottom: While incarcerated at Chino State Prison, Craig wrote a story called *The Little Lost Pup*. After he died of lung cancer, FFHM published it with my mother's viewpoint added. Many inmates throughout North America have received a copy.

In 2015, Chuck and I had the delight of dedicating a prayer chapel in Craig's honor at Rancho de Cristo. Whenever I'm there, I feel God's presence in a big way. (Notice the magnificent craftsmanship.)

Divine Intervention

While I was at the mission one day, someone introduced me to a young woman named Alma. She was there with her husband, Dr. Marco Angulo, who had become friends with Dr. Luc.

As the introductions were being made, Alma cocked her head a bit and looked at me in a curious way. It was almost as if she were studying me. Just as I was about to ask what she had on her mind, she said, "Hermana Charla, did you used to go by the Anza Theater in Ensenada about twenty-five years ago?"

Her question surprised me. "Yes, I did," I said. "I went by there often when we were doing legal transactions. Our attorney's office was across the street." Now I was the curious one—she would have been a small child at that time. "Why do you ask?"

"You looked so familiar to me," she said.

I noticed that the expression on her face had changed, and her eyes took on a distant look. It seemed as if her thoughts transported her to another time and place.

After a few long seconds, she lifted her head and met my gaze. "I knew it was you!" Her voice was barely audible as she said, "I was the little beggar girl on the corner."

Alma turned toward the window. Her eyes lingered on the happy children playing outside. They were fully clothed, well fed, and content. She watched as their house parents gave them love and attention and then asked me, "Why didn't you bring me here?" Her longing eyes could no longer contain her tears.

As we talked, I learned that her life had been typical of so many of the children and adults we ministered to—a life of unwantedness, brokenness, and abuse. How different her growing-up years could have been if she had been brought to our mission!

Before she was born, her father left the family. Because her mother didn't want the burden of another child, especially by herself, she attempted abortion—twice. Much to her mother's dismay, Alma survived.

She was given up for adoption to a couple with children of their own. The adoptive father died a short time later, and his wife focused on having fun, leaving the children to fend for themselves.

Drugs, alcohol, and shady characters invaded her home, and her personal space was violated repeatedly. Raped for the first time when she was two months shy of her sixth birthday, she didn't dare try to sleep.

"My mom's boyfriend molested me every single night," Alma said. "Life became a nightmare, so I escaped whenever I could."

They lived about five hundred yards from the city dump. "I would often run away during the day and hide in an old car by the dump. I'd try to sleep there." The dump dwellers taught her their survival skills. She learned how to forage for food and how to find "treasures" among the rubbish.

I asked Alma what was going on in her heart and mind at that point. "I wanted to be dead. If that kind of life was all I had to look forward to, why would I want to live?" she said. "One time I ran in front of a car. It hit me, but it didn't kill me."

She said she was in the hospital for a couple of days, and that's where she learned that drugs numbed the pain and helped her sleep. "I fell in love with drugs because they removed my fear and apprehension about this guy coming and jumping all over me. I could sleep for hours, and I thought that was a good thing to do."

Drug use became a habit for her. By the time she turned 12, she joined a gang and needed a way to support her addiction. Her older sisters were involved with prostitution, so she decided to go that route as well. She also stole for the gang and did whatever they asked her to do. For many years her life continued to spiral into the pit, and she didn't care.

Because she could carry money and drugs with ease, her gang leaders often assigned her to dangerous border crossings. She quickly learned many things from her customers and became fluent in English. Although she was beaten and jailed many times, no serious charges ever stuck. The police hated her for that.

Then one day her main supplier, Martin, said he was going to rat her out to save his back. She had twenty-four hours to find a place to hide.

Through a friend's suggestion, she ended up at a secluded commune that was tucked away in a canyon outside of Ensenada. She kept company there with a group of drug-induced hippies who philosophized about love and life, and that's where she met Marco. He treated her with kindness and respect and listened with concerned interest as she talked to him about her past. Their relationship grew close.

Months of communal life went by, and Marco returned to his family home in Ensenada. Alma promised to reconnect someday, but she had other things on her mind at the time. She wanted to visit her mother for awhile—it would be an eight-hour walk over the mountains—and then she planned to return to the commune.

However, she made the mistake of stopping at her brothers' house along the way. She found them sitting at a table, grinding stones of concentrated heroin. The distinct aroma of the fine powder pulled her in and held her captive again.

Sometime later, she ended up on Marco's doorstep.

Marco treated her with a tenderness she had never known. He promised to take care of her forever, but she didn't know how to receive love. "He was such a good man—too good to have his life ruined by someone like me," she said as she recounted her story. They got married, though, and had a baby girl.

Despite Marco's best efforts to care for her, Alma sank into a deep depression. The demons of bitterness, hatred, and unworthiness that had haunted her for years relentlessly repeated their ugly lies, and she went back to her old life of hustling on the streets. Marco left their daughter in the custody of his parents, and he attended medical school in Mexicali, returning once a month to visit. After a few years, the Angulos filed for divorce.

At one point, Alma became so hopeless that she acquired a gun and planned to kill herself. As the gun lay on the kitchen table, she began writing a letter to her daughter explaining the actions she felt she needed to take to remove the curse from her life.

But God intervened.

Just at that moment, she heard a car pull up and familiar voices outside. She quickly stashed the gun under the couch cushions and went to the door to find her old friends Benito and Rosa Maria. They had been the leaders at the hippie commune, which seemed to her like a lifetime ago. They looked different to Alma—almost as if they were glowing—and they had an aura of peace about them.

"Rosa Maria spoke about a dream she had," Alma told me. "In that dream I would stand up in front of her and say, 'I can't take it anymore.' Then I would shoot myself. She said the third time she had the dream, she realized it was God. So, they searched for me until they found me."

Alma said they started talking to her about Jesus. "They looked so happy, and I just thought they were using a new drug. But they said it wasn't drugs, it was the love of Jesus. Well, in my mind Jesus or God didn't exist at all. If He did, how could you explain a life like mine?"

Although Alma rejected her friends' message about how she could have a new life in Christ, something kept her from following through with her suicide plan, and she had a strange sense of restlessness in her spirit.

About two weeks after Benito and Rosa Maria visited, Alma headed downtown because she needed to make some quick cash. She also needed to find Marco and get him to sign the divorce papers that had just arrived.

But as she turned down a dark side street and cut across an auto repair lot, she heard singing. Her curiosity led her inside the door of a little store-front Pentecostal church, where about thirty people were enthusiastically praising and worshiping God. Alma recognized some of the tunes and certain phrases within the songs, and suddenly realized why.

When she was a child hiding away at the Ensenada city dump, sometimes a van painted with a dove or cross would wind its way through the mounds of decay along the hilly, rutted terrain. The people inside always handed out sandwiches and maybe apples or pieces of candy. Once the food was distributed, the van people told stories from the Bible and taught the gathered crowds a variety of songs about Jesus—some of the same songs Alma now heard as she stood inside that tiny church. The words spoke of God's great love and His wonderful offer of forgiveness, which caused her to have mixed emotions.

A preacher came to the pulpit, and Alma tried to sneak out as he began to talk. Someone detained her, though.

"Usually the police needed two of them to get me into a police car, but this little old lady made me sit down and stay for the whole sermon," Alma said. "And the whole sermon was about me! I thought Marco had come and talked to this guy. I was angry because he had no right to tell about my life."

As Alma's feelings festered and the sermon's message caused her to fidget, the preacher gave an invitation for people to come to the altar and pray. Alma looked around for an escape route and attempted to leave, but the little old woman detained her again. She insisted that Alma go forward and do business with God.

It was as if a mysterious force compelled her to walk to the front of the church. When she arrived at the altar, her previously impenetrable walls of resistance came crashing down. She desperately cried out to God, asking Him to change her life. "God, if You change my life, I won't sell cocaine anymore. No drugs. I'll sell Bibles instead. But please change my life." She challenged God to put her to sleep that night without taking any drugs.

"I don't remember what happened," she said. "But when I opened my eyes after going to bed, it was 6 a.m. The valium and cocaine I relied on still sat on the bedside table. I knew then that God was real."

Not only did God take away her need for drugs, but He also gave her a new outlook. A short time later, Marco had his own incredible encounter with Christ. God restored their marriage, and they began to build a financially successful life centered on their relationship with Jesus.

After Marco finished medical school with a specialty in family practice, he was sent to Jalisco to administer a medical clinic. In Jalisco, Alma and Marco started a small church with friends they had led to Christ. They moved back to the San Quintín Valley in 1994 to be near Marco's ailing father.

In the meantime, God was working out a beautifully-orchestrated plan. Alma reconnected with an old friend who now worked as a dentist at our mission. Marco tagged along with Alma on her second visit there and met Dr. Luc Chaussé. They bonded instantly.

Dr. Luc was just about to return to Canada after several years with us, and he considered Dr. Marco's timely arrival as God's answer to his prayers for a replacement doctor. Marco felt a strong calling to the position, but when Alma was hesitant, he asked God to give her a change of heart.

It was soon after that when Alma and I met. I'm convinced it was a divine appointment—one that confirmed she was right where God purposed her to be. God helped her to see His hand in bringing the two of them there.

Alma realized that everything she had experienced in the past would help her relate to the children at our home. Every child rescued from the dump, every child brought out of abandonment or abuse, was another child just like her. She knew their suffering. She understood their pain. She could love on them with deep compassion. And she could speak truth to their wounded hearts. Jesus had called her to make a difference in those children's lives.

Marco's and Alma's ministry at the mission was a good fit for them. Ever since becoming a Christian, Marco had wanted to be in full-time service for Jesus. He especially had a particular concern for the poverty-stricken indigenous people in the labor camps—the very people who filled the clinic each morning. While most of the Angulos' work was centered at the medical center, they often served in the camps.

One time, an indigenous woman Marco met in town pleaded with him to visit Las Choyas, a remote camp about two hours away. The hills, rough roads, and distance made it difficult for the migrants to walk to our clinic for help, and many were in great need of a doctor.

Dr. Marco assembled an assortment of basic medical supplies and headed to the camp. It didn't take long for a large crowd to gather around him. It also didn't take long for an angry ranch owner to arrive. He yelled at Marco, "Get off my property! You have no business here on my land!" The fierce tone of his voice caused the crowd to scatter and Dr. Marco to retreat to his van.

Later, many efforts were made to talk sense to the ranch owner—even a local Catholic priest got involved—but to no avail. Frank Ticknor, from our mission, visited the owner at his Ensenada home multiple times over the next couple of weeks. But the owner refused to allow a medical team to treat his workers.

Then one day, a farm worker walked more than twenty miles to our medical center in Colonia Vicente Guerrero and sought out Dr. Marco. He said, "You have to come! Our people are very sick." From what the man told him, Marco sensed the seriousness and urgency of the circumstances. How could he say no?

Marco loaded up his supplies and a good amount of medicine, and prepared for his return to Las Choyas. He asked Don Pierce, a male nurse and paramedic volunteer, to join him. I offered to go along to pray for the sick. Don drove our ambulance to the entrance of the camp, and after the chain was dropped so we could enter, we moved inside and settled in.

We discovered a population devastated by skin infections. Many of the people had high fevers, and all the children had festering, open sores that worsened daily because of their unsanitary living conditions.

Dr. Marco created a small dispensary in the middle of the camp, and most of the day he and Don handed out medicine and soap. He also gave instructions in good hygiene. Just as they started packing up to leave, a pickup drove in. The rancher sprang out of the truck, got in Marco's face, and raged at him. "I told you to stay off this property! You are a false church and are teaching lies to these people!"

"I am a doctor. These people are in desperate need of medical treatment," Marco said.

"I know what they need and don't need. You are trespassing!" He threatened Marco with combative words and his fist, and then shifted his weight to make the gun at his waist clearly visible. Don and I got in the ambulance and immediately prayed for wisdom for Marco to handle the hostile man.

After Marco started talking about God and the commonalities our mission had with the Catholic religion—something the rancher understood—a strange thing happened. His countenance softened ever so slightly, and he admitted to several heavy burdens he was carrying at the time. He shocked Marco by saying, "Would you pray for me?"

"Of course!" Marco wasted no time in lifting the ranch owner in prayer. It was a rare moment to watch as the hardened man wept in front of a stunned, wide-eyed crowd—definitely a divine intervention.

But faster than an eye can blink, the owner's heart turned back to stone, and he forced us to leave. "Get out! And don't ever come back!" he said. Marco warned him that he would one day answer to God for his decision.

Harvest time came and went, and Marco visited several other camps. One day, he recognized a familiar face. "Brother, how is your family? How is everyone at Las Choyas?" he asked.

The young man grinned. He explained that the camp no longer existed. "It was almost like a plague from God," he said. "All the other ranchers had a good harvest, but after you left, the Las Choyas rancher's fields were infested with blight. His 30,000 acres were the only ones affected." He went on to say that the rancher burned his fields and left, broken and ruined. His workers went to other camps.

That was just one of the many types of experiences Marco dealt with during the Angulos' time with us, showcasing the importance and need of our mission's outreach.

Another experience he had—an especially delightful memory for me—is that Marco delivered our great granddaughter while our granddaughter was a student at the Bible institute. He eventually took a call to Playa de Tijuana as a hospital administrator, and Alma got a job as a counselor. But they were with us for the celebration when my great granddaughter graduated from Stanford University years later. Marco and Alma hold a special place in my heart.

Alma made a powerful statement to me one time, and I haven't forgotten it. She admitted that the work she and Marco did at the mission was sometimes painful. "I don't just see a need. I see myself, and I feel what they feel. It would be easier to run away from it. But my personal feeling is this—you can't be a Christian and live like there's nothing going on out there."

She said it well. It's too bad everyone doesn't see it the same way.

God miraculously transformed Alma, a street urchin who lived at the garbage dump. She became Dr. Marco Angulo's wife, and together they served at the mission.

A Young Student and a Supernatural God

A note to the reader: Part of this chapter tells about María's encounters with the demonic in Yucuyi. Some readers may try to discount the incidents as absurd, but they are included because they actually happened. Although rarely acknowledged, demonic activity is a real thing.

W hile each of our Bible institute students is special, I want to tell you about María de Jesus Villa Pablo, because she has a fascinating story that showcases the power of God. She's one of the five remaining students from the year the big flood washed away our buildings. I introduced you to Glenn in a previous chapter, and I'll acquaint you with Raúl in the following pages. All of them went on to do great things for God.

María comes from a background steeped in darkness. Her father was a heavy drinker and womanizer, and he would disappear for days at a time, not at all concerned that his young family suffered from hunger. After he died from a tragic accident when María was an infant, her mother, Eugenia, took María and her sister, Galia, to her home town of Yucuyi in Oaxaca, where they lived with María's grandparents, aunts, and uncles.

Eugenia was pregnant with a third child at the time, and after she gave birth to a baby boy, her mother asked her to leave. She said, "We are very poor here. You need to take your children and go look for work."

With Eugenia's commitment to labor at least a year in the fields of Sinaloa, she and her children were offered a free bus ride there. After a year, they moved on to the Baja Peninsula, where Eugenia again toiled with migrants. In Sinaloa, she had the help of a couple of teenagers to watch her children, but now she was on her own. She also lacked food for her family.

One day, a woman who knew her situation said to her, "I've heard about a place that cares for children. They have many good people there. Why don't you go and ask if they can receive yours?" She also said, "They will have food for all of you."

Eugenia took the woman's advice and sought out the help of Hogar Para Niños. Because of a full house, we weren't able to accommodate the children immediately, but our administrator sent Eugenia away with groceries and a promise. Within a few days, our home for children had room for María—then about 2½ years old—and her siblings. They were uprooted from our care after nineteen months, when María's grandmother insisted Eugenia bring the children back to Oaxaca. We didn't have them under our umbrella very long, but long enough that God could plant precious seeds and memories deep within their hearts.

Eugenia left María and her siblings in Oaxaca with their grandmother while she went to live in the United States. Apart from their mother for seven years, the children were immersed in an environment filled with alcoholism and violence. Because of ongoing exposure to sorcery and superstition, María often faced evil spirits at night as their grotesque forms manifested around her bed. Like with so many children and adults in Yucuyi, fear tormented her.

Meanwhile in the states, María's mother had an encounter with Christ and began a dynamic relationship with God. Whenever Eugenia made her yearly visit to Oaxaca, she told stories to her children, sang to them, and prayed over them at night. María's fear would disappear, only to return as soon as Eugenia left.

By God's sovereign grace, Eugenia regained full custody of her children after her mother died. The four of them eventually made it back to Baja, where they lived once again in the labor camps.

Soon after arriving there, one of the girls in the camp asked María, "Do you want to go to a Bible class with us? They teach about Jesus, and they give us milk and peanut butter. Sometimes they give us candy too!" María was intrigued by the idea of peanut butter—she hadn't heard of it before—and she was excited to learn about Jesus.

Since becoming a Christian, her mother had told her stories about Jesus. Plus, María had a vague memory from her toddler years of drowning in a river current and being brought back to life. In her memory, a nice Man in bright white clothes told her she needed to return to her mother. (Years later, Eugenia told her it was Jesus who saved her.) Yes, she wanted to know more about Him!

She went to that class, and thanks to the two child evangelism teachers from the mission's outreach ministry—and the work of the Holy Spirit—María met her Savior. That day she gained liberation from the spiritual attacks and extreme terror that had paralyzed her in the nights. That day she also felt a strong calling to missions. She knew she needed to one day return to Oaxaca with the good news.

María continued to attend the child evangelism classes. She asked lots of questions and soaked up everything she learned. Soon she met Graciela Cordoba, who invited her to a discipleship class and to the mission church, where she learned even more. A year later, she was baptized.

And then when María was 14, Jon Cowpersmith said to me, "There's a girl out there in those fields who has really been born again, and she's witnessing to all those around her. She belongs in our Bible school."

I wasn't convinced, especially when I heard her age. "She needs to go to school, Jon. She's just a child! She doesn't need to go to the Bible institute."

But he insisted. "The call of God is on her life, Charla." After an interview with Graciela, the mission's pastor, and a few other people, María and her older sister, Galia, were invited to attend. They were the youngest students we ever accepted.

And Jon Cowpersmith proved me wrong.

After María finished Bible school, Minerva Trujillo invited her to take a special class in Tijuana that gave her training in how to minister to children. Then, on a two-month trip to Sinaloa, she worked with children in different churches. But she grew restless. She told the mission pastor, "Since I accepted Christ, a fire has been in my heart to return to Oaxaca and to tell the people that Jesus is the way, the truth, and the life. I want to go back."

"Tell me where you'd like to go," he said.

"In the place where I grew up. Yucuyi. There are no Christians, and it's a very dark place. That's where I want to be."

The pastor took trips to Oaxaca every year. He told her he'd check out Yucuyi and report back to her with his thoughts. After he returned from his visit there, he said, "You're only 16 years old. I don't believe it's the right time. You need to wait a while." She was disappointed, but he gave her some good news as well. "I found Christians in Juxtlahuaca, a place close by. I met several pastors, and they don't have a children's ministry. You can start there."

María moved to Juxtlahuaca and worked with pastors in the area to raise up a ministry to children. She started out teaching the children, and then months later trained others in the churches to do it. After three years, she felt like her time there had finished, but she didn't know what God wanted.

On her bus ride back to Baja, God spoke to her through a verse in Isaiah. In it, the Lord said, "Whom shall I send? Who will go for us?" María had a strong sense that it was time to return to Yucuyi to call out to God for her people.

Once she made the plans to go, a great battle began. Demonic spirits attacked her with nightmares, and evil voices hissed threatening messages. "Yucuyi is our territory. We will not allow you to affect it." She countered those voices with truth from God's Word.

Then the attacks intensified to cause physical harm. She asked her mother to pray for her, and as Eugenia prayed, María saw a dark creature with wings enter the room.

An all-out fight with oppressive forces continued as the rest of María's family was physically attacked as well. Throughout the night they all prayed, and María became even more determined to follow God's leading. She told her family, "It's a battle, and it won't be easy, but I know it's time for me to go. The enemy is defeated. I'm going."

At first, she lived in Yucuyi with an aunt and uncle. Her uncle was an alcoholic and beat his wife. It was hard for María to live in an environment like that, but she knew God had brought her with a purpose.

Then one morning as María talked with God, she heard Him say, "Pick up these rocks and walk up to the top of that mountain." She thought it was crazy, but she obeyed. Once she was there, God told her to build an altar with the rocks and to pour oil over it. Again, she obeyed.

As she accomplished that task, God said, "I want you to come to this place every day and call out for these people. Call out for this town." And that's what she did. Every morning she went to the altar, where she could see all the surrounding communities, and for half a day she called out for the people. In the afternoons, she taught reading and writing. She started giving Bible classes to the children as well.

Immediately came the opposition and accusations and shunning. "She's from the devil," people said. "She wants to change our religion. Don't talk to her. Don't listen to her. Don't receive her."

María prayed, "Lord, if they don't accept me, how will they accept the message I bring to them?"

The Lord said, "Continue praying and serve them. Don't preach My Word yet. The day will come for that. Just love them. Serve them. Let them see your life."

After a year without her being able to share the gospel, a group from the Bible institute—along with Alma Angulo, the school director at that time— came to Yucuyi. A medical team headed by Dr. Ramon Avitia joined them. Mario Cordoba, our mission administrator, was with them as well, and they all offered their support to María.

Because the townspeople didn't trust the group, and thought they were there to steal their land, not many came for medical consults at first. But one courageous woman stood up to the lies and proclaimed, "María hasn't done anything bad to us. She's done only good things." After that, more people were willing to receive medical help.

On the third day, Mario said to María, "It's our last day here. What can we do for you before we leave?"

Although the team had prayed against a paralyzing spirit of fear and the forces of evil day in and day out while they were in Yucuyi, María asked, "Can you go with me to the places where people see strange things?" She told them about a specific spot where every night at midnight a horse with a headless, chained rider was seen running through the town. "And there's another place—a fountain—where my grandmother took me when I was little to offer blood sacrifices."

The medical consults didn't finish until eleven o'clock that night, so it was late and dark when the group headed toward the town, praying all the way. As they walked among trees that took on the appearance of monsters, they heard voices mocking them and laughing at them. "You can't go against us," the voices said. "We're powerful. This place belongs to us." But the prayer warriors walked in faith, knowing that the all-powerful God was with them.

When they arrived at the area where the horse made its run every night, a pack of wild dogs rushed out and tried to attack them. One of the people in the group held up her hand and said, "In the name of Jesus, be quiet and go." The dogs immediately stopped barking and ran away.

In a Holy-Spirit-guided moment, María lowered to her knees and did what the prophet Daniel had done thousands of years before. She asked for forgiveness for that community. She cried as if she were the worst sinner, in representation of the town. The team members gave prophetic words over the place. And they finished by worshiping God.

Since that crucial night, the headless horseman has not returned to terrorize the community.

From there, they moved on to the fountain where María's relatives offered blood sacrifices. She cried out for forgiveness and for God's mercy on behalf of her family. And God gave her a beautiful promise as she finished. "I am breaking the curse!"

After that, they all went back to the home where they were staying and prepared for bed. Just then, the sound of a roaring lion shook the room. They all looked at each other and said, "Did you hear that?"

Someone asked, "Are there lions here, María?"

"No, not even one," she replied.

"The Lord showed me that the Lion of the Tribe of Judah has ordered the spirits that have held this place captive to leave," one of the women said. The group prayed through the rest of the night.

The next day, as the team was leaving, they experienced an incredible shift in the atmosphere. People came to them and said, "Can you pray for us? Do you have a Bible for us?" Once the enemy's influence over the villagers' lives had been removed, they begged to know about God. They could finally see their need.

María started having meetings in homes, and she had opportunities to share the gospel. She formed Bible clubs for children and taught adults to read and write. Out of the first group of believers, God raised up a young woman named Teresa, who has followed in María's footsteps. She went to the Bible institute and now serves full time ministering in various communities. Because she is able to speak the Mixteco language, she has a valuable advantage that María didn't have.

María then teamed up with Martin and Karen Arroyo, a missionary couple in Juxtlahuaca. Through the three of them, God birthed a church named Abundant Grace Family Christian Center. The church's focus is taking the gospel to those who have not heard the Word, including the remote communities in the mountains and also extending into the region of Juxtlahuaca. Their mission is to make strong disciples in Christ who can then make other disciples in Christ.

María spends a lot of time training others and assuring they have what they need to do the work. Her experiences in Yucuyi have given her great wisdom to share. In addition to evangelism, training, discipleship, and administration, María has also taken on the role of programmer for a radio station that transmits a great diversity of programming into areas that are unsafe or difficult to reach.

The needs continue to be enormous, and the risks are high, but she is a dedicated servant who joyfully gives her all for the sake of the gospel.

I shake my head in wonder as I remember the day I thought she was too young to enter the Bible institute.

María Villa Pablo is an anointed, humble servant of God. She was the youngest student ever accepted at our Bible institute and now ministers in the mountains of Oaxaca.

Due to Jon Cowpersmith's insistence, we accepted María into our Bible institute at the young age of 14. Not only was Jon instrumental in the ministry of the Bible institute and a spiritual advisor for the mission, he was also a man of many talents. (In this picture, he is playing a saw.) Jon's wife, Eleanor, served as office manager and in many other positions.

Abandoned, Broken, and Called

Raúl Garcia is a bronze-skinned, short-of-stature, Oaxacan man with an infectious smile and a warm hug. His sweet spirit and joy are known to all those in his presence. Because of the twinkle in his eyes, one might never realize he's endured horrible heartache in his life. God has done a mighty work in him and through him.

When he was just 3 years old, Raúl's parents abandoned him, and he was left with his grandmother. She decided she couldn't afford to feed him, so she gave him away to a widow with no children. He was 5 at the time. The widow used him as a serf and treated him as if he were an animal. Occasionally, she'd throw him a few scraps of food.

One day a stranger came through the village and noticed Raúl's situation. The stranger said, "Why don't you come with me? I'll give you a place to stay." With a ray of hope for a better life, Raúl followed him home.

His place to stay ended up being nothing more than a patch of straw in the barn with the animals. Each day he received a small pouch of food that barely lasted him beyond his morning hunger pains. Because the stranger's family didn't want to be seen with him, he spent his daylight hours among the sheep and cows in the hills.

He was abused by adults, mocked by other children, and encountered one set of bad circumstances after another. As he watched how real families interacted, his mind wandered. What would it be like to have a mother? He ached for the one he never really knew. Her absence had left a void in his life that couldn't be filled by anything else.

After hearing a group of boys talk about their plans of running away to Mexico City, a vague memory popped into his head. Several years earlier his aunt had told him that his mother lived there. That's all it took for 9-year-old Raúl to make a big decision. "I'm leaving here and going to Mexico City," he determined out loud. "I will find my mother."

That night he had a vivid dream. A Man robed in bright white garments with a gold belt around His waist stood before him. With His arms stretched toward Raúl, He motioned for him to come. Something about the Man gave Raúl a strange sense of comfort. He didn't know who this person was or why He appeared before him, but deep inside Raúl sensed that he was experiencing a supernatural presence. What is the meaning of this dream? he wondered.

A week later, Raúl met up with a couple of the boys who had talked of going to Mexico City. They hid alongside the road near a bend where cargo trucks slowed to a crawl, and they hopped on the first truck that came their way. The young stowaways laid low, so as not to be seen, and rode all through the night.

Raúl fell asleep and didn't notice that the others had deserted him, so when the truck reached its last stop at a busy terminal, he was alone. He crawled out of the truck bed and entered a scary new environment. As he looked around him, he got a sick feeling in the pit of his stomach. What had he done? In all his life he'd never seen such crowds! With the mass of bodies bustling around him, he realized that finding his mother was an impossible expectation.

He had nowhere to go, so he walked until he came upon a big city park—Alameda Central. The historic place had wide open green spaces, walking paths, and decorative fountains and statues throughout. At one time it served as the home of the Aztec marketplace and now was a hub of civic and recreational activity. Tired, hungry, and afraid,

Raúl found an empty bench and sat there to ponder his next steps.

Before long, he felt a tug on his sleeve, and a friendly voice drew his attention. "What are you doing here, amigo?" A dirty little boy in raggedy clothes sat down beside him.

One by one, other bedraggled children started to appear, and they bombarded him with questions. They were curious about his family, his plans, whether he had anything to eat, where he was going to sleep, and other important issues.

When a runny-nosed girl in a threadbare dress asked what he was going to do, Raúl hung his head as if defeated. "I don't know," he said. "I guess I'm going to die."

The children gathered closer around him and almost in chorus said, "No, you're not. You can stay with us." They shared their personal stories and comforted him with their common misfortunes.

That group of abandoned and runaway children became Raúl's family for the next ten years. They taught him how to make money from shining shoes and picking pockets. They also taught him where to sleep and how to bathe in the park's fountain. Although none of them had parents or guardians to nurture them, they learned how to care and look out for one other.

At the age of 19, Raúl met a group of bricklayers. They offered him a job and training. He saw it as an opportunity for a different kind of life, and after two weeks he received his first real paycheck. Because he slept at the job sites, he was out of contact with his park brothers and sisters. When he tried to find them so he could buy them all a hot churro with his newly-received wages, they were nowhere to be found.

For the next year, he spent his days off looking for his "family" without success. Then one afternoon he saw a familiar person. He hadn't seen her since he was 3, but he recognized her from a picture he kept in his memory. It was his mother!

He shoved his way through the crowd to reach her, got her attention, and hastily asked, "Are you María Lopez Jimenez?" She affirmed that she was. "Are you from Capulalpam de Méndez in Oaxaca?" He continued to ask questions that received positive answers. And then he said, "I am your son, Raúl!" He waited awkwardly for a response from the woman he had longed to share life with for so many years.

She turned fully toward Raúl, her eyes blazing as they stared into his. "You are not my son!" The rage in her voice increased as she continued her lie. "I found you in the garbage. Now leave me alone!" She spat in his face and walked away without looking back.

Despite the antagonistic encounter and his mother's apparent disdain for him, he wasn't ready to give up. The next day he collected his last paycheck and returned to Oaxaca. He went to his aunt's home and told her the story of finding his mother. She wrote a letter to her sister and, without telling her Raúl was there to see her, urged her to come home.

As soon as he got news a week later that she had arrived, he ran to his aunt's house, prepared with the words he hoped would convince his mother to change her mind. It didn't take long for him to realize something was wrong. His aunt stood in the yard. "Is she here?" he asked.

She shook her head. "No. She came, and once she figured it out, left on the first bus."

Raúl's drunk uncle emerged from the doorway and started ridiculing him, causing his already broken heart to ache even more. While the taunts continued, his aunt said, "You should have listened to her. She doesn't want anything to do with you."

His grandmother, sitting on a bucket and fanning herself in the shade of a tree, couldn't help but add to the agonizing chorus. "If she loved you, she would have stayed. Just move on."

In the distance, the sound of grinding gears as a truck labored up the mountain caught Raúl's attention. Knowing that the road led to Oaxaca City—where the bus station was located—he impulsively ran to the side of the road and lunged for the truck's tailgate as it drove by. He had to see his mother one more time and plead his case!

Once the truck reached Oaxaca City, Raúl jumped out and headed to the bus station. He found the one marked "Mexico City" and saw on the schedule that it would depart after dark. Lingering in the area as ticket holders loaded the bus, he waited until the coast was clear and then crawled into the cargo rack on the underside. It wasn't easy for him to squeeze between gaps in the luggage, but he was determined to do whatever it took to get his mother back.

For nine long hours, he inhaled exhaust fumes and listened to the loud roar of the motor. An empty stomach, a full bladder, and a throbbing head kept him awake the entire miserable trip.

When the bus finally arrived in Mexico City, the terminal was such a flurry of activity that no one saw him wriggle away from the luggage compartment. He stretched to loosen his cramped muscles and took several slow, deep breaths of fresh air. And then, as the passengers stepped out of the bus, who should he see but his mother! He hid in the crowd and followed her to her home.

The scene didn't play out as he had hoped. She was so enraged at his being there that she grabbed an extension cord and flogged him mercilessly. Blood oozed from his arms and legs where the prongs ripped away his skin. The lashing continued for a long while, until her husband intervened. "For your safety, you should go. She doesn't love you and obviously doesn't want you here." He almost sounded apologetic.

Raúl finally accepted the harsh reality that he was unwanted and unloved, shattering all his hopes. Over the next years, roots of bitterness, hatred, and unforgiveness began to grow in his spirit. He reached for alcohol to cope with his mother's rejection, and thoughts of murder possessed him. Because of his despondency, he joined the army, only to be dishonorably discharged after two years due to his drinking habit.

He returned to his hometown of Capulalpam de Méndez, where he found a job with the local police force. His drinking continued, and he gradually sank into isolation. It was during this lonely season that Raúl remembered his childhood dream of the Man robed in bright white. Not knowing anything about God other than that He existed, he began to cry out to the supernatural presence that had appeared to him so many years before.

Then one day, as Raúl napped in his yard, a stranger approached him. "Are you Raúl Garcia?" he asked.

Raúl's hand instinctively reached for the gun on his belt, and his questions came out in quick succession. "Who are you, how do you know my name, and what are you doing here?"

The man said, "The Lord sent me to talk to you about the gospel."

Suspicious of this unknown messenger, Raúl asked, "Who is this Lord you're talking about?"

"The Lord Jesus," the stranger said. "He told me your name, where you lived, and what you'd be wearing. You must go to Him and repent." Raúl didn't make it easy for him to complete his assignment. Finally, the man simply said, "Fine. I've done what God told me to do. It's on your shoulders now." He told Raúl where he could find him, if needed, and walked away.

A month later, Raúl had trouble falling asleep. All he could think about was the stranger and what he had said. He wondered about this mysterious Lord—the One who calls Himself Jesus Christ. After tossing and turning for hours, he eventually dozed off.

Once again, the Man in dazzling white appeared before him, just as had happened when Raúl was a child. This time He spoke. "I'm looking for you."

At that moment, pictures of his life flashed through his mind, and Raúl had a profound realization. He was an unholy man in the presence of holiness. Raúl cried out, "Oh Lord, I know You are Jesus! I have failed You. Please forgive me. From now on I want to follow You." It was an unexplainable experience, but it made complete sense in his spirit.

He knew he needed to tell people about his supernatural visitor. He knew he should attend church. Yet he also felt so unworthy. He struggled with the false mindset that church was only for perfect people, and he was far from that.

Even though his feelings caused inner turmoil, he walked three hours on Christmas Eve until he arrived at the church door, where several men greeted him and warmly invited him in. He sensed immediately that he had found what he'd been looking for his whole life, but he left the service confused, wondering how God could accept a person like him.

He returned home with a Bible, which he tried his best to read. One night in January, as he fell asleep, he was talking to God about his conflicting thoughts. For the third time, he had a supernatural visit.

"Get up!" The voice startled Raúl, and he promptly sat up. He saw a man at the foot of his bed and another at the head. Both of them had dark faces, similar to his, and they were immersed in brilliant white light. One of them delivered a message and then instructed Raúl to open his Bible. Raúl did as he was told, and the pages fell to Ezekiel 33:12—the exact passage of scripture his nighttime visitor had quoted.

The words went straight to his heart. He was overwhelmed by a powerful sense of God's grace, and he wept for joy as he felt a freedom he had never had. When he looked up again, the men were gone, but the memory of the encounter stayed with him. From that point on, he was a changed man.

Eventually, Raul ended up in the San Quintín Valley. He lived in the Rancho Milagro camp for migrant workers and freely shared the gospel with others. So many came to Christ that they formed a small church. He dreamed of attending a Bible institute, but dismissed it as being a far-fetched reality and tried to put it out of his mind.

Then one day a pastor arrived at the camp. He asked around for Raúl Garcia and, with the help of some of the people there, finally found him. Raúl didn't know the man. In fact, he hadn't had any contact with pastors since he arrived there. So, when the pastor approached him, Raúl asked, "Who are you, and why are you here?"

The man said, "My name doesn't matter. The Lord says you are going to study in the Bible school. Here are some papers." He handed Raúl a brochure and an application.

At first Raúl thought he was crazy and didn't believe him. When the pastor said he'd fill out the application for him, Raúl said, "I don't have money to pay for Bible school." The pastor assured him it wasn't a problem and told him that he'd return before September to take him there.

Raúl had a heart-to-heart chat with God after the pastor left. He said, "Lord, what is this about? That man said he was going to take me to a Bible school. They won't accept me. I don't have a pastor or anyone else who can provide a reference. No one knows me." He offered several other reasons why he couldn't attend. Then he said, "But I have one thing— You. If You go with me, I'll go. If You don't go, I'm not going."

The pastor picked him up at the indicated time and drove Raúl to our Bible institute at Chilpayates. His dream had come true! The assistant director greeted him and said, "Are you Raúl?" Raúl nodded. "We've been waiting for you. The Lord revealed to us that you were going to come."

Raúl graduated at the top of his class and then served as an intern in our outreach program, teaching and preaching in the migrant camps and leading many to Christ. Because of so many opportunities to visit families, he started praying for a wife. He knew it would be easier to reach out with a helpmate. And that's when Florentina (Flor), a young Mixteco girl, came on the scene. He met her at Camp Garcia.

He wanted to invite her to the mission church, but didn't know the traditional steps required for asking permission.

She said, "First, you must ask my father. Then you must bring your mother to see him."

"But I don't have a father or mother," he said.

"Can you bring another mother?"

"The only mother I have is Hermana Charla, and she speaks only English."

Flor asked how they communicated. "I don't know how I talk to her, but I do."

Raul asked me to vouch for his character and to negotiate an agreement with Flor's father. The request delighted me. Of course, I said yes. Together, we went to their cardboard hovel and sat on 30-gallon buckets. I noticed the simple woven floormats on the ground and learned later that they were their beds.

We exchanged greetings with Flor's father, who was obviously surprised to be talking with a white woman. Then he started in on the questions—and there were a slew of them! "How does he get his money?" "Is he a drinker?" "Is he an angry man?" "How will he support Flor if they get married?" Apparently, I answered the questions satisfactorily because he allowed Flor to attend church gatherings with Raúl.

While they were courting, I had a speaking circuit in Alaska. During a Sunday morning service at an Assembly of God church in Sitka, someone placed a diamond ring in the offering. That was a first for me! Lorraine Barter, our bookkeeper and my good friend, felt strongly that we should give it to Raúl to use as his pledge of fidelity to Flor. Six months later, they married. She has been God's gift to him, and together they make a great team.

Raúl and Flor faithfully served as house parents at the children's home in addition to outreach work and other responsibilities at the mission. Eventually, God put a desire in Raúl's heart to return to Oaxaca. Raúl asked God what He had in mind. Here is the message he received: "You need to open a work for the people of the mountains. They have need. This is why I've brought you here."

The Lord went on and impressed these words from Acts 26:16–18 upon Raúl's spirit. "Now get up and stand on your feet. I have appeared to you to appoint you as a servant and as a witness of what you have seen and will see of me. I will rescue you from your own people and from the Gentiles. I am sending you to them to open their eyes and turn them from darkness to light, and from the power of Satan to God, so that they may receive forgiveness of sins and a place among those who are sanctified by faith in me" (NIV).

Raúl asked, "What do I do now?"

"Write down what I tell you and leave it in the office." Raúl did as God directed. He claims that even now he has no idea of what he wrote on that piece of paper, but he gave it to Mario, and God put His incredible plan into action.

That vision led to a special work in Oaxaca that is way beyond what we at FFHM could have ever imagined. (I'll tell more in the next chapter.) Raúl also established La Loma Esperanza (Hill of Hope)—a Bible school in a remote area of the Oaxacan mountains, where he trained and discipled pastors and leaders, some who walked hours just to attend classes. Flor taught literacy to the people there.

Although he later had to return to the Baja mission because of health issues, the ripple effects of his obedience to God's calling are far-reaching in magnitude and scope.

Sometimes people try to give Raúl credit for what he's accomplished. He tells them, "It didn't happen because I was trying to do something. When God pulls you, you have to fulfill His purpose."

To that I say, "Amen."

Top: Raúl and Florentina on their wedding day

Bottom: Raúl is someone who was abandoned, rescued, redeemed, and blessed. His smile says it all.

A Home Base in Oaxaca

Hundreds of years before Christ, the prophet Habakkuk had a conversation with the Lord. He poured out what was on his heart, asked lots of questions, and waited for God's reply. Here's what God told him:

> *"Write down the message I am giving you.*
> *Write it clearly on the tablets you use.*
> *Then a messenger can read it*
> *and run to announce it.*
> *The message I give you*
> *waits for the time I have appointed.*
> *It speaks about what is going to happen.*
> *And all of it will come true.*
> *It might take a while.*
> *But wait for it.*
> *You can be sure it will come.*
> *It will happen when I want it to."*

(Habakkuk 2:2–3, NIRV)

As God spoke to Raúl Garcia in his dreams and impressed on him that it was time to do a project in Oaxaca, Raúl inquired of the Lord, "What do I do now?"

God responded in a similar way as He did to Habakkuk. "Write down what I tell you and leave My message in the office."

Although the vision wasn't completely clear to Raúl, he obediently recorded it and delivered it to Mario, the mission administrator. After praying about it, they made a presentation to the board. Before long, plans started falling into place for FFHM to start a work in Oaxaca. God didn't reveal the big picture all at once. Instead, He has shown us His will one step at a time.

The first step was to establish a home base—a place where we could offer support for our missionaries, pastors, church leaders, and teachers who serve faithfully in the mountains of Oaxaca—a place where we could build them up, cheer them up, and stir them up. Anything we could do to equip and empower those doing the work of reaching the unreached would help us fulfill our purpose.

Frank Ticknor, the host at our Baja mission, caught the vision for the project and volunteered to go with Raúl to explore the land. What an unlikely pair the two of them made—they were opposite in every way! Frank was a tall, fair-skinned, silver-haired man of Swedish descent and Raúl, a Oaxacan with raven black hair and dark eyes, whose head barely reached Frank's shoulders. But they were a great team. Frank was a visionary with a pioneer spirit; Raúl knew the land, the culture, and the language.

Our list of requirements included a level, centrally-located property that had access to water and electrical power. It also needed to be near enough to an airport where people could fly in and out easily. At the time, we didn't have any funds set aside for the project, but we knew God had a great track record, and we trusted Him to provide.

With their marching orders in mind and the prayers of a multitude embracing them, the men loaded up a little pickup truck and set out for Oaxaca. Once there, they researched, asked questions, and combed the region for a suitable and affordable retreat-center spot. Because property there is traditionally passed down from generation to generation, and it's not normal for people to sell their ancestral land, they had few choices available to them.

Finally, after thousands of miles traveled and eighteen months of searching, they identified five sites with potential. Dr. Ernesto Cano (the head of our Mexican board), Mario, and I made the trip south to check out the options.

Mario and I fell in love with one of the spots on the list, and we both agreed that it would be a fabulous place to live once we retired. I've never seen a more gorgeous property in my life! It had a sparkling stream running through it, mango and avocado trees filled with low hanging fruit, and the ruins of an old mission on site. Unfortunately, it wasn't practical for our purposes because of the need to travel ten miles on an unpaved mountain road to reach it.

But another one of the properties kept drawing our attention, and we returned to it five times in the two weeks we were there. It seemed to have many advantages—the biggest being that it was right off the Pan-American Highway with a paved road in front, and it was only about an hour's drive from the airport in Oaxaca City. The twenty acres just outside the town of Tlacolula also had a well and access to electricity.

At the forefront of the land stood an unfinished two-story building that had seen better days. It looked as if the cement floors were sagging, and we were unsure whether it was even salvageable. A jungle of overgrown thorn bushes—most of them eight to ten feet high—covered the rest of the property. They looked like one continuous tangle. And those thorns were huge!

A beautiful, low-level mountain range served as the backdrop to the property. Within those mountains is a rock formation that bears the resemblance of a woman sleeping on her back. Everyone in the area knows her as "The Sleeping Lady."

One day a Presbyterian minister, a roving evangelist, came by the site while we were there. "This is sacred land," he said, and went on to tell us some of the fascinating native legends about the woman. "People say that when she awakens, she's going to deliver a message that brings peace to the land." His words gave me goosebumps.

On our third visit to the site, we learned that the property belonged to El Pacto, the Evangelical Covenant denomination in Mexico. They had originally planned to use the building as a retreat center, but something got in their way of completing the project. Knowing the twenty acres was owned by a group of Christians factored into our decision to buy it.

Frank, Mario, Dr. Cano, and I met with a delegation of eight indigenous Covenant pastors and church leaders at Taco Brown, a restaurant in Tlacolula owned by one of the men. They were surprised to be negotiating with a woman!

The asking price for their land was $50,000. "Will you take $30,000?" I said. "It'll take us $20,000 to finish the building and clear the property." At that point, we still hadn't secured funds for the purchase, but I spoke with confidence, knowing God would provide. I just wasn't sure how.

"We'll need to pray about it and talk to our advisory board before we can answer," they said.

In the meantime, as we awaited their yes or no, I sent a fax to our office in the states. I wanted our FFHM team to know we had made an offer on a piece of land. "Please pray," I wrote.

The return fax delighted me. "We just received a donation of $50,000 designated toward the purchase of land in Oaxaca," it said. I learned the gift had come from a woman who lived in Newark, Illinois—a tiny farming community. It was the first (and last) time she ever sent money to our mission. Because we don't normally receive gifts that large, and the timing was so perfect, it was obviously God's hand at work. What a good God He is!

After a few days, the Covenant delegation got back to us. They agreed to accept our offer. Mario took care of all the legal documents and worked with the proper authorities to transfer the property into our possession—a huge undertaking, especially in Mexico.

Through each step of the process, God made His presence known, and three months after we closed the deal, He again affirmed to us that we were in the center of His will. He did it in an extraordinarily amazing way.

Pastor Dwight Nelson of Bethany Covenant Church in Mount Vernon, Washington, had asked me to bring the morning message on a Sunday in September. Our friend and medical advisor to the ministry, Dr. Gary Johnson, is a member of the church and helped with the arrangements.

As was my routine, I scheduled several events to make the most of my time while in the area, and that evening I was booked to do a presentation for a Lutheran church. I'm not sure of their reason, but the Lutheran church cancelled the service at the last minute. The situation frustrated me. If I had known earlier, I could have lined up another venue.

When Gary became aware of the circumstances, he said, "Why don't you and Chuck come to our place for lunch and spend the afternoon with us? We're hosting a couple of missionaries. They're going to tell us about their recent trip to Oaxaca." His invitation piqued our curiosity, of course, and we readily accepted.

After church, Chuck and I joined the small group at Gary's house and enjoyed chatting about the place that is near and dear to our hearts. The missionary ladies told us about the vacation Bible school they held in a town so tiny it could barely be found on a map—Tlacolula. *Hmmm . . . interesting coincidence.*

They continued talking about their Mexican adventures, and one of the women said, "While we were in Tlacolula, we visited a piece of property a few miles away. It had an old shell of a building on it."

As she described the building and the setting, Chuck and I turned toward each other and shared a knowing look. I whispered to him, "Sounds familiar, doesn't it?" We both grinned.

And then the missionary said something that just about took my breath away. "We walked the land, and the most amazing thing happened. The power of the Holy Spirit came upon us, and we felt the overwhelming presence of God in that place." I don't remember ever hearing a member of the Covenant church speak that way.

The excitement in me bubbled over. "You're probably not going to believe this, but we just purchased that property!"

What are the chances of that happening?

If the engagement at the Lutheran church hadn't been cancelled, we would have missed out on the blessing God had for us that day. He encouraged us and assured us that His anointing was on the chosen land. All of us in the room sensed His smile, and we had a glorious time of rejoicing together.

In the following days, God continued to guide us, and we moved forward with His leading one step at a time. Chuck Mills went down to inspect the building. "It's salvageable," he said, so he started making plans for repairs and construction. Word got out that we needed help. And what a response we had!

Our first work group came from The Church of Glad Tidings in Yuba City, California. Ted Holmes, who had served at the mission previously, led the group that included three other general contractors, plumbers, electricians, carpenters, cement block layers and finishers, welders, and painters. They worked from sunrise to sunset and beyond. What they accomplished was nothing short of a miracle! My Chuck came down and helped lay the cement. Another construction team followed, this time from Valley Vineyard of Reseda, California, led by Pastor Bill Dwyer and Roberto Muñoz-Flores.

A sweet older couple from Centralia, Washington, who were vacationing in Oaxaca, volunteered to clear the land for us—all twenty acres. They parked their trailer on site and then over a three-month period cut down the thorn-bush jungle with machetes. It was a huge undertaking! (They returned the next year to do it all over again.)

While the details for this big project in Tlacolula were playing out, Almighty God had another plan in the works. It took me by surprise and, to be honest, I balked.

Somehow, Frank Ticknor and Chuck Mills met an American missionary from Texas. Because of health issues and other circumstances, he offered to give our ministry five acres of land in Etla, a city one hour to the north of our new home base in Oaxaca. The "gift" included an orphanage with thirty-nine children aged 2 to 12. A young woman in her early twenties cared for them with the help of a teenaged girl.

My response? "No! I-Am-Not-Interested-In-An-Orphanage! Exclamation point!" We had already done the children's home thing—Hogar Para Niños in Baja and another that we just opened in Morelia. My focus was geared elsewhere now.

When we began our exploration of Oaxaca, I was single-minded in purpose, with a passion to reach all the unreached people groups in Oaxaca—and beyond—with the gospel of Christ. Our missionary base and the services we provided there would help accomplish my dream. Not once had the idea of a home for children entered my thoughts.

"But, Charla, they need our help," Chuck Mills said. "We have to care for those children!"

Our FFHM board decided to accept the property sight unseen, and Frank took Corrine and me out to look at it. "I need to deal with some other business," he said as he dropped us off. "I'll return later to pick you up."

But he didn't. Frank "forgot" us for two days! How is that possible? I have a hunch his memory loss was intentional because he knew our compassion for God's precious children would win us over. And that's exactly what happened.

Most of the little ones interned there came from prison. In parts of Mexico, it's a common practice for children to accompany their incarcerated parents, and nowadays social workers are giving more effort to assigning guardianship to a relative or children's home. One can only imagine the atrocities those poor children have suffered in their short lifetimes. My heart breaks for them.

The L-shaped, single-story structure they lived in was nestled into the hillside. It had been made with a Gunite-type material used for quick building. (Gunite is a dry-mixed form of concrete that is applied with a sprayer over wire-mesh and steel-rod reinforcements.) At the lower part of the property sat a three-bedroom house, which flooded every winter due to the downhill water flow.

Although the facility itself was in fairly good shape, the children's living conditions horrified me. When we got there, Eunice, the young lady in charge, was outside trying to cook a pot of beans over an open flame. Because of lack of funds, they had run out of butane in the kitchen and only had beans and rice available for food. Niche (Eunice's nickname) was picking up sticks to fuel the fire while the children busied themselves catching grasshoppers to serve with the beans.

The children wore tattered, mismatched clothes. Many of them had shoes rubber-banded together to hold the soles in place. Inside the home, mice scampered across the red tile floors and cockroaches marched up and down the walls. Bedbugs infiltrated the children's mattresses.

If that weren't enough, all the shower water and everything that went through the toilets drained into a five-foot-deep trench that ran through the center of the property. It was only about twenty or thirty feet from the building. Thick swarms of little black bugs hovered above it.

I don't know how Niche survived. Despite the scarcity and hardships, she did whatever she could to show God's love to the children. She taught them the Word and had devotions with them every morning and evening. She taught them the power of prayer. She taught them the value of gratitude. I've never seen anyone so committed. And the children obviously loved her.

But the circumstances were more than I could tolerate. During my fitful attempts at sleep that night, I cried out, "Lord, how can this be? How can these children live like this?" (I also reminded Him that I had no desire to take on another children's home.)

By morning, the only thing on my mind was, "These children need your help, Charla." And I surrendered to God's will.

When Frank finally came to pick us up, my thoughts were racing with plans that needed to be implemented immediately. But the first requirement on the list involved getting the property legally transferred to us.

The owner from Texas flew down and met with Frank, Mario, and me at an attorney's office in Oaxaca City. He signed all the paperwork, and everything became official within a week's time. That's unheard of in Mexico!

Once it was in our hands, I sent an SOS to Larry Swayze, a septic system contractor I knew in Canby, Oregon. "Larry, we're in desperate need. The children in this orphanage are living in a cesspool." Four days later, he arrived with a crew of five guys. First, they dug a huge hole. And under my Chuck's expert tutelage, they started laying block. In two days, they built a 6,000-gallon septic tank. By the time they left a few days later, we had a fully functioning system.

Valley Vineyard also came and built a new kitchen and bathroom. Another crew replaced the leaky roof. We had two beautiful houses built for staff as well. Our supporters donated funds for the furnishings.

God provided the work groups, an excellent staff, and everything needed to transform the Etla home into a smooth-running, well-equipped place. It became a safe and healthy environment that offered new experiences and opportunities for the children.

Little did I know at the time how God's master plan would play out in the days ahead.

Because of all the activity in Tlacolula and Etla, the mission needed a permanent administrator in Oaxaca. Mario and Graciela moved their family from the Baja mission and took on that responsibility.

God soon made it abundantly clear to us that He had much more in mind than just a conference center for the Tlacolula property. Before long, Peter Bianchini, the chairman of our board, had designed some beautiful new buildings. He traveled monthly from Chicago to oversee the construction.

People prayed. God sent the funds, the skilled labor, and lots of volunteers. Within a few years, we moved the children from Etla to a fabulous new 40,000 sq. ft. mission home on our twenty acres. We now have a children's home, a school, a multipurpose auditorium, and a church on site. It also includes staff/guest housing, a maintenance/warehouse building, administrative offices, and a playground. It truly is a crown jewel.

And our precious Niche is still with us. She has served as a housemother, the director of the children's home, and is now involved in local outreach. What a gift she is to the children and to us!

As we were relocating to our new facilities in Tlacolula, we noticed construction happening on several buildings across the highway—prison buildings! It was just another part of God's amazing master plan.

The vision God gave Raúl Garcia about starting a work in Oaxaca has evolved into an incredible, far-reaching, life-changing ministry. If I would have understood the magnitude of it at that time, I might have been too overwhelmed to do anything about it. But God is gracious. All He desired was our trust and obedience to one small step at a time. I know He has much more in store for us there.

As He continues to show us His ways and teach us His paths, we will walk forward, hand in hand with Him. And He will receive all glory, honor, and praise.

Top: Raúl Garcia and Frank Ticknor spied out the land in Oaxaca.

Bottom left: Dr. Ernesto Cano has been the president of our Mexican corporation (Cristo por Su Mundo) for five decades. He was with Mario and me when we checked out the available property options, and he helped with negotiations and details. This is a more recent picture of us together.

Bottom right: Niche (Eunice) has been with us since we "inherited" the Etla orphanage. She's a joy and a priceless member of our ministry.

Top: This is the property we purchased just outside of Tlacolula, Oaxaca.

Bottom: Peter Bianchini is sitting at the table and reviewing the plans for our property with the foreman. Elaine and Ian Croft, who helped supervise the project, are standing behind. I can't count the number of times I've praised God for Peter. He was chairman of our board, is a master builder, and was the designer of the Oaxaca mission. His skills, generosity, and vision brought beauty to our home base in Oaxaca. He's also the one responsible for the redesign of our Bible institute in Baja after the flood.

This is our beautiful Oaxaca property today. Notice the backdrop of "The Sleeping Lady."

These are some of the precious children who live at our home in Oaxaca.

Some of Our Heroes

Lucio

Sixteen-year-old Lucio, a Oaxacan boy from one of the camps, was shot in the head and left to die on a desolate beach. A caring passerby noticed his lifeless body and took him to El Buen Pastor Hospital in San Quintín. Thanks to the Good Samaritan's help and the intervention of doctors, Lucio survived. But he lost his sight and suffered damage to his brain.

Because his family was unknown and there wasn't much hope for an indigenous boy in his condition, a physician at the hospital, aware of our work at the mission, released Lucio to our care. We took him in and gave him tasks that he could handle. The mission's pastor taught Lucio how to sweep the church floor by pushing a large broom along the walls. Lucio also learned to sweep the patio and many of our walkways.

Our children quickly grew to love Lucio. He was a kind and gentle soul and always seemed happy. Shortly after he arrived, a revelation occurred to one of the boys. "Lucio's name means light," he said. "With a name like that, he shouldn't be blind." And from that point on, the children, who were intimately acquainted with a big God, frequently prayed for him.

Then one day a couple of the young prayer warriors observed Lucio as he worked. They noticed that he stopped sweeping and stooped to use a piece of cardboard as a dustpan. He carefully brushed a small pile of dirt and trash onto the cardboard and threw it away.

That set off an eruption of excitement. "Lucio can see! Lucio can see!" The children who witnessed Lucio's actions darted toward the home, shouting all the way. "Lucio can see! Lucio can see!" They didn't stop until everyone had heard.

Lucio couldn't explain what happened. He only knew that his brain function and eyesight were restored. He simply stated, "I was blind, but now I see."

His unforgettable healing miracle brought revival to the work of the mission. Word spread rapidly. Before long, our small chapel, which we used primarily for our children and staff, could no longer hold the incoming crowds. We moved our services to the old theater building, and a thriving, community-based church was born.

Multiple satellite churches were planted in surrounding areas, and eventually we constructed a building on site where a thousand worshippers gather each week. The ministry increased far beyond anything Chuck or I had ever asked or imagined.

One thing that brought me the greatest joy at that time was Lucio's testimony. He cultivated his faith under the umbrella of our mission and then took his light to the darkness of the Copala region of Oaxaca. He became our first missionary there.

Lucio confidently shared the life-changing message of God's amazing grace with the Triqui people. Sadly, not everyone welcomed that message, and hostile villagers stoned him to death.

As I think about Lucio and the unreached people groups of Oaxaca, I can't help but be reminded of these words from Isaiah 9:2. They refer to a different time and population, but they offer hope that God's plans will prevail. "The people who walk in darkness will see a great light. For those who live in a land of deep darkness, a light will shine" (NLT).

Those who martyred Lucio might have thought they could extinguish the light he carried, but it still shines through the sparks he ignited and through those who came behind him to fan the flames.

⚬∞⚬

Edgar Rivera Guerrero

Several of the people I mention within these pages could have an entire book written about them. Edgar is one of those. He has endured unspeakable things. And he is a warrior whom God has used in amazing ways to bring the light of Christ to a dark place.

At the age of 11, Edgar joined a gang, and it was the first time he stabbed someone. By the time he turned 15, many of his friends had already died. He didn't depend on drugs or alcohol to perform his terrible deeds. Instead, he did things consciously and without emotion.

When he was 16, he knew he was either going to die or become crazy, and he realized that he needed to change his life. One day he came across a childhood friend, and that friend invited him to church during special Holy Week services. It was a good church. They loved God and preached the gospel. But when Edgar showed up, they weren't ready to receive a young man with a background like his.

Edgar wanted the peace the pastor spoke about, but he didn't see it displayed in church members. He saw only their hypocrisy. Despite their unwillingness to accept him—and the truth is that Edgar didn't always make it easy to do so—he continued to attend services.

His experiences as a congregant had more downs than ups, causing him to become angry at God and to question Him about many issues. Eventually, though, God broke through all the barriers he raised.

During one of the meetings, the pastor made a public call for those who wanted to surrender their life to God and serve Him full time. Edgar went forward. A while later, the pastor started mentoring Edgar, and he grew in the gospel.

As he was walking to church one day, he saw a prostitute friend who was "on duty" at the time. He shared his story with her and invited her to go to church with him. He was thrilled that she agreed to go. However, after she entered the building with him, the people treated her much the same way they had treated Edgar. They shunned her. They stared at her and gossiped with each other about the way she was dressed.

This behavior continued throughout the service. When she finally had enough, she grabbed Edgar by the hand and said, "Get me away from here! You told me they'd love me, but they're treating me worse than the drunk men I work with."

Ouch.

Edgar took her out of the church and never saw her again. He doesn't know what happened to her, but that day he said to God, "I want to preach to those the church will not preach to. I want to talk to those the church won't talk to."

His life experiences uniquely qualified him to reach out to the unsavory individuals whom others weren't prepared to reach. He said, "If I can do nothing other than trip people up, then I want to trip people up on their way to hell. I want to block their path." That passion defines his ministry.

After he got married and started a family, he heard about a medical team that had planned a trip to a place with a horrible reputation and where there were no known Christians. It was in Oaxaca. Edgar and his wife, Lettie, both immediately sensed that God wanted them there, so they sold all their belongings and followed His lead. Along the way, God confirmed for them again and again that He wanted them in the mountains of Oaxaca.

As Edgar and Lettie began sharing the gospel message in one area of Oaxaca, a church started to grow. But when some in the community realized what they were preaching, they reacted aggressively. Only three months had passed when the first Christian was killed, and Edgar was blamed.

They went on to other towns, and their work began to flourish. Within six years, they had planted eight indigenous churches, and twenty-two communities had Christians living in them.

When they moved on to yet another area, they encountered horrific opposition. The townspeople removed all the belongings from Edgar's house and burned everything down. At least eight times while they were there, the villagers tried to kill Edgar. He had no choice but to flee with his family.

Although they saw God's hand at work in many ways during their mountain ministry, the pressure and safety issues for Lettie and the children became too much, so they moved to the city of Oaxaca. Edgar got involved with Alas de Socorro, an affiliate of Missionary Aviation Fellowship (MAF). The name means wings of help (or relief) in Spanish. They fly into the mountains and come back out, which allows him to continue his contact with the churches and to reach the unreached.

Through Edgar's and Lettie's search for a good school for their children, they discovered our missionary base and children's home in Tlacolula. Our school readily accepted their children, and Lettie volunteered in the kitchen.

As he got to know people there, Edgar realized that our mission had a similar vision to his—we reach out to those whom others won't reach out to. Since then, he and his family have been a vital part of our FFHM ministry. He encourages and supports our missionaries. He maintains contact with the churches in the mountains. He coordinates care and emergency medical help through Alas de Socorro. Not only that, but for a time he also served as the pastor of our Tlacolula mission and was instrumental in bringing healing and spiritual growth to the community.

Bob Sundberg, a missiologist who researched and studied all the unreached people groups in Oaxaca, thinks very highly of Edgar. In his little book, which I keep in my Bible, Bob claims that Edgar is the greatest missionary ever to reach out to those groups. Because of Bob, I learned about

Edgar long before I knew him. And what a gift he's been to us!

When I told Edgar that he is one of our heroes, he lowered his head and said quietly, "I just get to see what everyone else does, and then I cry."

⌒∞⌒

Modesto Velasco Yescas

Modesto was born and raised in Las Cuevas, which is in the region of Santiago Amoltepec. According to the government, it's considered the most violent area of Oaxaca. Because of how far away it is from the capital city, it also has extreme poverty. That's where Edgar first started his mountain ministry and met Modesto.

Because Modesto's parents abandoned him when he was a child, he lived with his grandparents. They didn't want him to go to church, but sometimes he'd go anyway and then receive a beating when he returned home.

Edgar had a special affection for the boy, who had impaired vision. Modesto was diagnosed with congenital cataracts at a young age, but nothing hindered him from doing what children with healthy eyesight could do. He played along with them on the basketball court, running, dribbling, and attempting to throw the ball through the hoop. (Every town in the mountains has a basketball court.) Even though he didn't always have success, he had determination. That showed through in whatever he did. He also had a desire to serve God.

Something Edgar stressed to church members was the importance of visiting others. From spending time with Edgar, Modesto learned that lesson as well. And he took it to heart. On a regular basis, he and a few other children would show up to Edgar's house at five in the morning. They'd all walk for several hours to reach another town in the mountains in order to preach the gospel. In the afternoon, they'd walk back—singing, playing, and cutting fruit from trees to eat along the way.

One time, Modesto met in the early morning with the group of children at Edgar's house, but Edgar wasn't there. Lettie, his wife, said, "Edgar hasn't returned from his trip to the other town, so he can't go today." When the children left, Lettie assumed they had gone back to their homes. Instead, they went on their own to do visitation as they always did.

The children walked six hours to cross four or five mountains to get to the town of Las Tortugas. Once they arrived, word spread that the children were there and that it was time for the church meeting to start. Of course, the townspeople thought Edgar was along with them.

Eleven-year-old Eluderio (the oldest of the children), Modesto, and some of the others started to sing the worship songs. Eluderio preached. They prayed for the congregants. Once the service was over, they ate, filled up their bags with fruit, and went back home. The people couldn't understand what had happened. These were the same children who had walked six hours to get there, children who had been playing in the mud the whole way!

As soon as they returned to Las Cuevas, Modesto and the others went to Edgar's home. One of them said, "We're back!" Edgar asked where they had been. "We went to Las Tortugas," they said. The news amazed him.

The children made such an impact during their visitation that the Las Tortugas congregants gathered on their own the next day. They acknowledged that they should be the ones responsible for leading their services. So, one of the men led the worship. Another one preached. The church grew. And it was all because a courageous, dirty group of children taught them how to do it.

When Modesto was older, he told Edgar, "I want to prepare for ministry." Edgar knew he had the character to complete his calling, but he also knew Modesto wouldn't be able to enter any Bible schools because he hadn't studied. He had very little education. And he was almost blind. (He can't see out of one eye at all, and the other eye is just shadows.)

So, knowing that one of our goals as a mission is to give to those others wouldn't give to, Edgar called our Bible institute in Baja. Three days later, Modesto was on a bus headed for Colonia Vicente Guerrero.

Despite our administrator Mario's having to look for Modesto everywhere, this young man graduated with top academic honors and was loved by all.

When he arrived in Baja, he had only one change of clothes in his backpack. He wore a rope around his waist to hold up his pants. But even with the rope, his huge pants hung loosely on him.

I saw Pastor John Foss, a very thin Lutheran pastor I knew, at a meeting and greeted him by saying, "I need your clothes." For some reason, my statement startled him. Again, I said, "I need your clothes. I have a wonderful plan for them." I explained what I meant, and Pastor John came to the rescue. The following week he showed up with a box of clothes for us to send to Modesto.

After that, the pastor occasionally came to me and asked, "Does your son need more clothes?" Each time that I said yes, he gave me another box filled with shirts and pants. In fact, Modesto graduated in a suit Pastor John gave him. God is so good to always provide just what is needed.

Modesto is now working in Oaxaca where his pastor was martyred. He walks several hours through the mountains to visit different communities. He evangelizes. He encourages the brothers and sisters in the churches. He teaches the Bible. He disciples new Christians. And then he comes back. He speaks to the people in their Mixteco language because many of the older ones do not understand Spanish.

He also helps out with the pastoral work at his church in Las Cuevas. He visits the sick, helps the widows, preaches, leads worship, and whatever else is needed.

For a time, the FFHM board wanted to help him out with transportation. A board member gave him money to purchase a motorcycle with the idea that a church brother would drive him to and from his destination. But Modesto was so accustomed to being independent that he would take the motorcycle by himself. One day, someone came looking for him. He found Modesto at the edge of a cliff, trying to see the light of the river so he'd know where to go. That's the day we agreed he needed to walk, and we took the motorcycle away from him.

Modesto is unstoppable when it comes to reaching others with the good news of Jesus Christ. He bears the fruit of someone who loves God with passion and lives with a purpose. Oh, that we would all be the same!

Pastor Edgar Rivera Guerrero (far left) has planted many churches and done much work in the remote mountains of Oaxaca.

These missionaries (Modesto, Esteban, Yadira, María, Tere, and Glenda) serve the Lord in the mountain regions of Oaxaca in very primitive and often dangerous circumstances. Modesto is legally blind, yet he walks the remote mountains sharing the good news.

Reaching the Unreached

My missiologist friend, Bob Sundberg, has identified at least 157 people groups in the mountains of Oaxaca, and my dream is that we would one day reach all regions of this diversified state. But in many of the villages, foreigners aren't welcome. The people there are also especially antagonistic toward Christians. Vengeance and killings are rampant in these pagan, hostile areas.

Our Oaxacan ambassador, Frank Ticknor, got a little taste of that when he visited one of our Bible school graduates who is now a missionary in a mountain community. He heard shots, but didn't realize his pickup had been hit until he saw the holes in its door.

It isn't easy, but with God's guidance, we've discovered that the best way for us to break down walls of resistance is to offer opportunities, practical helps, and much-needed services. Once relationships are established, and people have seen the love of Christ through actions, they are more receptive to hearing about Jesus.

A huge percentage of Oaxacans are at a disadvantage because they can't read or write. I know from experience how that can negatively affect a life.

With that in mind, I said to Mario, "We need to find someone to go to the mountains and teach people how to read using the Bible." We've seen how when the Bible is used as a primer, people are able to read in a way that's miraculous. Plus, it allows for many Holy-Spirit-led conversations.

Before I ever brought it up, God had already been at work behind the scenes orchestrating His plan. A dear young woman with a heart to teach was serving as a house mother at our Etla home. When Yadira first started there, she was in her first year of a three-year Bible school. Mario had asked her at the time, "Sister, why are you studying in a Bible school?"

She answered, "Because I want to serve the Lord."

"You're already doing that," he said.

"Yes, but I want to do something different. I want to go to the mountains of Oaxaca where others don't want to go, where there's not a church, where missionaries don't want to enter." As Mario listened, he tucked that information into his memory banks. She continued, "I don't know how it will happen, and I don't know where it will be. I just know that's what I want to do."

"Okay," Mario said. "You have two more years of classes. That'll give us enough time to pray." And that's how the discussion ended.

When she was halfway through her last year of Bible school, Mario asked what she did on her rest days. "I teach two men from my church how to read and write," she said. He also asked if she had made plans for her next steps after graduation.

"No, not yet. I've been praying, but God still hasn't given me an answer."

"I know what you are to do," Mario said. "A while back, Hermana Charla came to me and said we needed to look for a person to teach reading and writing in the mountains. I believe you are that person."

After graduating, Yadira took special training, and then went to a town in the Istmo region of Oaxaca. She looked for adults who wanted to learn to read and write, and set up classes with them. She stayed for six months and from there went to another town in the same region. It was there that she had what she calls her "test of fire."

Cactus and beans were her only food choices. To go to another town to purchase food required too much effort—two hours on horse and then two hours in a van. One day someone gave her a little piece of beef. The meat was bad, and she became horribly sick. Bacteria in her intestines caused serious damage to her liver and internal organs. She wondered whether the person had intentionally tried to harm her.

She ended up being brought back to the mission home base and received medical treatment for about three months. When she felt better, she returned to the town. Mario tried to reason with her and keep her from going, but she said, "I have a group of women waiting for me. I promised them they'd be able to read and write within a certain amount of time, and I need to keep my promise."

After she accomplished her goal in that community, she went to a town in the Pineda region of Oaxaca. The pastor of a small Christian church there prepared his congregation for her arrival. "A missionary is coming to evangelize the people," he announced through the microphone. Because the church was at the top of a hill, the sound carried to the village below. The message wasn't well received.

Once she got there, Yadira went from house to house to find women with a desire to read and write. They asked, "Are you from the church at the top of the hill?" When she answered yes, they shut her down.

Yadira started praying that the Lord would open doors for her ministry. Soon after that, the town doctor connected with her. "You're new in town, right?" She said yes. "I assume you're here for one of three reasons—religious reasons, drug-trafficking reasons, or political reasons."

"You could say I'm here for religious issues," she said and explained that she wanted to teach people to read and write.

The doctor offered to help her. At a gathering of the town's women, he made an announcement. "If you want to change your religion, it's a personal decision. But if you want to learn to read and write, this is an opportunity you shouldn't pass up." With his next words, he gave them a lot to consider. "Who's going to come to your houses? Who's going to come to your town to teach you? You owe it to your children, your husband, and to future generations. It's your choice."

Yadira had a notebook with her. After the doctor spoke, she said, "If anyone is interested, I'll take your names." More than one hundred women stood in line to sign up.

It was a miracle how it all came together. So many women showed a desire to learn that Niche came to help Yadira for a few months. They lived with terrible conditions—a tiny room next door to a pig pen, very little food, and no budget. But they persevered through the challenges, and God used them to transform lives.

One special woman—Dorothy—captured Yadira's heart. Born with only one leg, Dorothy faced shame and ridicule every day. At 40 years old, she had never gone beyond her home. If she sat on the patio outside, children mocked her and threw things as they passed by. She'd never been to the center of town. She'd never been to a school. She'd never been to a medical clinic. She didn't even attend her father's mass and burial because she wasn't allowed.

When Yadira showed up to her door one day, Dorothy backed away, too embarrassed to be seen. Yadira persisted and talked lovingly toward her, something Dorothy hadn't experienced before. "Would you like to learn to read and write?" she asked. "I will come to your house to teach you."

"I can't. I don't have money to pay you."

She assured Dorothy there would be no charge. "I will provide your books as well."

Yadira started working with her, and over time, as Dorothy warmed up to her, the door of her heart cracked open. Her many years of suppressed pain flowed out in her emotions. She wept as she talked about how she'd suffered for so long.

Yadira grieved for Dorothy's deep pain and spoke truth to her soul. "God isn't punishing you," she said. "He hasn't put a curse on you. You have great value, and He loves you more than you can imagine, just as you are." She prayed that Dorothy would be able to see herself as God sees her.

After six months of lessons, the day of graduation came. Although Yadira had encouraged Dorothy to attend, she declined. "No, I've never left my house," she said. But God stirred in her heart, and just an hour before the celebration was to begin, she decided to go. She asked that Yadira accompany her.

When Yadira arrived at her house, Dorothy met her at the door with a broad smile—one like never before. "Are you sure you want to leave?" Yadira asked. "What if people insult you?"

"It doesn't matter," she said. "I want to be there because no one has given me more love than you."

Yadira told her that Jesus loves her more than anyone. "I'm just His arms. But He gave His life for you." That day Dorothy received Jesus as her Lord and Savior.

I attended the graduation ceremony held at the basketball court and was so moved as Yadira honored her students. She called on many of them to read out loud. Dorothy was one of them. The pride she exhibited because she had value and because she could read caused me to cry tears of joy on her behalf. I remembered the shame I felt during my childhood when I couldn't read and write. Thanks to a special fifth-grade teacher, my life was changed forever. Literacy is such a wonderful gift!

Although offering that gift helps us gain entrance into rebellious communities, great risk is often involved. Yadira told me once that she faces difficulty wherever she goes. And then she said, "But I like that, because it is when things are the most difficult that God most shows Himself."

She started a children's club in an extremely poor area. Every Saturday the children came to a small wooden room and huddled around her on the dirt floor as she told them Bible stories. One day, she was midway through the story of Jesus's raising Lazarus from the dead when two men appeared in the doorway. They were big, and they were ugly. One of them said, "Is this where there's a dead person?" She shook her head and said no. Then he opened his jacket and brought her attention to the gun at his waist. "We know why you're here," he said. "This is just a warning."

One of the townspeople told Yadira that the men are hired to kill Christians. She strongly encouraged Yadira to flee for safety's sake. Outsiders who were familiar with the town's history also pleaded with her to stop going there.

She didn't know what to do, so she had an honest discussion with Almighty God. "Lord, I'm scared. Did You really bring me here just so they could kill me? You know I can't leave these women. I can't leave these children." She asked God to protect her and then surrendered to His will. She said, "But Lord, my life is Yours. If it's Your will that I die, so be it. In the end, it's all about You."

After that, she was extra cautious when entering the town. Instead of taking the shorter route and walking among the trees for covering, as she normally did, she started walking on a wide path more out in the open.

One day, while speaking to a group of women, one of them asked, "Teacher, do you have a husband?"

Yadira said, "No, why do you ask?"

"Because every time you come to town, I see two men waiting for you. When you get here, they start walking with you—one on your left side, the other on your right." Yadira insisted she must be mistaken.

"No, I know you. You're my teacher. You always have your backpack. You always have your tube with the flannelgraph stories. My husband and I work on the other side of the road where there's a fence, and we see you. I know it's you."

Some of the other women told Yadira they had seen the men as well and described them to her. "They are very tall and white. Their hair is not the same color as yours. They look like Americans."

The situation baffled Yadira. When she arrived back to the town where she lived, she made an appointment with her pastor. She didn't want people thinking she was with men!

As Yadira told him her story, the pastor had an aha moment. "Yes, now I understand!" he said. "The men the people see are not men. They're angels God sent to protect you. You don't see them, but everyone else does—especially those who want to harm you." He told her to keep walking and to continue doing what God has called her to do in that place.

Since that time, Yadira has married Esteban. Together they oversee the missionary outreach in Oaxaca, where they often travel to remote and dangerous territories. Their dream is that FFHM would one day have a missionary in each region of the state of Oaxaca. With God's help and strategic planning, that dream will come true.

∽∞∾

Another way we're able to gain entrance in some of the communities is through medical help. In a previous chapter, I mentioned Edgar and how he works with Mission Aviation Fellowship. With their assistance, we can provide a valuable service.

Many of the mountain regions are physically difficult to reach. If someone has a medical crisis, it's almost impossible for them to receive urgent care. A trip in a good vehicle with good tires on a good mountain road could take fourteen to sixteen hours—and that's if it's not the rainy season. The person could die in the meantime. But Edgar can arrange for a pilot and medical team to fly in and get the patient needed help in a fraction of the time.

The ability to offer this service gives us leverage with the village authorities, and we can use it as a way to support our pastors as well. For example, in one community, hostile villagers threatened to "eliminate" a pastor. Edgar confronted the mayor and said, "That's our brother, and we come as a package. If you oust him, we won't fly for you."

Because they didn't have an emergency exit without Mission Aviation Fellowship's help, they backed off. That provision has allowed us the opportunity to enter the village, and when we enter, we bring the hope that comes through Christ.

∞

For many years, we've also had the blessing of teaming up with volunteer groups at our Baja location for medical outreaches. Heaven in Sight is an organization based out of Valdosta, Georgia, whose mission is to share the love of God and provide medical care in impoverished areas of the world. Under the leadership of Dr. Mark Eanes, an ophthalmologist, they would annually bring a team that includes dentists, oral surgeons, eye surgeons, orthopedists, nurses, and more. With the assistance of our medical center's staff, they were able to treat hundreds and hundreds of patients during a seven-to-ten-day period.

Pastor Bill Dwyer and Roberto Muñoz-Flores from the Valley Vineyard Church in Reseda, California, have a passion to reach the unreached, especially Oaxacans. The church has been greatly supportive of our ministry and has sent teams of volunteers to help us many times. In 2012, they scheduled an outreach trip to the mountains of Oaxaca. I was along on that trip as well as my good friends Pastor Leland and Marcia Lantz.

Our group arrived early at the mission base in Tlacolula to prepare for the arrival of the Heaven in Sight medical team. Right away we got to work. We erected an awning to shelter patients from the intense sun as they waited outside, and set up chairs that we had rented beforehand. Rooms were cleaned and stocked with supplies.

Dr. Eanes and his dedicated team were due in the following day. However, we got word that the Popocatépetl volcano had erupted and grounded all flights in and out of Mexico City. Our volunteer doctors were stuck in the states! That was a real problem, especially since we already had hundreds of people waiting for the opportunity to receive treatment. We couldn't let those dear people down!

Because Roberto Muñoz-Flores's father was a noted physician in Mexico, he had clout, so he went to the military base in Oaxaca City and recruited an ophthalmologist. Dr. Chapas worked late into the night over a two-day period and performed countless surgeries. Little did he know when he came that he would leave a changed man. Roberto shared his testimony with the doctor while he was there and led him to a saving knowledge of Jesus.

Finally, Dr. Eanes and his team arrived, and we eventually headed north and west to the mountain region of Juxtlahuaca, where María Villa Pablo ministers. María and our team prepared a primitive facility where the doctors and medical staff could examine patients and treat illnesses and disease. We stacked up bricks and put planks of wood over the top to serve as beds and operating tables. We placed reclining lawn chairs in rooms for the dentists and oral surgeons to use. The setup wasn't fancy, but it would work to provide much-needed medical help to long lines of underprivileged Oaxacans.

The doctors did surgical procedures and gave out corrective eyewear and medications. The blind received sight, the lame walked, and the poor heard the good news of Jesus Christ.

At the end of one of our very long days, I struggled to breathe and thought the altitude was affecting me. When I became sick to my stomach, I realized I was having a heart attack. My precious friend Marcia lovingly cared for me and listened as I weakly reflected on my past. "If only I had given more," I said. Then I started in on my end-of-life instructions. "Try to convince them to bury me in Juxtlahuaca. That way they won't have the expense of dealing with my body."

Meanwhile, Dr. Avitia (one of our doctors on the trip from the Baja mission) and Pastor Bill Dwyer went in search of oxygen. Someone directed them to a wealthy man who lived in the region. He had oxygen in his home as well as a small tank in his car. He allowed the men to borrow the tank "to help the American lady," but asked that it be returned.

Once they showed up with the oxygen, we made the way-too-long trip to Oaxaca City. From there I flew back home to Southern California, where I was admitted to the hospital upon my arrival. Thankfully, with many prayers lifted on my behalf and the help of excellent cardiologists—one who was a Messianic Jew—the hospital released me after a few days, and I was able to return to my mission duties.

One of the first things I did was to email María with a thank-you note for the generous man who loaned me his oxygen device. I expressed my deep appreciation and asked how I could ever repay his kindness.

He responded quickly, telling me he was honored to have helped. He went on to say that health complications required his moving to a lower elevation. "Would you be interested in buying a radio station?" he asked.

I almost fell over in my seat! For years I had dreamed of a radio station that could carry the good news to the people of that area, particularly in Copala where FFHM had lost three missionaries to martyrdom. Could this be God's answer to my prayers?

Right away I sent off a note asking if the airwaves reached the Copala region. "Yes," he answered.

"How much are you asking?"

"Ten thousand dollars," he said.

I didn't know how the money would come, but I did know that I have a big God. I had witnessed His supernatural ways for many years, so I started praying and trusted Him to provide.

Soon thereafter, I received a phone call from an investment counselor friend in Laguna Beach, California. "What's on your heart today, Charla?" he asked.

I was straightforward with my answer. "I want a radio station. It costs $10,000."

"A check is in the mail," he said. He had never donated to our ministry before. What a gift!

We now operate a radio station that broadcasts Christ-centered messages to the Mixteco and Triqui peoples in distant villages. María is the programmer.

I praise God that we've been able to reach the unreached through literacy, medical help, and now radio. Only He could use a heart attack to bring about His master plan.

Every day my heart beats for the lost people of Oaxaca who so desperately need to know Jesus. My fervent prayer is that we would continue to reach even deeper into that land until every region has heard about the life-changing power of Christ.

Yadira (in the plaid shirt) has taught hundreds of people to read.
Here are some of the women in her literacy program.

Some of the special people we minister to in the mountains of Oaxaca

My good friends Pastor Leland and Marcia Lantz, of Lutheran Church of the Cross, accompanied us on an outreach trip to Oaxaca in 2012. They ministered to me the night I had a heart attack in the mountains.

Caring for Those
with Special Needs

Dirk and Mary Kos came to the mission in February 2000 as chaperones with a group of students from Edmonton, Canada. When asked on the first day about his occupation, Dirk said, "I make specialized equipment for the physically challenged."

That's all it took. Our team took them into the community, where they learned of the great needs of our neighbors, and from Monday afternoon until Friday evening they were introduced to people with physical challenges. With pages full of notes, Dirk and Mary returned to Canada and got to work assembling the parts to accommodate specific circumstances.

Dirk needed twelve wheelchairs in different sizes for children and adults, and with a variety of adaptations. He wondered where he'd find good quality chairs in so many sizes. After praying about it, he contacted a wheelchair store in Edmonton, explained what he needed and why.

They surprised him with their answer. "We just cleaned out our inventory of pre-owned wheelchairs and have a heap of them that we're going to throw away. You can have all of them if you can use them."

The pile had twelve wheelchairs and included every size Dirk needed. That special provision from God confirmed a new path of ministry for the couple, and they returned to the mission many times to volunteer their expertise, to teach, and to help with those in the community.

With permission of our FFHM board, Dirk set up a small work space inside the carpentry shop. All the tools needed— even a welder—were provided through a fundraiser their niece in the Netherlands held. He trained Angel Baeza to build, service, and repair wheelchairs, and with that the wheelchair shop was born. (Angel was one of our first children at Hogar Para Niños and with our help had many surgeries in the states for his crippled condition. His story is told in *Charla's Children*. He now uses a wheelchair.)

On one particular trip to Baja, Dirk made a call to a mother and her sick child at the hospital in Ensenada. What he observed left him angry and frustrated. They couldn't afford a change of clothes. They couldn't afford food. Yet, for her child to live, the mother needed to fill the prescription she held in her hands. It was an impossibility for her. Dirk blessed the concerned woman by providing for her needs that day, but he returned to the mission with an unsettled spirit.

After praying for answers, he did something he'd never done before. He grabbed his Bible and let it fall open. He decided that he'd accept whatever text his eyes landed on as God's message for him in that moment.

Here's what he read in Isaiah 58:10–11: "If you spend yourselves in behalf of the hungry and satisfy the needs of the oppressed, then your light will rise in the darkness, and your night will become like the noonday. The LORD will guide you always; he will satisfy your needs in a sun-scorched land and will strengthen your frame. You will be like a well-watered garden, like a spring whose waters never fail" (NIV).

As he mulled the words in his mind, Dirk felt a tugging on his heart that he needed to do more. He knew the direction God was leading, but he wanted Mary to sense God's direction as well.

A year later, Mary had an experience that prompted a similar tugging. She visited a girl with special needs who was locked up every day in a tiny camp compartment with no window and only a small light. That broke her mother-heart.

On the drive back to Canada from the mission, Mary shared an idea with Dirk. "Do you think we could start a day-home for children with special needs? We could pick them up in the morning, have some type of program for them during the day, and drop them off at their homes in the late afternoon."

She talked about finding Mexican people who could lead the program and how she and Dirk could support it by continuing to help part time. But Dirk let it slip that he sensed God was calling them to full-time ministry.

"Full time?" Mary said, shocked at his comment. "I can't do that! We can't just pick up everything and leave the family behind! That would be too hard."

Dirk and Mary had a quiet ride after that, with both of them praying and searching for answers. Then, as they drove through endless fields in Utah, they spotted a small sign. It had only two words on it: "Trust Jesus." And that's what they decided to do.

They sent me their request to start a day-home program, and with the approval of the board, they left their life in Canada in July of 2006 and came to Mexico with the Lord's promise to be with them.

We granted them permission to live in a larger apartment on the mission grounds, and Mary started her "day home" in the kitchen with four children. Once the initiative began, the number of children grew rapidly. Soon we moved them to a room at the back of the medical center, but it needed an extensive renovation that required money and workers.

In God's wonderful way, I received a call right about that time from a church in Washington. They asked, "Do you have any special projects at the mission that are in need of fundraising and hands-on laborers?" Indeed, we did, and God provided for the renovation as He had so many times before.

The day-home program continued to grow. We let them expand into several rooms, and even the hallway was used for one-on-one education. But eventually that space became too small as well.

We floated around a new idea. What about building an entire school completely geared to children with special needs?

Plans were drawn up, the board discussed the possibilities, and we told Dirk and Mary that we were in favor of the project. "But we need at least sixty percent of the approximate cost to be in the bank before we can even break ground," we said.

After two weeks, I called Dirk. "The money's in the bank. We can start building."

What a joy to give a fabulous facility as a gift to our children with special needs from a group of anonymous donors! The children celebrated by imprinting their names and handprints in the concrete in front of the entry door. They serve as a reminder of God's faithfulness and care.

So many good things happened after that. With the opportunity for online access, they were able to use the internet as a teaching and research tool. They had six computers for the students that were used consistently. The children were able to receive government-approved certificates to pursue higher education. And the Lord provided one committed and caring teacher after another.

Then one day Dirk and Mary had coffee with the principal of Strathcona Christian Academy in Sherwood Park, Alberta, Canada. He had one question for them: "What is your dream for your program at the mission?"

Dirk shared some personal wishes to create a few small classrooms connected with the workshops we have at the mission so that he could teach carpentry, auto mechanics, and metal working. But the principal pushed them for a bigger, more God-sized dream.

With that, Mary poured out the desires of her heart. "I'd love to have more classrooms with computer access for our students with special needs. The children in the home need more computer access as well."

So, from that little meeting, Dirk and Mary were tasked with designing a building with four extra classrooms, an office, and a computer center with twenty-four computers.

Our board approved of the plan, Dirk and Mary humbly sent a cost estimate to the principal, the school in Canada accepted it, and the fundraising began. By the end of the school year, the fundraising amount had surpassed the estimate by fifty percent, which allowed for the purchase of quality items without the need to cut corners.

In addition to that, a large group of teachers and their spouses came to the mission the following spring to build the 70 ft. x 30 ft. education center. Experts in every part of the building process assisted Tony Baeza, the contractor. (Tony is Angel's brother and one of our first children at the home.)

God worked all the details together in a beautiful way and provided a high-tech learning facility and program for our community's children with special needs.

Because of a health issue, Dirk and Mary found it necessary to return to Canada in 2017, and Esther Torres took over as director of the program. It continues to thrive.

Today, we have a fleet of accessible buses that are used to transport the students from their homes and back again. We have excellent teachers and helpers who get the students up to high school and college levels of education. And God sends provisions of learning materials and supplies, such as diapers for the incontinent, through our faithful supporters.

Dirk and Mary never imagined that their first trip to the mission would lead to such an important ministry of caring for the community's children and adults with special needs, but I have a sneaking hunch that God had it planned all along.

∽

We have so many stories to tell of how God has used our special-needs ministry and learning center in the lives of the students and their families, but one in particular stands out.

A request came in for an 18-inch-width electric wheelchair for Juanito, a young man with muscular dystrophy who lived in one of the work camps with his sister and brother-in-law. When Dirk delivered the chair and a ramp to help with accessibility, Juanito greeted him with a wide smile. His excitement over the life-changing gift showed in his abundance of thank-yous.

Then, with the help of a translator, he expressed a deep desire to Dirk. "Please get me out of here," he said. "I want to study the Word of God. Is it possible that I can go to the Bible institute and become a minister?"

Dirk promised to get an answer for him, knowing that his whole family would need to accompany him as well. That would require a wheelchair-accessible two-bedroom unit in the living quarters of the Bible school.

Immediately after Dirk asked on Juanito's behalf, permission was granted. And within days, a church group with first-class craftsmen ready for a project came to the mission. Before the week was over, a newly renovated place, where Juanito and his family could stay while he attended school, was ready.

After two years of difficult studies, Juanito completed his course. A true evangelist, he had a yearning to go into the mountains of Oaxaca and minister to his own people, but his condition made him unable to do that.

Eventually, his muscular dystrophy took more and more of his energy. One day he made a special request of his wife. "I'd like you to take me into the mountains," he said. That would require her to push him in a regular wheelchair on rugged terrain, an almost impossible task.

"Why do you want to go there?" she asked.

"Because a man lives there who does not yet know the Lord, and I need to talk with him," he said.

Some time went by and Juanito died. We later learned from Juanito's wife that the man he visited that day took over the leadership of a church in that area of the mountains.

To that I say, "Now glory be to God, who by his mighty power at work within us is able to do far more than we would ever dare to ask or even dream of—infinitely beyond our highest prayers, desires, thoughts, or hopes" (Ephesians 3:20, TLB).

That's the continuous story of His Ministry in Mexico.

Dirk and Mary Kos started a day-home program for children with special needs. Here they are with one of the children they helped with a wheelchair.

Their dream for the mission was to have a learning facility for children with special needs, individualized education, and to assist students at the secondary and high school level where the computer is the tool to learn and do the required homework. Thanks to the fundraising efforts of Strathcona Christian Academy in Sherwood Park, Canada, their dream came true.

Casa de Mefiboset

Welcome to Casa de Mefiboset (Mephibosheth's House)!

The painting of Jesus and the children hangs on the wall of our learning center.

Charles Curtis and a Journey of a Lifetime

Our family had a dear church friend named Ruth Story. I referred to her as Remarkable Ruth because she was so much like Dorcas in the book of Acts, where it says, "This woman was abounding with deeds of kindness and charity which she continually did" (Acts 9:36, NASB).

Ruth made her home—a small, four-room house on an acre of land—in what was then a rural area in the San Fernando Valley. She lived frugally so she could give to others, and she did so at great personal sacrifice. The mainstays of her diet were tea, fruits, and vegetables. Yet she anonymously treated the staff at the Baja mission to a bountiful Christmas dinner at Don Diego's Restaurant in Colonia Vicente Guerrero "so they could sit down and be served for a change and not have to do the dishes."

When a house fire struck one of our church families, and their little girl suffered severe burns, word got out that they had no insurance to cover her medical expenses. I went to the church office and tried to make a donation to help, but the secretary said, "Oh, it's already all been paid for by an anonymous giver." Yes, it was the same "Story." The bill was more than $10,000.

Then there was the Siberian Seven, a persecuted Pentecostal family who sought asylum in the basement of the US Embassy in Moscow from 1978 until 1983. When the Vashchenkos were finally allowed to leave for Israel on a tourist visa, guess who paid for the visa? None other than our generous friend Remarkable Ruth. The family of seven eventually settled in Texas, where they received a $29,000 home—donated by an anonymous giver. Again, the same old "Story."

Ruth's winter clothes came out of moth balls in October and returned to moth balls in April. Our Zapotec son, Charles Curtis, adored Ruth and delighted in the never-ending source of candies from the deep pockets in her unusually aromatic woolen coat.

She cherished Curtis and prayed for him regularly. As he grew older and faced ongoing temptations, she stepped up her prayers even more.

One day, during his junior year at the Lutheran high school, I learned that Curtis and some of the other boys had been drinking beer in the parking lot at lunch time. The news infuriated me, and I marched into the pastor's office to get some answers. "What's going on?" I asked. "How can these boys get away with drinking on school property?"

He tried to downplay the situation and made it seem like it wasn't a big deal. "Now Charla, I'm sure Chuck has a beer when he mows the lawn on a hot day."

I ended that nonsense right away. "He most definitely does not," I said firmly as my anger rose. "And you certainly should know that Curtis probably has a propensity toward alcohol, because so many indigenous people do."

We allowed Curtis to finish the school year there, but we moved him to North Hollywood Continuation School where he completed his senior year.

Curtis became a binge drinker and left our home because he knew it was "killing his dad." But at 23, he returned and asked for help. The next Sunday that we went to church, Curtis was with us. Ruth saw him and couldn't contain her emotions. With tears streaming down her cheeks, she slid away to one of the Sunday school rooms and wrote a lengthy letter, which she gave me along with a check for $1,000.

Once we got home, Chuck and I read the letter and then placed it on the dresser. In it, Ruth said she felt strongly that we should reconnect Curtis with his biological mother. At the time, I knew only two things about the young mother: (1) Her first name was Marta, and (2) she came from a remote Zapotec village in Oaxaca. Finding her would be almost impossible, but Ruth believed in the impossible and gave us the check to help fund that important search.

The following Wednesday, as I was walking out the door to go to midweek church services, the phone rang. Chuck and Curtis were already waiting for me in the car. I didn't want to be late, but I answered it anyway. A woman on the other end of the line spoke timidly in broken English. "I don't want to cause you pain."

"Please tell me who this is," I said.

Again came the words, "I don't want to cause you pain."

The voice was Curtis's birth mother, Marta! She told me that God had spoken to her in an audible voice, saying, "Charles Curtis is in trouble."

"Would you like to speak with him?" I asked.

Her response was the same. "I don't want to cause you pain."

I asked her to hold for a moment while I went to the car to talk with our son. "Charles Curtis, your biological mother is on the phone, and she'd like to speak with you."

"You're the only mother I have," he said.

Then I remembered Ruth's letter and the check on my dresser and told him about it. "Ruth Story gave me a letter on Sunday and said I was to find your mother." Curtis loved Ruth and knew she had a prophetic gift, so he agreed to talk with Marta. After a brief conversation, he handed me the phone.

"Where are you calling from, Marta?" I asked. To my surprise, she was working as a domestic in Beverly Hills. I invited her to dinner the next night.

What have I done? What if she's an alcoholic, or a con artist, or . . .? My creative imagination led me down all kinds of crazy paths, so I prayed.

The next day, Marta took a bus and arrived at our home promptly at six. Many years had passed since I last saw her. Now, her beautiful dark hair showed tinges of gray at the temples. She wore a lovely dress and treated us with great respect. But the thing I noticed most is that her eyes and face radiated Christ.

Over time, Curtis and Marta developed a precious relationship. A few years later, she moved to Kansas. As her health declined because of terminal cancer, her whole family gathered in the hospital waiting room. And what should appear on the television there but *The 700 Club*'s broadcast of the story of Charles Curtis's adoption, which led to our founding the mission in Mexico! They could sense God's warm smile.

At the age of 51, Charles Curtis accompanied us on what was his first trip to the mainland of Mexico. It was an extraordinary adventure. Not only did he get to stay at our beautiful mission base there and experience many of the Oaxacan customs, as well as the various ministries we have, but he also had the opportunity to search for his extended biological family.

The southern state of Oaxaca is a rugged land full of diversity and contrast. It's made up of numerous spoken languages, cultures, and ethnic groups. We knew Curtis's family came from a small village called Yatzachi el Bajo, but we had searched every known map for the location without success. The quest to find it seemed insurmountable.

I thought of my missiologist friend. "If anybody knows where it is, it would be Bob," I said. Bob Sundberg had given ten years of his life assessing the situation in Oaxaca and learning of the groups that were still unreached for Christ. He drove to as many of the remote pueblos as he could, and when he couldn't get there by car, he walked. He created a booklet detailing his research, which I keep in my Bible for prayer.

We contacted him and asked for his help. He said, "I not only know where Yatzachi is, but I will also be happy to take you there!"

So, on the third day of our Oaxacan adventure, we headed to the mountains with Bob. Following many stops to ask for directions through the rough mountainous terrain and curvy dirt roads, we finally arrived after an arduous, four-plus-hour journey. The village was across a stream, perched on the side of a hill. Everyone agreed it was a miracle we even made it. Praise God for His direction and for giving us endurance every mile of the way.

We stopped at the first tiny roadside store we saw, hoping to find gas for our return trip. What we found instead were carbon copies of our son Curtis. The resemblance was amazing, but even more amazing was learning that the owners of the little tienda were Charles Curtis's first cousins. What a beautiful, God-ordained moment!

After we explained the reason for our trip and got the introductions out of the way, Curtis's cousin asked, "Would you like to see your grandparents' home? It's only a short distance away." My heart leapt with joy at their offer to take us there.

The simple, two-room adobe dwelling remained untouched by time. A shelf along the wall held stacks of Christian books, covered in thick dust. We also saw a Zapotec Bible and hymn book. Learning that his grandparents were Christians deeply impacted Curtis. But something else we discovered was even more significant. Curtis's cousins told us that from 1936 to 1940, Wycliffe translators actually lived in his grandparents' home while they translated the New Testament into the Zapotec language.

The sense of God's presence in that moment filled us with awe. We were no longer standing in a humble little adobe home—we were standing on holy ground.

Later that day, we met Curtis's uncle, Pastor Telesforo Lopez, who had received the Lord in 1974. He pastored La Roca (The Rock), an evangelical church of thirty-four in

Yatzachi. Mario Cordoba took us to an evening service, and Curtis shared his testimony in that special sanctuary. He wept as he told his story of God's redemption, how he was born to an unwed mother, and how his adoption led to the founding of our home for children—children just like him.

At the conclusion of the service, we returned to the mission's home base in Tlacolula. A Missionary Aviation Fellowship pilot was in the area and offered to fly us to Amoltepec the next day. That was a wonderful gift for us, because the flight takes only half an hour as opposed to fourteen hours of driving.

We visited Modesto, a graduate of our Bible institute, along with his wife, their baby, and their small congregation. Though the people there are extremely poor, they graciously welcomed us and shared what little food they had. Mario and I had the opportunity to encourage them and to lay hands of blessing on the village children.

The following day we flew to the beautiful colonial city of Morelia, Michoacan, to visit the pristine children's home and Christian school founded in 1998 by one of our beloved Hogar Para Niños children, Ana Laura Haire. (FFHM helped her with the organization and management of it until 2016, when it became independent.) The administrator there was a former fisherman and treated us with a feast of freshly caught fish and lobster.

Each part of our eight-day journey was memorable, but especially more so for Charles Curtis. He was able to connect with relatives he'd never met and learn about his birth family. He also had his first experience at our Oaxaca and Morelia homes for children, met many of our missionaries who came to surprise us, and joined us as we ministered to the inmates in two prisons. By the time we were ready to return home, he couldn't help but add his voice to the thousands who have visited our missions and said, "I will never be the same."

Top: Charles Curtis (far right) with us and his pastor-cousin, whom he had just met

Left: Bob Sundberg, my missiologist friend, was happy to help us find Yatzachi el Bajo, the city in Oaxaca where Charles Curtis's mother lived.

Bottom: This is painted above the dining room door at our Oaxaca mission. Just like so many others, Charles Curtis left Oaxaca and said, "I will never be the same."

God's Workers
and His Ways

W hen Apostle Paul wrote his letter to the Philippians, he started out by saying, "I thank my God every time I remember you" (Philippians 1:3, NIV). I echo his words when it comes to the fabulous team God has put together to accomplish His work in Mexico. Because of the involvement of people from all of North America and abroad, what began with a vision of a home for children has now evolved into a multifaceted, far-reaching ministry.

Although there's no possible way I could name each individual who's had a part in our mission over the decades, I can point to the different groups God has used. All of them have played a significant role.

Our Board Members: Through the years, we've been blessed with many dedicated board members who have given untold hours of their time without compensation and often at great personal expense. The original board was comprised of those who were part of our Friday night prayer group. Later, others came to serve. We also have a Mexican board. Each member has a devotion for missions.

Our Missionaries and Staff: We often say that the real heroes are those who serve on the field. They have sacrificed in countless ways to be part of the ongoing work in Mexico. Many are far from their homes and families. They minister to children who suffer with abandonment, abuse, anger and resentment, disease, fears, loneliness, hopelessness, and so much more. They reach out to prisoners, those with addictions, the underprivileged, the poor, and the needy. They endure sleepless nights, lack of comforts, heartbreak, death, and suffering all around them. They do battle with spiritual forces. Truly, these are the light of the world, bringing the love of Jesus to the destitute and hurting.

Our Prayer Warriors: How grateful we are for the army of warriors who intercede for our many needs! They do the most important work. Without them, we wouldn't exist.

Our Donors: These generous souls give of their little or much to make all of our ministry possible. They sustain us.

Our Volunteers: We're often asked how it's possible so much has been done with so little. The answer to that is our phenomenal volunteers. They are a gift from God! Each year, thousands arrive from the United States and Canada (and sometimes overseas) to offer their time, energy, and talents to do tedious, behind-the-scenes tasks. Their help frees up our staff and enables us to expand our outreach even more. Our valuable volunteers come in all shapes and sizes, colors, ages, and backgrounds, and they include individuals, families, snow birds, retirees, church groups, youth groups, ministry organizations, and lots of others with servant hearts.

Throughout this book's pages, I've told of God's amazing ways and His perfect timing of bringing together just the right people to fulfill His master plan. Now, I want to highlight how He's used volunteers by telling about a special couple who came to help us with a project and ended up staying with us for seventeen years.

Here's what happened—

I had appeared as a guest on Gary Randall's half-hour daily television talk show in Oregon a few times, and when the date for their fundraising banquet approached, they wanted me as a speaker. The gathering was held at the Red Lion Inn in Portland.

A friend there pointed out a tall, stately man and his lovely wife standing across the room. "See that man over there?"

she said. "His name is Chuck Mills. He's a church builder for the Assemblies of God. You should go talk to him and show him your plans."

My friend knew I was on the lookout for a builder. She also knew that I always carried a set of plans in my bag with the hopes of one day having a divine appointment.

Because of a revival in our Colonia Vicente Guerrero community due to blind Lucio's healing miracle, people started flocking to our little chapel. We had to remove the windows so those standing outside could hear. Then we relocated our services to the old theater building and continued to have overflowing crowds. We were in desperate need of a larger church!

So that night, after my speech—armed with the knowledge that a builder was in the room—I became a woman on a mission! I wound my way through the banquet hall, keeping my eyes on my target. Not to scare him off immediately, I started with a brief introduction and chitchatted for a minute or two. Finally, I said, "I hear you're a church builder."

"Yes," he said. "I take time off work each year to build churches in foreign countries—mostly Latin American countries. So far I've overseen the building of seventeen churches."

During our conversation, I learned that the second-generation brick and block mason had been inspired by this message from a guest evangelist at his church: "God doesn't just want a tithe of your money. He also wants a tithe of your time and all of your life."

That bit of information delighted me, and I got right to the point. "Mr. Mills, I have a wonderful plan for your life! Would you consider going to Mexico to build a church? I just happen to have the plans with me."

I took the plans from my bag and spread them out on the table in front of us. At first glance, he said, "Oh, that's bigger than what I usually build. I normally just put together a crew of men, and we throw up some walls and top it off with a roof."

He tried to downplay his skills, but I didn't let it deter me. "You really should visit our mission and experience the situation," I said. "The current building is packed corner to corner, and people are standing on the outside. We need help."

Praise God, he agreed to make the trip and take a look. When the timing worked out, he and his wife, Phyllis, got in their little camper truck and headed south. He walked the grounds, assessed the situation, and felt God's tugging on his heart. "Okay, I'll do it," he said.

And that's how we got our master builder.

Chuck quickly endeared himself to everyone there and became lovingly known as Carlos. He stayed several months at a time, and over a period of three years—with the good help of volunteer labor—erected a beautiful church with Sunday school rooms where a thousand worshippers gather every week to glorify God and study His Word. Amazingly, the completed project cost only $29,000.

A funny thing happened while Chuck was at the mission. He fell in love with some children, so he thought he would hang around for a while.

Then the pastor of the church needed a three-bedroom home, so he lingered a bit longer.

A clothing room was needed, then a bunkhouse for our teen boys, so he stayed.

Carlos's "kids" were getting older and ready for university or trade school, and our student home in Tijuana needed an addition. So, guess where he spent his weekends?

The ministry continued to grow, and we had a desperate need for staff housing. Two-story duplexes would best meet the need. Carlos just kept laying blocks.

Months grew into years, and the Mills's little motor home didn't grow any bigger, so he built his bride of forty-six years a house. Even the roof was made of cement blocks. What else?

The kitchen storage, the dining room, and the sala all needed to be enlarged. Again, he kept laying blocks.

He built a bell tower in honor of his buddy Chuck Pereau, and an administration building with a full attic for storage.

Our Bible institute buildings were washed away in the devastating floods of January 1993. He placed one block on top of another, rebuilding on higher ground.

A clinic to serve the destitute. A warehouse. School classrooms. A rehab center. A retreat house. Guest housing. The conference center at our site in Oaxaca. The list goes on and on. He just kept pouring cement and laying blocks.

Chuck's accomplishments were many. His love for God's work and God's people, huge. His investment of time, resources, and talent at our mission in Mexico continue to have an eternal impact years after he's gone. As I fondly remember him today, these words from Matthew 25:21 come to mind: "Well done, good and faithful servant!"

⁂

I have hundreds more God stories I could tell about His workers and His ways. Here are a few that demonstrate God's remarkable responses to specific needs in His perfect timing. Outsiders might attribute what happened to coincidence, but we know better.

One time the administrator of an old nursing home in Pomona, California, made us an offer we couldn't refuse. We could have their beds and all the stainless-steel kitchen equipment, including cupboards, sinks, and counters, if we demolished the building and cleared the site. It would require a lot of hard labor, but how could we pass up all the free stuff?

My Chuck and three other men—Dave Taylor, Bill Moffett, and Nick Andruff—accepted the challenge and went to work. They disassembled everything in California and then took load after load of equipment and parts to the Baja mission with just a pickup truck. Although the project often seemed overwhelming and required countless hours and an abundance of energy, they didn't give up.

However, when the time came to install everything, nothing fit. No one had a clue how to transform the stainless-steel pile into the fabulous commercial kitchen that Mary Peterson, a member of our board, had designed. And it required someone with specific training to cut, weld, and assemble stainless steel. So, it sat there for two years, just taking up space.

Finally, I told Chuck, "We have to quit salvaging and filling this place with junk. It's all going to end up at the dump."

But Chuck saw it a different way. "You really don't understand the value of stainless-steel equipment, do you? This is expensive stuff!"

"If we can't use it, it's junk!" I said.

Then one day a Winnebago pulled into the mission's parking lot. The driver walked to the office and introduced himself as Eugene Suta from Oregon. "I'm headed to Cabo San Lucas for vacation. I saw your sign and turned off the highway out of curiosity," he said. "May I have a tour of the facility?" The hostess was happy to show him around.

When they came to the unfinished kitchen, Eugene saw the stainless-steel equipment and said, "What are you going to do with all of this?"

She was a bit embarrassed to answer him. "Well . . . we have a design, but nothing fits, and it takes a skilled tradesman to rework it. So, it's been sitting here for a long while."

At that, he made an astounding statement. "Maybe I can help. That's what I do for a living, and I happen to have all my tools with me in the Winnebago."

Eugene changed his vacation plans and worked until every cabinet, counter, and sink had been properly cut, welded, and installed. Only God . . .

A similar thing happened a short time later. Osborne Neighborhood Church in Arleta, California, collected a special Thanksgiving offering to provide our mission with a prefabricated, commercial, walk-in refrigerator-freezer. Anthony

Arnold, our building overseer, ordered a really nice one from a restaurant supply catalog.

We had the refrigerator-freezer. We had a kit to put it together. And we had the plans with instructions how to do it. But over the course of several days, the process of doing it turned into a fiasco.

Each of our staff members who attempted to install the large unit had an opinion about how it should be done. The combination of male stubbornness, pride, and perceived qualifications resulted in a power struggle among them. They argued a lot, and a couple of them even walked off the job because they couldn't handle the frustration. Eventually, the rest of them gave up, and the project came to a halt.

Then God sent Barney Coones, an angel from British Columbia. He was another one who was headed south and noticed the sign for our mission. He pulled off the highway and asked for a tour of the property. When the hostess showed him the kitchen, he became curious. "What's going on here?" he asked.

Our hostess explained the situation, and during the course of the conversation she asked him what line of work he was in. "I'm a caulker," he said.

She wasn't familiar with the term. "What in the world does a caulker do?"

"I install commercial refrigerators."

What can I say but wow? Our angel stuck around, and within twenty-four hours we had a professionally installed walk-in refrigerator-freezer. I'm in awe of God's ways.

Another instance of our being wowed by God's provision of the right person at the right time happened after Chuck went to the building supply store in North Hollywood. He came home giddy with excitement. "I found this incredible deal at the store!" he said. "They were selling beautiful ceramic floor tiles for a dollar a foot, and I bought three thousand feet!"

I wasn't so giddy with my response. "You just spent $3,000 on tile?" I made sure to emphasize the amount. "We don't have that kind of money sitting around! Who do you think is going to pay for it?"

"But it was such a good buy!" he insisted.

Of course, God was behind the scenes orchestrating His plan. The next day, a check arrived in the mail from an unknown donor in the Midwest. It was for the exact amount of Chuck's purchase and was designated for the medical center's floor. I shouldn't have been surprised because Matthew's gospel tells us that our Father knows what we need before we ask Him.

On Chuck's next trip to the mission, he hauled the tiles with him and left them there. A man who drove from Oregon to the Baja Peninsula with plans to fish stopped by our property because he saw the sign. He just happened to be a skilled tile layer. He cancelled his vacation and laid all the tile in the medical center.

As I mentioned before, I have hundreds of stories with similar scenarios.

Here's the bottom line: FFHM is His ministry. God will provide His workers and meet every need in His amazing ways and His perfect timing—all for His glory—for He is great and greatly to be praised.

Chuck Mills served the mission as a master builder for seventeen years. His wife, Phyllis, became the head cook and oversaw the activities of the sewing room. He and my Chuck were amigos, and in 2005 he built a bell tower to honor him. The plaque on the tower says, "Constructed by Carlos Mills, Master Builder, in honor of his buddy (amigo) Chuck Pereau, co-founder of the Mission."

In addition to many other projects, Chuck Mills oversaw the building of our fabulous mission church, which has a capacity of one thousand.

Looking Back

The nineteenth-century Danish philosopher Soren Kierkegaard said, "Life can only be understood backwards; but it must be lived forwards."

In November 1961, God surprised us with a 2-day-old Zapotec baby. Then, in October 1966, I had a life-changing experience with God. He gave me an incredible vision as I stood on an arid plot of land in Colonia Vicente Guerrero, Mexico, surrounded by a few old adobe buildings. I didn't understand what it meant or entailed. I only knew that I needed to move forward in trust, one step at a time.

Here's an excerpt of what I wrote in chapter six about that vision:

> "Then I looked outward, and instead of an expanse of desert flora and rocky, sandy soil, I saw a golden field of waving grain. Immediately, words from the Bible filled my mind: 'The harvest is plentiful, but the laborers are few.' Although I didn't know what was going on, God certainly had my attention."

Little did I realize the magnitude of the vision at the time. Now, here I am decades later, and I can look back and see God's big picture. I'm overcome with awe at what He has so beautifully orchestrated. Much has been accomplished, and the work continues to grow, but it's not because of Chuck's or my efforts. We were simply the facilitators.

Foundation for His Ministry began with the establishment of Hogar Para Niños in Colonia Vicente Guerrero.

Since that time, we've consistently expanded our reach into new regions and new areas of ministry. We have three initiatives that guide our overall mission: rescue children, restore the broken, and reach the lost. We start with practical love, because that's what Jesus did. But in every ministry our hope is for the spiritual renewal of all people.

Below is a glimpse of our bountiful harvest as well as a few more stories of God's amazing ways. I'm humbled by how He's used so many elements of my life—even the difficult ones—to affect positive change in Mexico.

⌀

Children's Homes: As I look back to my early influences, I think about my mother who opened her heart and her home to the fatherless. Even though we were poor, she had a reputation for "taking in strays." I also will never forget spending the summer with Reid Lunsford and his family when I was 12. Reid oversaw the ministry of the Eliada Orphanage in North Carolina. Those experiences made a lasting impression on my life, and God gave me deep compassion for children in need.

Since childhood, the words of Jesus from Mark 9:37 are always fresh on my mind. "Anyone who welcomes a little child like this on My behalf welcomes Me."

I'm delighted that we've been able to make a difference in children's lives through our two beautiful homes in Baja and Oaxaca. Each provides love, shelter, food, clothing, education, and Christian discipleship to those who have been abandoned, abused, or orphaned.

The majority of children who come to us are like withering plants that haven't seen sunlight and water. They carry with them the wounds of rejection, neglect, malnourishment, disease, and so many other spirit-breaking issues. Their haunting eyes are mirrors of their pain.

Because they arrive with a history of trauma and tragedy, many of them are emotionally immature. And many of them are confused, angry, and fearful. It's hard for them to trust other people. But over time, God brings healing, and love wins out. What joy to eventually see them bloom with new life as we pour God's living water and sunshine into them!

We strongly believe that education is one of the greatest tools we have for succeeding in life and for breaking the cycle of poverty, so we work hard to provide an excellent education while teaching our children how to be followers of Jesus. Each of our missions has an elementary school on site. The children are also taught to speak English, which gives them an advantage as they get older.

With the help of volunteers, we're able to provide music instruction and teach vocational skills such as sewing, auto mechanics, carpentry, and more. Generous donations from our supporters allow our children to attend either summer camp or youth conferences.

Newborn babies through 2 years of age (until potty trained) are cared for in the nursery until they graduate into one of our household families. Our purpose is to give them love, protection, and encouragement in the absence of their biological parents.

In 1998, we also helped establish a home for children, locally known as Casa Hogar, in the state of Michoacan. It's located in one of the poorest suburbs of Morelia—a large city with more than a million people—about one hundred miles west of Mexico City. We built a school there as well, which became an evangelistic outreach to the community. In 2005, Casa Hogar was recognized as the best in the nation, and the children were invited to celebrate at the presidential palace.

The seed for the Morelia mission began many years earlier when a recently widowed mother took the four youngest of her fourteen children to our home in Colonia Vicente Guerrero. Anna Laura (Reyes) Haire was 2 years old at the time. After fourteen years, her sister invited Ana Laura to come and live with her and her husband. Her sister had married an attorney, and he provided wealth and security for them.

Ana Laura became a Christian in her teens. She grew in her faith and, in her early twenties, felt God's calling to build a children's home in her hometown suburb of Morelia.

On a plot of donated land at the end of a pothole-filled, desolate road, and with the help of generous work teams, gifted volunteers, financial supporters, and praying people, the doors to the bright yellow building opened and immediately began impacting lives for Jesus. FFHM oversaw the work there until 2016, when it became independent and self-supporting. Praise the Lord!

At the time of this writing, plans are in the works for establishing a children's home in Tijuana as well. Jill Smith, our director of Mexican operations, and the FFHM board are seeking God's guidance and clarity in every part of the process.

TJ House: In the early years of our ministry, we had two teenaged boys at the home who were extra special. They had natural musical talents. Both could play piano, string bass, and guitar by ear. Both were unusually bright and had what it takes to be outstanding leaders. But they had finished the highest schooling available in the area, which was eighth grade. I wondered what their lives had in store. "God," I prayed, "give us the vision and the means to equip these children, Your children of promise, to better face their futures."

On August 16, 1977, I spent a hot, sultry day in Tijuana searching for a Christian home where our teenagers could board and attend classes to help them reach their full potential. God had encouraged me with a promise: "Behold, I set before you an open door, and lo, I am with you always." But after hours of exploring, I found nothing. That afternoon, Hurricane Dora turned Tijuana into a sea of mud and rocks.

I felt defeated. As I made a harrowing eight-hour trip south to the Baja children's home in my little Volkswagen, I cried out, "Lord, this does not look like an open door to me!" It was certainly a day to remember.

Exactly one year later—August 16, 1978—God granted my desire to prepare our young people for their futures. We moved a group of twenty students into their new home in Tijuana, where they would be able to attend trade school, preparatory school, or the university. Hannah and Mark Larson were the first house parents.

The story has a wonderful twist to it, revealing God's behind-the-scenes activity. We purchased the place from the man who built it. He had taken out a permit to construct a four-room house in a lovely area of Tijuana. For some reason, he didn't follow the original plans and just kept adding rooms—fourteen rooms plus baths, to be precise. It was far more than a single family could use, so he put the unfinished home up for sale. I sensed God's smile when we learned from the legal papers that the owner took out his building permit on August 16, 1977. Yes, it was a day to remember for sure.

Since that time, hundreds of our children have made their home at the TJ house and received higher education for careers in mechanical engineering, linguistics, business administration, nursing, medicine, and more. How gratifying to see these young people become responsible, productive Christians and break the cycle of poverty or addiction that has impacted them so harshly!

The TJ house has been a center for Christian outreach, Bible studies, prayer meetings, and student fellowships. Over the years, as it's become outgrown, we've added several additions.

Community Outreach: Every day, our outreach team is in the community, being the hands and feet of Jesus. We meet the unique needs of families, children, and broken-hearted, extending to them resources, fellowship, and, above all, God's wonderful love.

We evangelize, disciple, instruct, and give guidance with basic life skills. We offer literacy classes and medical help. We hand out clothing, food, blankets, tarps, water, and other supplies to make their lives better. We rescue, restore, and reach.

In our child evangelism program, we play games, sing songs, perform skits, and hug the children. We pray, tell Bible stories, and provide a big glass of milk and a large scoop of peanut butter for each child. Many hundreds of impoverished children in the community enjoy the blessing of this ministry.

Through loving our neighbors, we've witnessed the transformation of countless lives.

Day Care: The Baja mission's day care serves and disciples thirty preschool-aged children who would otherwise be left unattended while their mothers and fathers work in the fields in the surrounding community. The program provides a bath, food, education, and transportation five days a week.

In the fall of 2018, Mexican social services approached us about establishing day care in the farming area of San Quintín. They gave us a new facility with a capacity for one hundred fifty children and allowed us to run it our way without any restrictions. For the government to want our involvement shows how much they trust our ministry.

We thank God for the hours we get to spend with each of these little ones. It gives us a wonderful opportunity to teach them about the love of Jesus, which they in turn take home and share with their parents. Our prayer is that Jesus, and their time with us, will impact their future in positive ways.

Special Needs: The disabled children's learning center at the Baja mission provides schooling for thirty children with special needs who otherwise would not have educational opportunities. They are transported daily to our site and are trained in life skills. We care for their medical needs and give spiritual instruction as well. Some go on to higher education.

Bible Institute: The Bible institute equips Mexican nationals to serve as future missionaries and pastors. We offer three years of intensive biblical training to our students, who learn how to minister in the poorest communities throughout the nation. We especially have a heart for working with the largely unreached indigenous people groups from the state of Oaxaca. A number of our graduates currently live and minister in Mexico. Several have built churches and are pastoring congregations in remote areas.

Missionaries in Remote Regions: We support eight missionaries in the mountains of Oaxaca. These heroes of the faith are living and serving in towns where people have not yet heard about Jesus or where no church exists. They are willing to face persecution to bring light to the darkness. Our dream is to support a missionary in each of the nine regions of Oaxaca.

Medical Care: Medical, surgical, dental, and optical needs of thousands are met through our Baja mission's medical center. We have a great team of practitioners who give excellent care, and we're blessed with the help of specialists who provide services that aren't available anywhere else in the nearby community. We also host medical missionary teams who come in and volunteer their time for a week or two each year.

Emergency Services: In 1997, our Baja mission established a fire, paramedic, and rescue service. We have the only fire department in the area, and our volunteer emergency team responds to calls as far away as Ensenada, 110 miles from the mission. Our men have had extensive live-saving training. They are even equipped for accidents requiring the Jaws of Life.

Rehabilitation: After Glenn Almeraz graduated from the Bible institute, he purchased land in Zapata with money received as a wedding gift and deeded it to FFHM to use for a drug rehabilitation center. His history with prison and addiction, coupled with God's powerful work in his life, uniquely equipped him to be the director of the center. It started as a pegboard shanty and was later replaced with a block building that houses up to eighteen men.

In a beautiful act of Christian love, Navajo believers from churches on reservations in Arizona and New Mexico came to help lay the foundation and raise the walls. (Hans Benning had long been serving the southwestern Native Americans in the name of Jesus and inspired them to reach out and serve as well.) To watch the Navajos encourage their Mexican brothers—who were once enemies—and to hear their prayers for the rehab center was a deeply moving experience.

In addition to the center in Zapata, we broke ground in 2006 to build Rancho de Cristo, another place where troubled men can be delivered from the bondage of drugs and alcohol through the power of Jesus Christ. Juan Carrillo, who worked at the mission for multiple decades, gifted the land to FFHM when he retired. The five acres of beachfront property north of Camalú provides a picturesque setting and a peaceful environment for the men to heal.

Hans Benning took over the leadership of Rancho de Cristo at that time, and since then he has made bi-monthly trips there to build (with the help of the brothers) what it is today—a beautiful village with a church, a prayer chapel, housing for the men, a spacious kitchen and dining room, and four workshops where the brothers can learn skills to prepare them to return to normal life.

The residents participate in a one-year program that includes literacy as well as the vocational training. They are taught trades such as construction, woodworking, leathercraft, metal work, auto repair, and also some gardening. But above all, they learn that Jesus loves them and has a plan for their lives. They have morning and afternoon devotions to teach them God's Word.

Hans loves the brothers and plans to continue what the Lord has called him to do as long as he's able.

Rancho de Cristo is very near to my heart. After my son Craig died, a prayer chapel was built and dedicated in his honor. I sense God's presence there.

Garbage Dump Ministry: Men from our outreach team in Baja visit the local dump to minister to the men living there. A majority of them are paralyzed by drug addiction. Our staff feed them, give them clean water, share the gospel with them, and encourage them to consider entering our men's rehab, Rancho de Cristo.

Prison Ministry: I have an interesting background with prison ministry that goes back to 1973. When I arrived for a Women's Aglow speaking engagement at a hotel in Santa Maria, California, a gentleman greeted me in the lobby and introduced himself. He said, "I pray for special events and those who are ministering in our city. On Thursday, I saw your picture on the religion page of the newspaper, and I've been praying for your meeting today."

I'd never heard of anyone doing that and thought it was unusual, but the idea intrigued me. Then he said, "As I was praying for you, the Lord revealed to me that you would be going to prison." He saw the panic on my face and said, "Oh, not as an inmate, but to minister."

At the time, I was a throw-'em-in-the-slammer-and-forget-'em kind of person and wasn't interested in anything related to prisoners, so his statement seemed outlandish to me. But I was polite and listened to what he had to say. "I felt so strongly about this that I brought you a box of books for distribution to inmates," he said. I thanked him, took the books, and excused myself.

Once I got home, I carried the big box to the service porch. My teenaged son Dana asked, "What are all these books, Mother? They're all about prisoners!"

"I'm not sure," I said. "Some nut in Santa Maria gave them to me. I'm going to call Art Reardon and see if he can get rid of them at the Los Angeles County Jail."

The prophet and the prophecy were all but forgotten until seventeen years later. Reverend Percy Gutteridge, an old friend of our family, scheduled a speaking itinerary for me in British Columbia. I reviewed the schedule and noticed a maximum-security prison on the list. "What's this?" I asked. "You show me going to Matsqui Prison. I don't do prisons!"

"Well, now you do," he said. "I went through a lot of trouble to get it approved, and you can't back out." He gave me a bit of background on the prisoners. "Most of the inmates are first nation—they're indigenous. They need to hear the miraculous story of how you adopted a Zapotec baby."

I had never been in a prison and had no desire to be in a prison. I balked, but Pastor Gutteridge wouldn't back down. Finally, I decided it wasn't worth the fight and gave in.

The guard who met us didn't appear happy about my being there. He obviously wasn't used to having a woman speaker in an all-male prison. After going through the too-intimate-for-me inspection process, we walked from one yard to another. And with each gate that clanged shut behind us, my fear increased.

Then God gave me a word: "This is that." I pondered what it might mean. Once again, I heard the words clearly. "This is that."

Suddenly, I thought of the story in Acts 2 when, following the first Pentecost, Peter had said, "This is that." God reminded me of the crazy man in Santa Maria who told me years earlier that I'd be ministering in prisons. I knew this day was preordained.

Hardened criminals filled every seat in the auditorium, the majority of them native aboriginals. As I looked into the audience, I felt a heart connection. I talked about Charles Curtis and how his adoption resulted in our ministry to the indigenous people of Mexico. After my talk, I invited the men to come forward for prayer, and at least forty received Jesus as their Savior.

But the story didn't end there. Some years later our son Craig was incarcerated, and we spent the next eighteen years visiting him in various California prisons. We also started a letter-writing ministry to his fellow inmates. In addition, I've had invitations to speak in other prisons. For example, my friend Linda Strom invited me to speak at a women's correctional facility in Gatesville, Texas. So, I wasn't surprised at all when the prisons were built right across the street from our new mission in Oaxaca, or that some of our precious children's parents are incarcerated behind those walls.

I'm delighted about the many opportunities our outreach teams have in the Mexican prisons. We're able to share the love of God, lead Bible studies, present church services, provide practical helps, teach literacy, and offer medical attention. Thanks to the Bennings and Tito Quiroz, the inmates in Ensenada also have the opportunity for music lessons. (Hans and the brothers from Rancho de Cristo built a beautiful music room inside of the prison walls. It is still being used today in many different ways.)

We've been blessed to witness miraculous healings and changed lives. When inmates are released, our mission teams often help make arrangements with local pastors for them to be welcomed into God's family, and the ministry continues with regular visits in their homes.

I'm especially pleased that one of the young men Craig led to the Lord while incarcerated is now part of our team in Oaxaca. What joy that gives me! Because of all these God-ordained experiences, I'm a different woman than I was that 1973 day in Santa Maria. I have a deep compassion and love for inmates and their families.

And this is that.

Sinaloa: Culiacán, Sinaloa, located in northwestern Mexico, is an extremely dangerous place. It's home to the Sinaloa Cartel, which is the most powerful drug trafficking organization in the world and Mexico's predominant organized crime group. Because of its ideal weather conditions and fertile soil, it is also what is considered the "breadbasket" of Mexico. Not only is the physical harvest great, but opportunities for a spiritual harvest are as well.

More than 250,000 workers from all over the nation come every year to labor in the agricultural fields. They live in crude migrant camps bordered by chain link fences that are topped with barbed wire. Nearly one hundred of these camps are in Culiacán alone, with up to three hundred families living in some.

The laborers work long hours and return to their meager conditions exhausted. Their inadequate compensation leaves little room for improvement and offers no hope for retreat. These circumstances, along with the abundance of drugs in the area, contribute to the breakdown of families and lead to tragic outcomes.

Since 2010, our ministry has been active in these communities. We purchased a house to create a permanent base in 2011 and built dorms on our property to accommodate visitors and additional staff.

The needs in Sinaloa are never ending. FFHM is present and doing what we can, but we're eager to do more.

Other: A couple of other things worthy of mention are our macadamia orchard that helps support our mission and employs some of our neighbors. We also reach countless people through our mission churches and satellite churches.

⌘

Yes, in looking back I see a great harvest. Yet as I observe the fields before me, they are still ripe for the picking. Much is left to do.

All those years ago, when God revealed to me a golden field of waving grain and impressed on me that the harvest is plentiful and the workers are few, I didn't understand His intentions. As I processed the vision and realized it involved me, I had what I call a Moses moment. I asked God, "Who am I? Can't you send someone else?"

But as I trusted His guidance and walked obediently hand in hand with Him, He proved to me the truth found in 1 Thessalonians 5:24: "Faithful is He who calls you, and He also will bring it to pass" (NASB).

∽⦿∾

After Janelle Keller graduated from Moody Bible Institute, she followed the leading of the Lord, which eventually took her to Oaxaca, Mexico. She served competently and effectively in building the FFHM outreach ministry there. After four years, she returned to the states to pursue other avenues of service. However, part of her heart remained in Oaxaca. In time, she called me from Chicago and asked if we had any opportunities for her to return and work with FFHM.

It just so happened that the executive assistant at our San Clemente office had resigned one hour prior to Janelle's telephone call. "Can you be here tomorrow?" I asked. And she was! Janelle served as my executive assistant until 2015, when it was time for me to turn over the reins as executive director to her. I have committed the leadership of FFHM to Janelle with joy and confidence. She will continue to build on the foundation of what God has accomplished with new vision for all He intends to do in the future.

If you'd like to keep up to date with what's happening through Foundation for His Ministry, consider visiting our website at www.ffhm.org and signing up for the newsletter.

In 2015, I turned over the reins as executive director to Janelle Keller. She has a heart for the people of Mexico, a heart for God, and a huge vision for things to come.

Rancho de Cristo is a place where troubled men can be delivered from the bondage of drugs and alcohol through the power of Jesus Christ.

In looking back over our ministry years, I think about all the gifted people God provided to establish and sustain FFHM. Competent, consistent, supportive help has been one of the biggest blessings—and continues to be. It's impossible to mention everyone here, so I've decided to highlight just a handful on these next few pages.

Top left: Eva Schiaffino Quick, Olive Thayer (my mother), and Ann Mills were my personal encouragers. These three continually reminded me that it's always too soon to quit.

Top right: Minerva (Minnie) Trujillo has been a precious, faithful servant in our ministry for many years. Filling numerous roles—including house parent, teacher, administrator, translator, mentor, and more—she is always willing to step in where needed.

Bottom left: For decades, Dr. John and Doris Lucas of Maranatha Evangelistic Association have served in significant ways to facilitate the ministry of FFHM. John is our Canadian director.

Bottom right: Carl and Jan Holter were friends of FFHM since its inception. Carl served on the board of directors. Jan was a concert pianist and taught piano to a multitude of children.

Top left: Olive Kieler caught the vision of bringing work groups to the Baja mission, and her husband, Larry, drove the bus. For more than forty years, they've gathered up young people from all over Canada who would have their lives changed forever by their trip to Mexico.

Top right: Terry Northrop was an assistant administrator at the mission. His wife, GiGi, gave birth to two children at our medical center.

Bottom left: Paul Juss served as a charismatic leader at the mission for one year before establishing large congregations in Grand Prairie, Alberta, Canada. He has been a consistent friend of the mission ever since.

Bottom right: Ted Holmes is a general contractor who remodeled the Tijuana house and participated in many other building projects. His wife, Mary, is famous for her German chocolate cake.

Top left: Greg Rush and Les Leadke faithfully distributed candy for "Night in Bethlehem," an outreach production done each year at the mission.

Top right: Terry Thatcher served for five years as assistant administrator. His wife, Madelyn, taught piano. They also sponsored Antonia (pictured with them).

Bottom left: For thirty years, Tom and Georgia Klebau have joyfully and generously served FFHM as board members and volunteers for the monthly mailing.

Bottom right: Bob Bond was an electrician; his wife, Dorothy, was a quilter. For seventeen winters they left their home in Cottage Grove, Oregon, and served at the mission in Baja. Many other snowbirds (too many to mention) have come to help over the years as well. They are all unsung heroes of the faith.

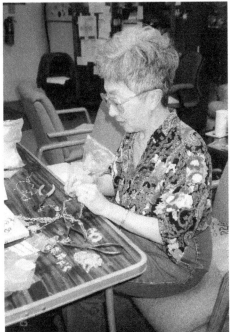

Top: Michiko Kus has been a supporter and sponsor of children for many years. In this picture she is making jewelry that she sold to help finance the building of the hair salon at the Baja mission.

Bottom: My granddaughter Christi is a hair stylist and served for a time cutting hair in the mission's salon.

Top: Gerry Witt lived part time in Baja and worked as a mechanic at the mission. He had a word from the Lord for Abby-Jill Braun that led to her salvation.

Bottom: Abby-Jill (left) was called to become the executive director for FFHM, but cancer struck a few months later. Carolyn Libby (right) took Abby-Jill to all her appointments and greatly supported her in many ways.

The writer of Hebrews talks about running the race God has set before us with endurance, which can be accomplished by keeping our eyes on Jesus. That's something I've tried to do over the years. One time I had the opportunity to run a different kind of race on behalf of Jon Cowpersmith. Because of cancer and a heart condition, he had been hospitalized at Saddleback Memorial Hospital in intensive care for eleven days. His wife, Eleanor, expected an astronomical bill, but she never received one.

Each Memorial Day the hospital sponsors a half-marathon race to raise funds. In appreciation of their free care to Jon, I ran. Pictured with me is an unidentified runner who needed assistance.

Last Words

I had a dilemma. Several hundred women were gathered at the Castaways Restaurant, overlooking the San Fernando Valley, for the Women's Aglow meeting. I was the scheduled speaker, and as I drove into the parking lot at the restaurant, I had not yet received the mind of the Lord for my presentation.

"Lord," I cried, "I need Your help. I'm just going to open my Bible and trust You to give me a message to share."

When I held up my Bible, the pages fell open to the end part where I had written the words to Andraé Crouch's song "Through It All." It was my testimony and the testimony of countless others who have had tragic lives. I used Andraé's words as the outline for my talk.

The sponsors for the event, Pastor Jack Hayford and a black Pentecostal pastor, sat at the back of the room. After my message, the elderly black pastor waited patiently until he could greet me. "Do you know who I am?" he asked.

"No, I don't think I've had the privilege," I said.

"I'm Andraé Crouch's father."

He told me that Andraé had recently made some poor decisions and had backslidden. At the time, our son Craig had just been incarcerated for four years. Pastor Crouch and I embraced each other and wept without shame, knowing that our Redeemer lives. A short time later, he graduated to heaven, but I will always cherish that memory.

The truth in the song's words came full circle for Andraé, and for so many years they've provided needed encouragement for people around the world. As I write this final chapter, they are fresh in my mind once again.

"Through It All" pretty much sums up Chuck's and my marriage and our ministry together. What a journey it's been.

Now that you've read our story, you know about our challenges, our pain, and our joys. You've learned what God has done in our lives because of our Zapotec son and the vision God gave us. You're aware of the harvest in Mexico and what God has accomplished through the laborers He's provided.

Here's a nutshell version of our experience (thanks to Andraé).

We've had . . .

- tears and sorrows.
- questions for tomorrow.
- times we didn't know right from wrong.
- times we've felt all alone.

But we can thank God for . . .

- the mountains.
- the valleys.
- the storms He's brought us through.

Because we've learned that . . .

- God will console us in every situation.
- in our lonely hours, He will remind us that we are His own.
- if we never had problems, we'd never know God could solve them.
- our trials serve to make us strong.

But best of all, we've learned . . .

- to trust in Jesus.
- to trust in God.
- to depend upon His Word.
- And we've learned what faith in God can do.

I can't count how many times I've cried out to God for help in the midst of the challenges we faced. Sometimes I didn't know if I'd be able to hang on. But my heavenly Father, in His sweet way, would often comfort me with the words in Psalm 121, reminding me of His faithfulness and loving care.

I lift up my eyes to the mountains—
where does my help come from?
My help comes from the LORD,
the Maker of heaven and earth.
He will not let your foot slip—
he who watches over you will not slumber;
indeed, he who watches over Israel
will neither slumber nor sleep.
The LORD watches over you—
the LORD is your shade at your right hand;
the sun will not harm you by day,
nor the moon by night.
The LORD will keep you from all harm—
he will watch over your life;
the LORD will watch over your coming and going
both now and forevermore.
(Psalm 121, NIV)

Through all our years of ministry, the Lord has never let us down. He's done a magnificent work. He's also taught us that He specializes in things thought impossible. Over the course of many decades, we've walked a seemingly impossible path. Oh, the amazing miracles we've witnessed, thanks to Him!

Time has a way of moving quickly and catching us unaware of the passing years. It seems like just yesterday Chuck and I were young newlyweds embarking on our new life together. Yet, in other ways, it seems like eons ago, and we wonder where all the years went. Writing this book has bubbled up uncountable reminders of days gone by and given us glimpses of what got us to where we are today.

Chuck and I were babies when we married. He was 19; I was 17. The only marriage counseling we had was from my mother. She was such a wise woman, and she continued to bless us with her wisdom until she died.

Here is some of her advice to me: "Stay married." "Feed the brute." "Stay in the same bed." (Our mattress sags toward the middle, by the way.) "Keep short accounts." "At the end of each day, pray the Lord's prayer together."

Mother's advice must have worked, because at the time of this writing we've been married seventy-one years!

In addition to Mother's counsel, Chuck reads the Word of God to me each morning. We're able to start the day with our eyes fixed on the Lord. How good it is to be saturated in truth and to be able to depend upon His Word! That's how we've endured. That's the solid rock on which we stand.

Now, as I've come to the conclusion of the book, I'm pondering last words.

I read that at the end of his life in 1965, Prime Minister Sir Winston Churchill said, "I'm bored with it all."[2]

I'm in the twilight hours of my own life, and I wonder how it's possible he could say that. My perspective is quite the opposite. As long as I have breath, I will be excited about the work God has given me to do. It's a delight and honor to serve Him and to praise His holy name.

I'm more in line with what General William Booth, the founder of the Salvation Army, said three months before he died in 1912. He addressed a crowd of seven thousand Salvationists in what would be his final but most notable speech. Among his last words were these:

"While women weep, as they do now, I'll fight. While children go hungry, as they do now, I'll fight. While men go to prison, in and out, in and out, as they do now, I'll fight. While there is a poor lost girl upon the streets, while there remains

---

2 https://www.nytimes.com/1965/02/02/archives/churchills-last-words-i-am-bored-with-it-all.html

one dark soul without the light of God, I'll fight. I'll fight to the very end."[3]

The passion and purpose he shared that day resonate so much with what's on my heart and what I've fought for all these years. General Booth's words are especially meaningful to me because of the significant role the Salvation Army played in my childhood. Back when I was just a little girl, God was already laying the groundwork for what was to come.

I also think of the last words of Jesus, known to us now as the Great Commission. He met with His disciples on a mountain in Galilee and said to them, "Go and make disciples of all nations, baptizing them in the name of the Father and of the Son and of the Holy Spirit, and teaching them to obey everything I have commanded you" (Matthew 28:19–20, NIV).

Jesus gave a promise at the end of His commission, and it's a promise that's emphasized many times throughout Scripture. "Surely I am with you always, to the very end of the age." Every step of the way, in every part of our calling, He's been with us. He's been faithful. He's been good. That is my testimony.

As Chuck and I face our few remaining days, we sense God would still have us focus on what matters the most— His commission to reach the lost with the message of Christ and His charge to believers in Matthew 25: feed the hungry, provide drink for the thirsty, give shelter to the homeless, clothe the naked, care for those who are sick, and visit the prisoners. This is the foundation on which we built His Ministry.

Our involvement is different today, and we're not physically able to do everything we once did, but our hearts, prayers, and efforts will always be with the dear people of Mexico. No matter our age, there is still a work we can do.

---

3 https://www.salvationarmy.org/nhqblog/news/2012-05-09-ill-fight-100-years-since-booths-final-address

One day years ago, I shared a devotional message at the Baja mission, and I mentioned several names of those who had given a significant portion of their lives to His Ministry: the Davises, the Arnolds, the Taylors, and others. No one seemed to know of whom I was speaking, which gave me a strange feeling.

The experience reminded me of what the New Testament writer James said. Our life is just a vapor that quickly vanishes. Even though Chuck and I have devoted decades of our lives to the ministry, we too will soon be forgotten.

That causes me to consider the importance of our legacy, our posterity. We're here on this earth such a short time, but we have the responsibility to make this world a better place. With that in mind, I think about theologian Francis Schaeffer's famous question, "How should we then live?"

As for me, I plan to live in the now. And, following the advice my mother gave me when I was a 13-year-old child (who boldly proclaimed she wanted to do great things for God), I'll continue doing the kindest thing I can do today and leave the rest to the Lord.

Chuck and I may not be remembered, but the lives of those who have been touched by His Ministry will tell the story for years to come.

May God be pleased.

Praise the LORD.
Praise God in his sanctuary;
praise him in his mighty heavens.
Praise him for his acts of power;
praise him for his surpassing greatness.
Praise him with the sounding of the trumpet,
praise him with the harp and lyre,
praise him with timbrel and dancing,
praise him with the strings and pipe,
praise him with the clash of cymbals,

> *praise him with resounding cymbals.*
> *Let everything that has breath praise the LORD.*
> *Praise the LORD.*
> (Psalm 150, NIV)

Hallelujah!
Thank You, Jesus!
Praise the Lord!

Through it all,

we've learned . . .

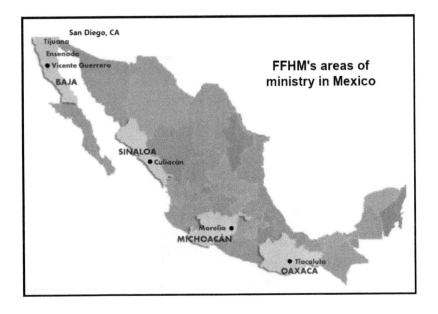

"For I was hungry, and you fed me. I was thirsty, and you gave me a drink. I was a stranger, and you invited me into your home. I was naked, and you gave me clothing. I was sick, and you cared for me. I was in prison, and you visited me."
(Matthew 5:35-36, NLT)

About the Authors

Charla Pereau and her husband, Chuck, adopted a Zapotec baby in 1961, causing her to develop an ever-growing love and compassion for the Mexican people. Although she considers herself an ordinary woman, her faith in an extraordinary God led to her doing a great work on the Baja Peninsula, the mainland of Mexico, and into the mountains of Oaxaca through Foundation for His Ministry, an organization she founded after receiving a supernatural call and vision in 1966. She has now dedicated decades of her life there to rescuing children, reaching the lost, and restoring the broken. In that time, she has witnessed and experienced God perform countless miraculous deeds. Learn more at www.ffhm.org.

Twila Belk is a writer and speaker who loves bragging on God. She is the author or co-author of eight books—including the devotionals *Raindrops from Heaven* and *The Power to Be*—and she's contributed to many other titles. The mother of three grown children and grandma to four little ones, Twila is recently widowed and lives in Iowa. For more info, visit www. gottatellsomebody.com.

CPSIA information can be obtained
at www.ICGtesting.com
Printed in the USA
LVHW021314070921
697193LV00010B/558

9 781953 114044